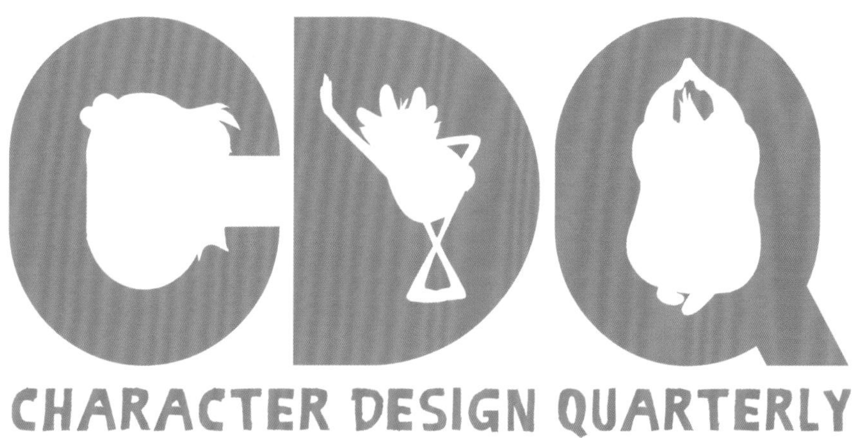

CHARACTER DESIGN QUARTERLY

CONTENTS

04

BEHIND THE COVER ART

Learn how Simone Grünewald put together the cover artwork

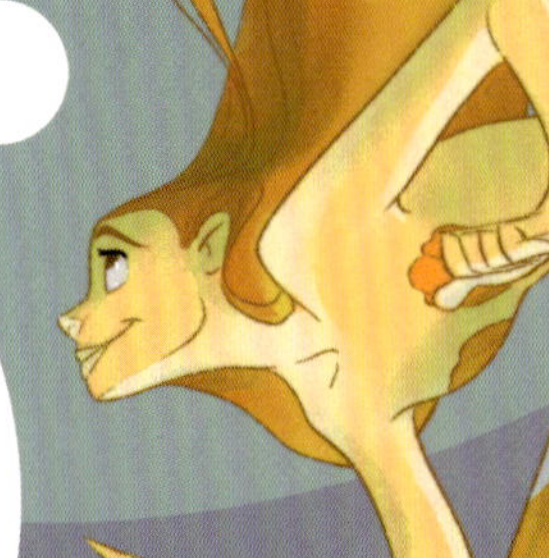

18

MISSION POPO

Jennifer Wu shows us how she created her award-winning short film

32

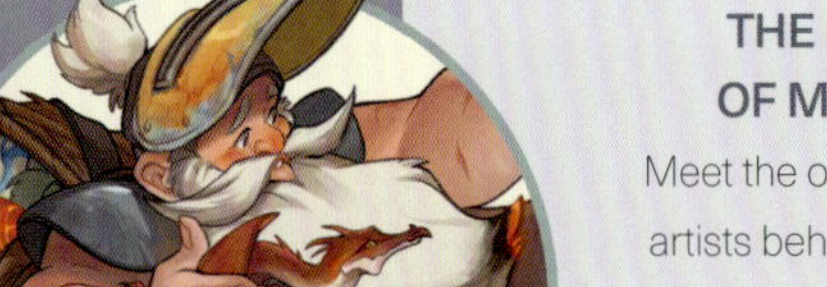

THE MAGIC OF MERMAY

Meet the organizers and artists behind the social media sensation MerMay

WELCOME TO *CHARACTER DESIGN QUARTERLY 32*

Whenever we speak to artists, it's clear that the impact of social media on their careers is often huge, and with AI art flooding the internet, being seen is harder than ever. That's why we were delighted to be able to speak to Lauren Barger and Whitney Pollett, who between them run the incredibly successful MerMay, a month-long social drawing challenge that promotes inclusivity and boosts work by a wide range of incredible artists – all of it made by actual humans! We also speak to the recent winners of the competition to hear what MerMay means to them.

This issue's tutorials cover a wide range of different topics: we have a lighting masterclass with Chelsea Blecha, a guide for preparing a character turnaround for animation with Sheryl Yap, and a detailed look at preparing designs for comic books from Marco Ferraris.

With our usual in-depth cover feature, this time featuring the incredibly talented Simone Grünewald, and much more besides, we're sure you'll find something to inspire you – and maybe we'll be featuring you as a winner of MerMay one day!

SAM DRAPER

EDITOR

48

DEVELOPMENT GALLERY

Grace Tran shows us how she created three separate characters

LIGHTING THE WAY

Learn how to effectively light characters with Chelsea Blecha

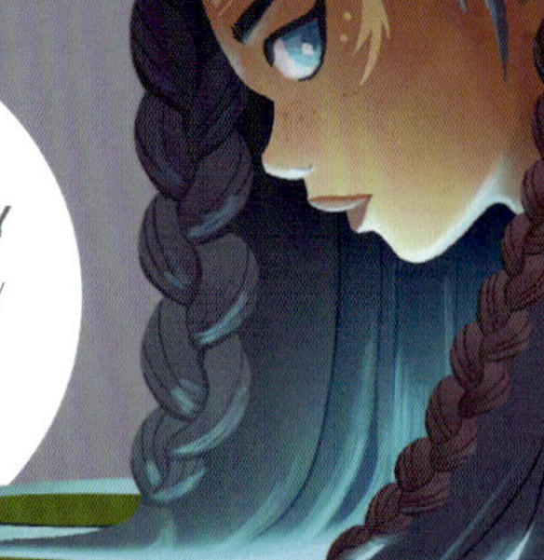

52

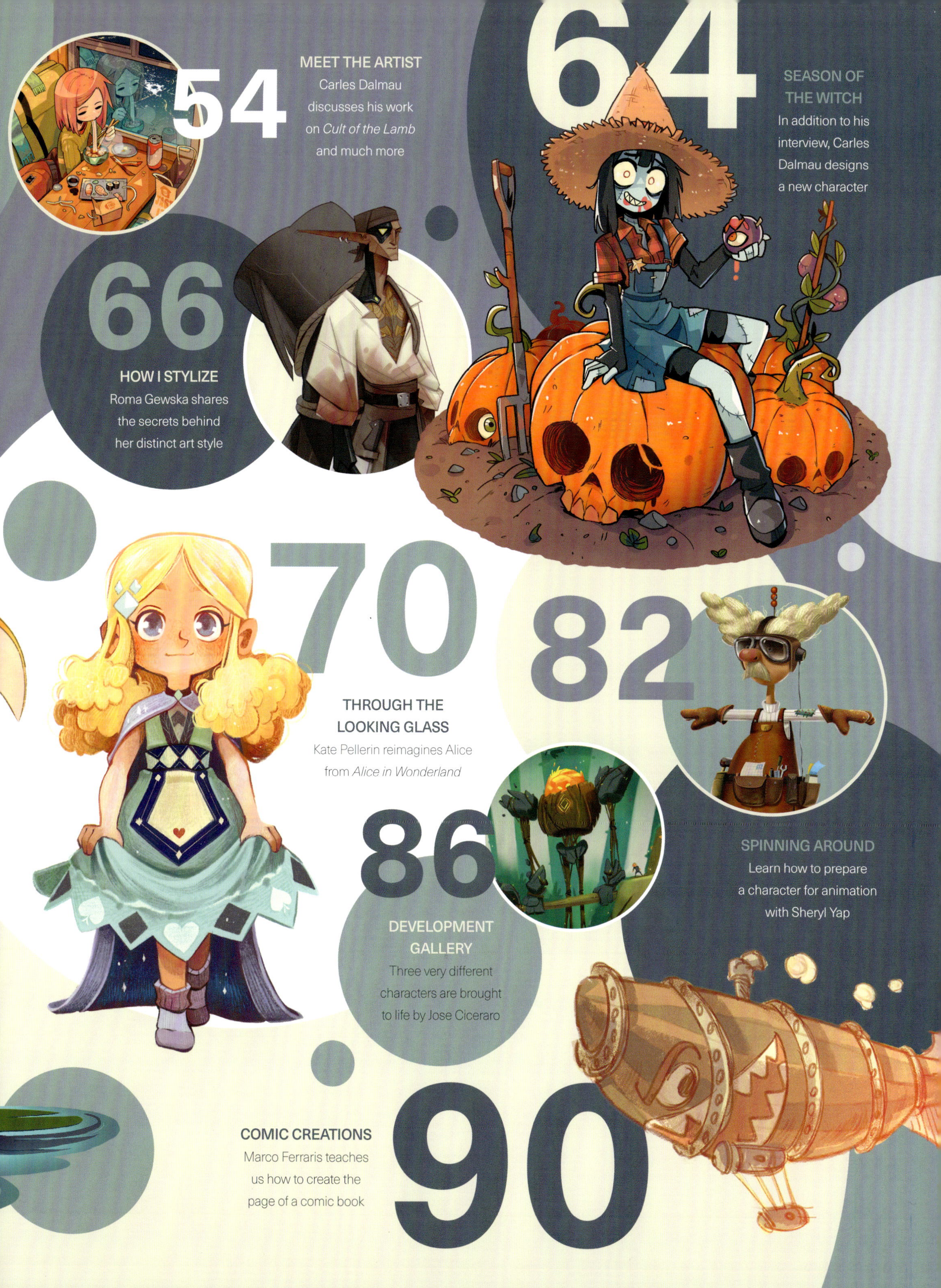

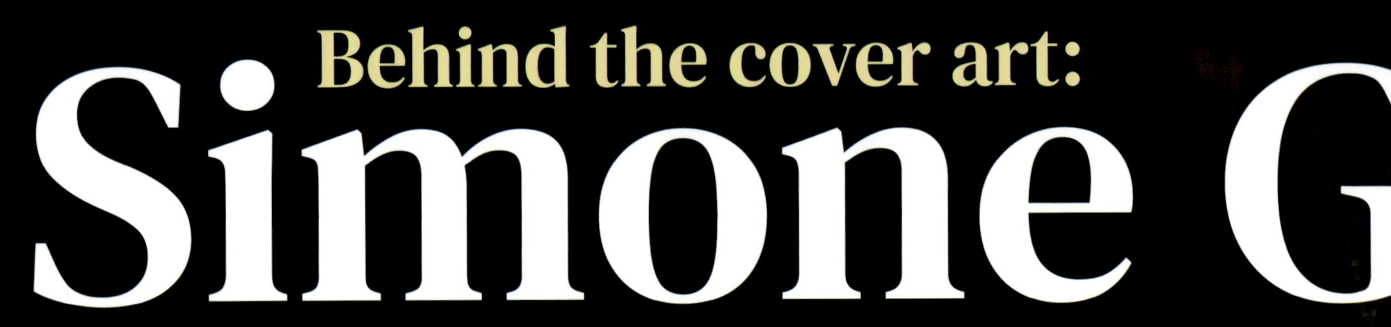

Behind the cover art:
Simone G

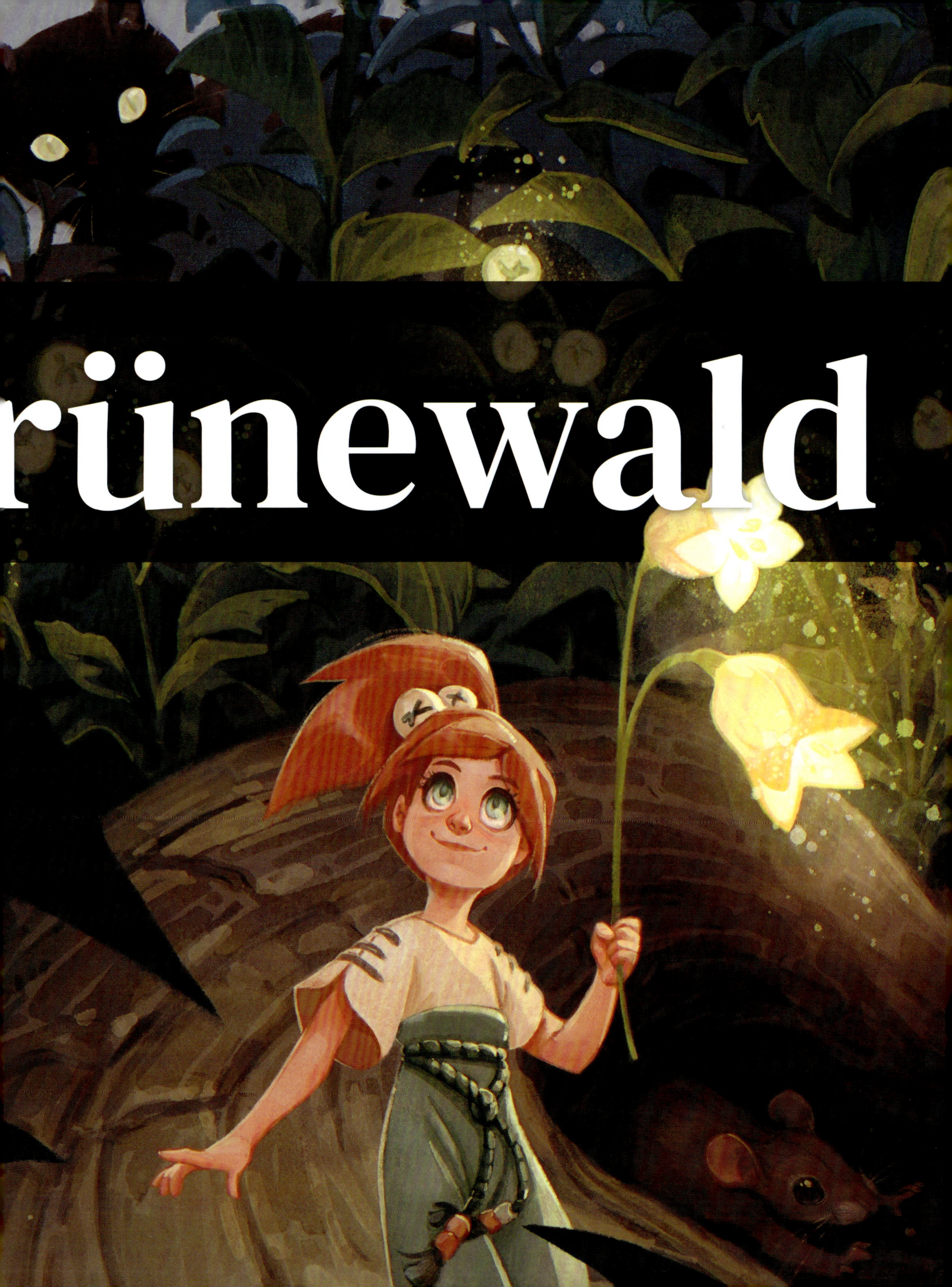
rünewald

Hi Simone, welcome back to *CDQ*! What have you been up to since we last spoke?

I feel like a lot has happened since then! I launched 'The Cosy Art Club', a newsletter and blog where I share insights and tips on healthy artist habits. I really want to build a community where we can all complete challenges together, motivating one another along the way. Everyone who joins gets my 'Easy Art Essentials' pack, a huge collection of resources that makes it as easy as possible to get started with creating.

My husband and I also got a publisher for our video game, *Under the Island*, which we've been working on for six years now. We plan to release it in 2025, which is super exciting for us! I also went to Madrid and recorded a Procreate course with Domestika, which went live this February.

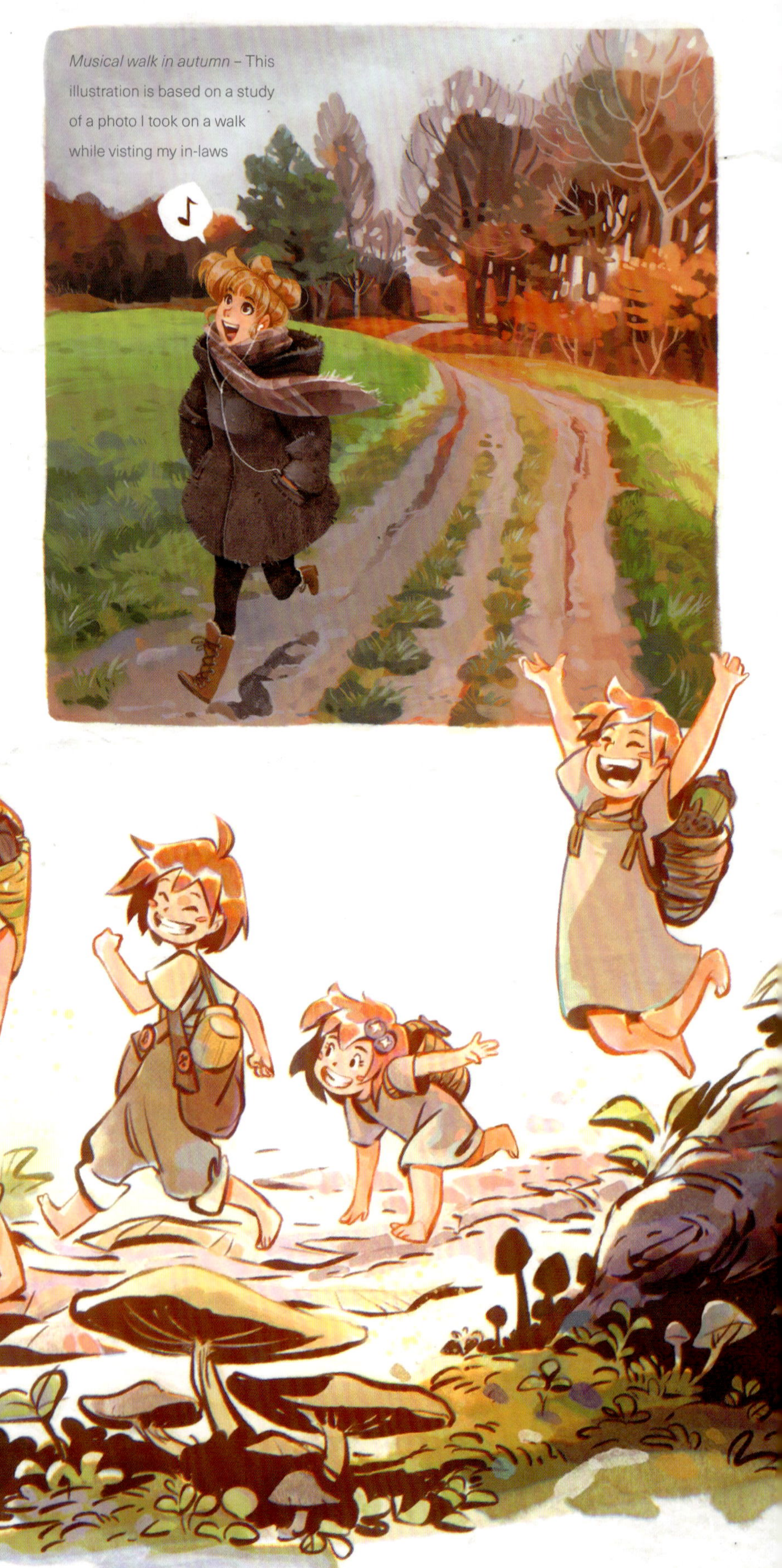

Musical walk in autumn – This illustration is based on a study of a photo I took on a walk while visting my in-laws

Can you tell us a little about the inspiration behind the cover art?

I've been exploring the world of my small folk for quite a while now. I'm fascinated by miniatures and the ensuing size changes of things, and painting nature makes me happy, so marrying these two in an illustration is always fun. Throw in some interesting lighting and the hint of a narrative and I have myself an illustration that excites me!

Family foraging –
Like squirrels, my small folk
are very busy in autumn
preparing for winter

How has your art style evolved over time? Is it still evolving?

Yes, it's always evolving. I think of my style as a big bubbling pot into which I'm constantly throwing topics, hobbies, fashion, and all my other interests. Just as I keep evolving as a person, so does my style, and I hope it always will.

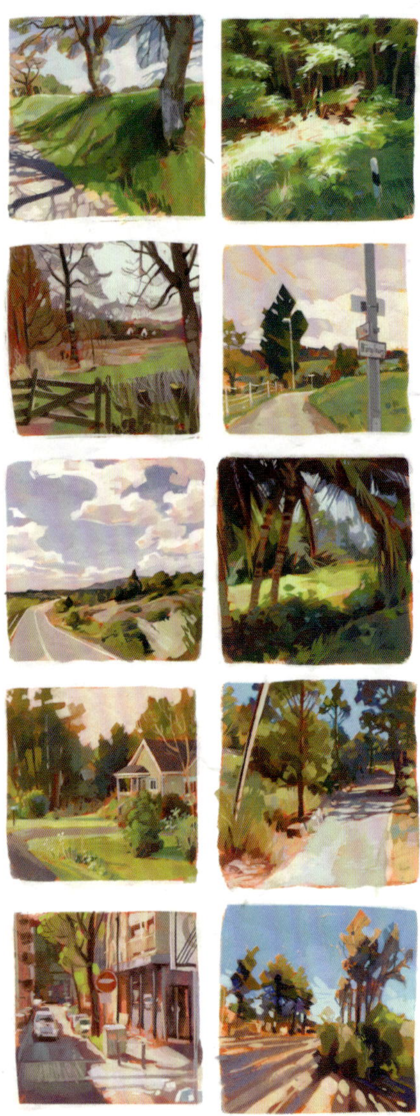

Mapcrunch Studies – Nowadays I love doing studies from Mapcrunch.com. To keep myself from getting lost skipping through the world, I try to sketch the first location that is suggested

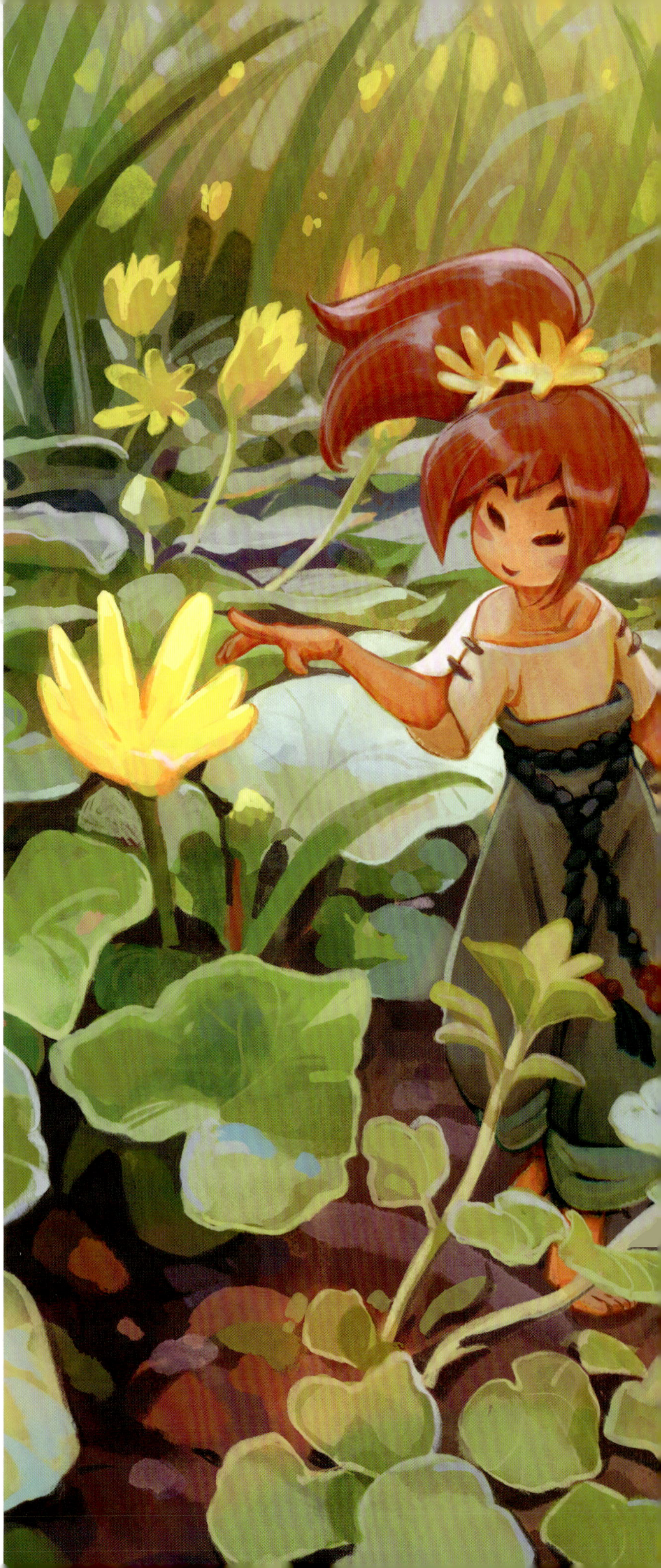

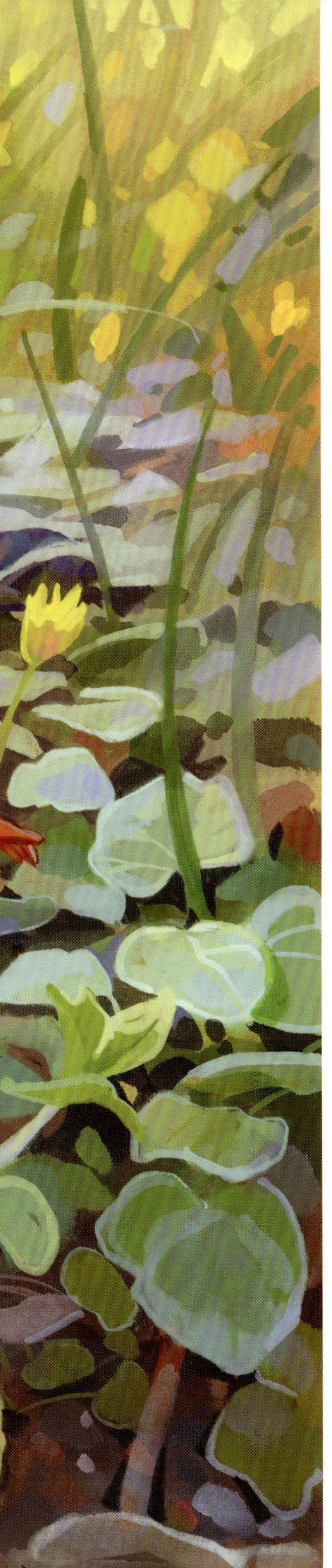

Your Instagram is constantly updated with new sketches and illustrations – where do you find the ideas and inspiration for your drawings?

My sketchbook is the place where I pin down ideas that flash through my mind from time to time throughout the day. I follow a thought, iterating on an idea, letting the story unfold, seemingly by itself. My last chain of ideas started last autumn with a sketch of a small person of mine arranging leaves in a pattern. A couple of days later, on impulse, I picked up four ginkgo leaves on my walk. That, in turn, led to a collection of sketches and illustrations inspired by them.

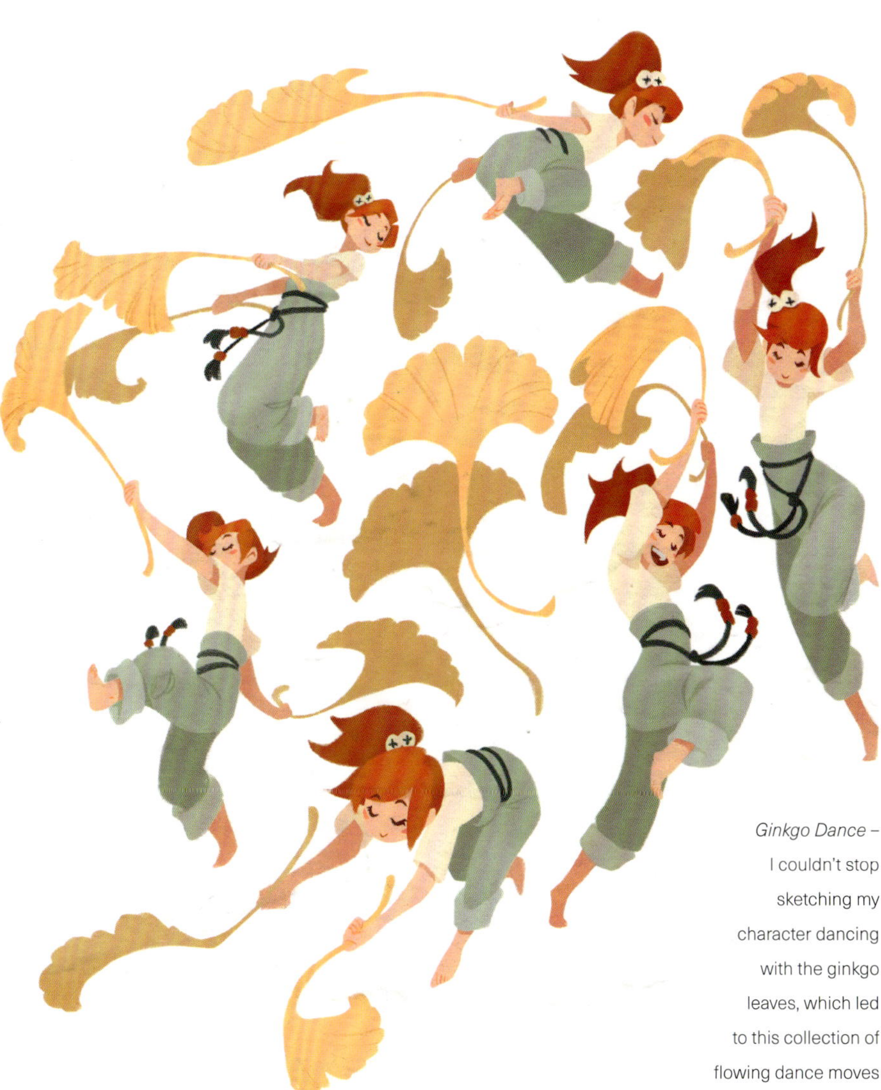

*Ginkgo Dance –
I couldn't stop
sketching my
character dancing
with the ginkgo
leaves, which led
to this collection of
flowing dance moves*

Have you got any tips for artists on how to keep motivated and busy?

I think that one great piece of advice is that you need to get your head right. What that means is going to be different for everyone, but taking the pressure off, leaving room for play and curiosity, is a good place to start. Keep a 'bad' sketchbook if the 'good' one seems too intimidating. For ideas, I find ways to trick myself into starting on a project, for example, by working on a study and allowing other thoughts to develop. Forcing ideas rarely works, but doing something else (like starting an art study or going for a walk) and intentionally leaving space for thoughts to flourish often works for me.

Thanks for chatting with us Simone! Is there anything coming up we should be looking out for?

The one big thing I've been planning this year has been an art book featuring my little people – I have sketched and painted them so much that all I need to do is assemble them. The process is fairly slow, though, since other jobs that pay my rent keep interrupting it, but I'm certain I will finish it sometime next year!

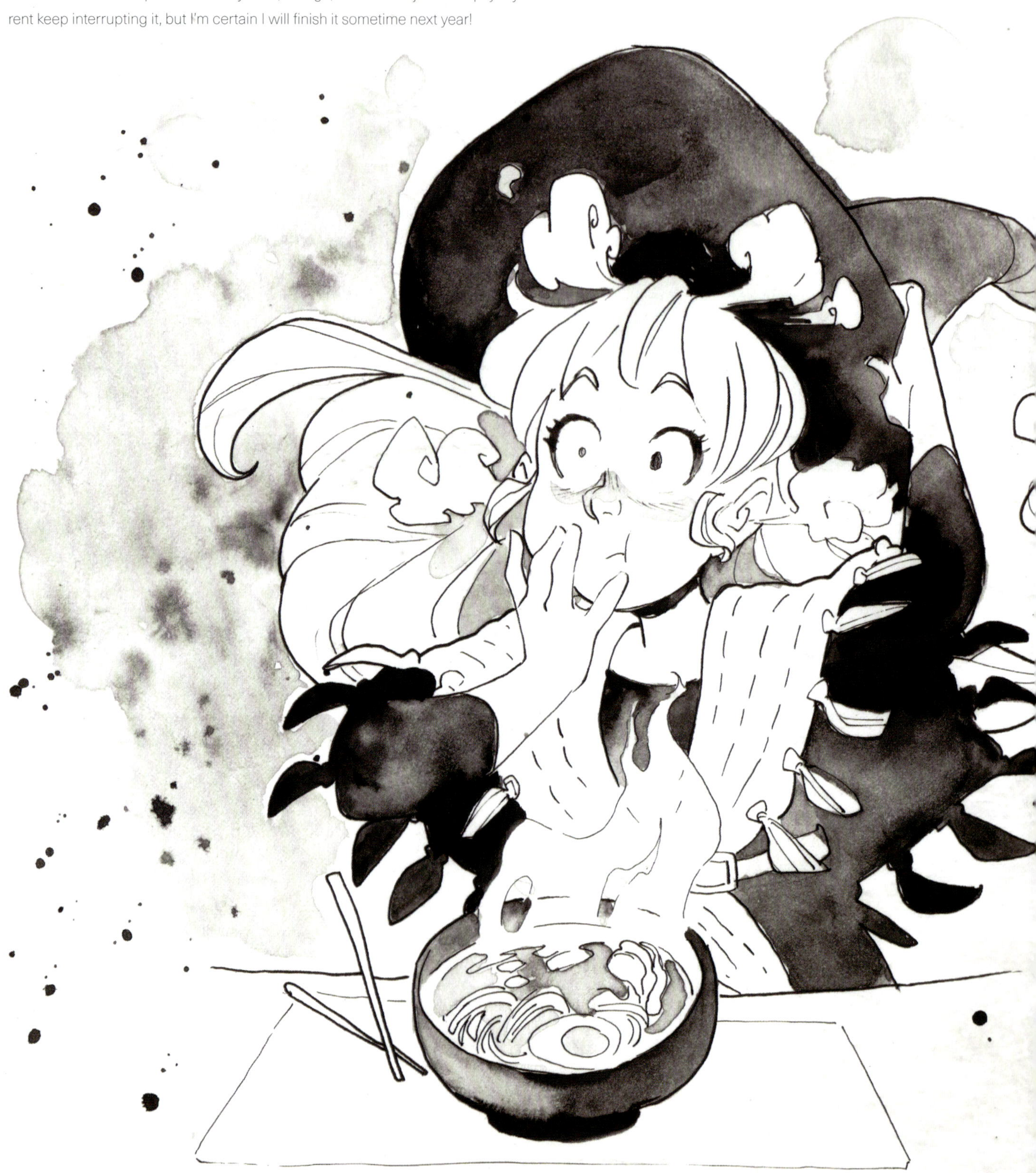

Hot Food is Hot – I really like how I interpreted the 'hot' prompt for Inktober here. Everything about the character is reacting to the heat.

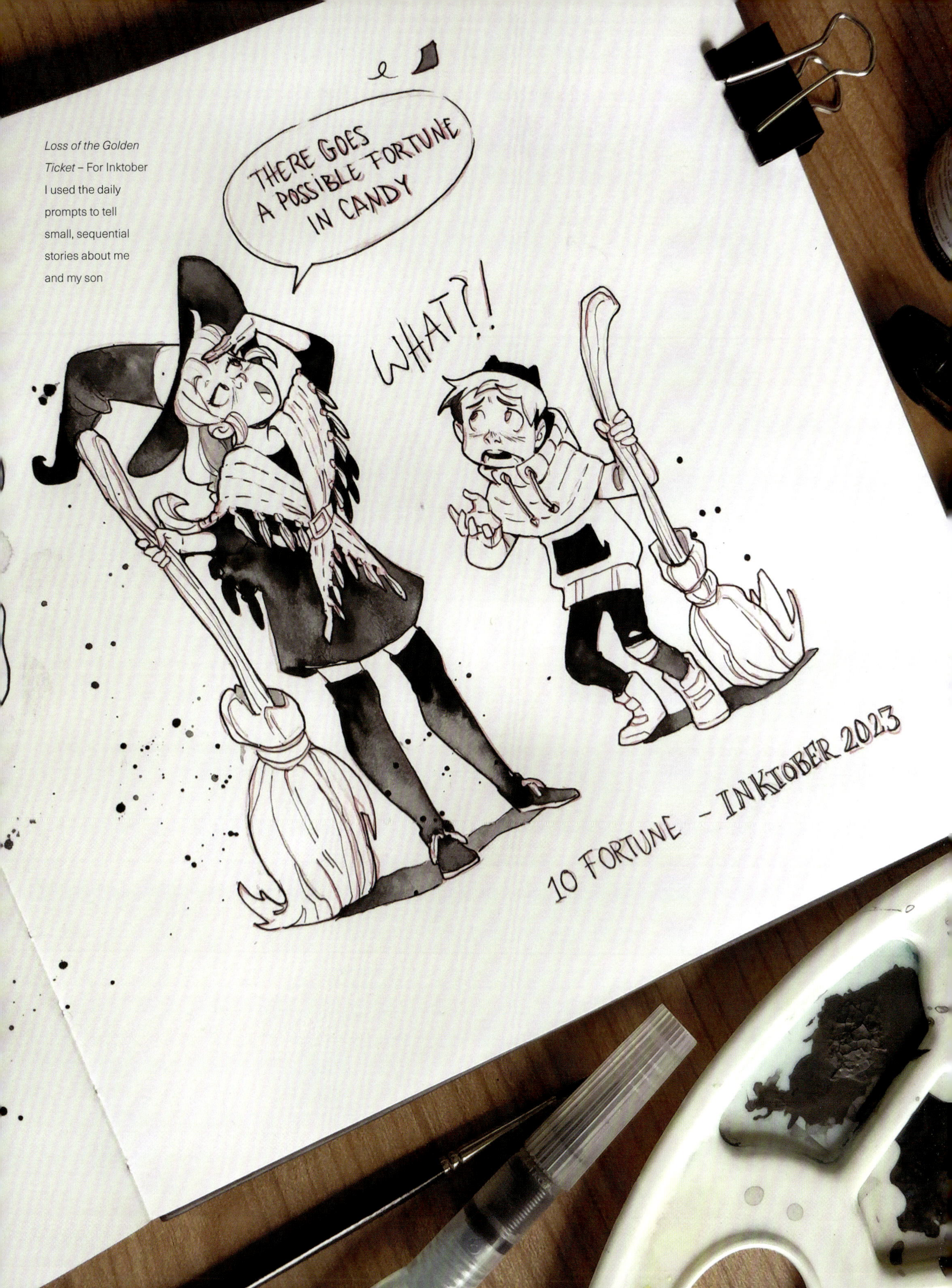

Loss of the Golden Ticket – For Inktober I used the daily prompts to tell small, sequential stories about me and my son

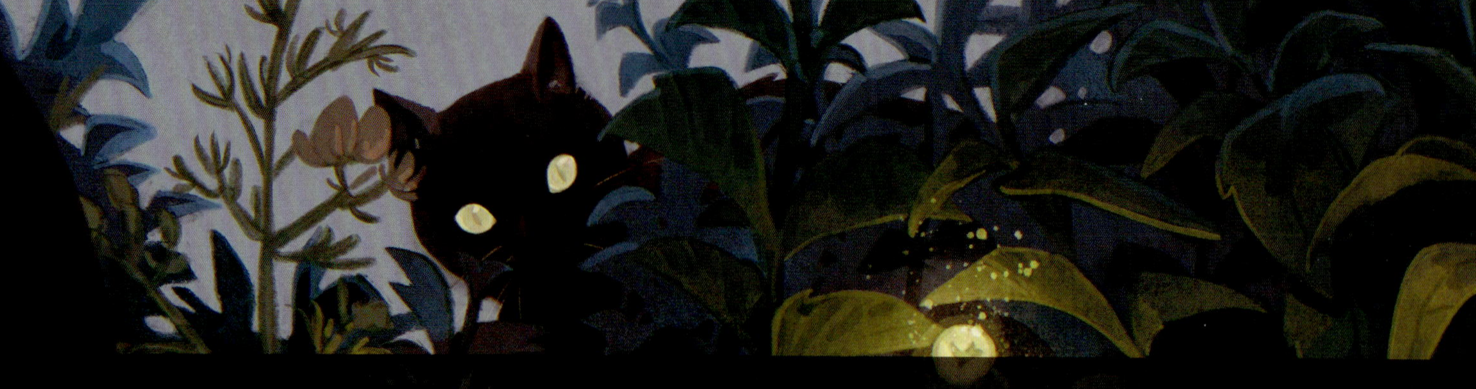

Crafting
the cover

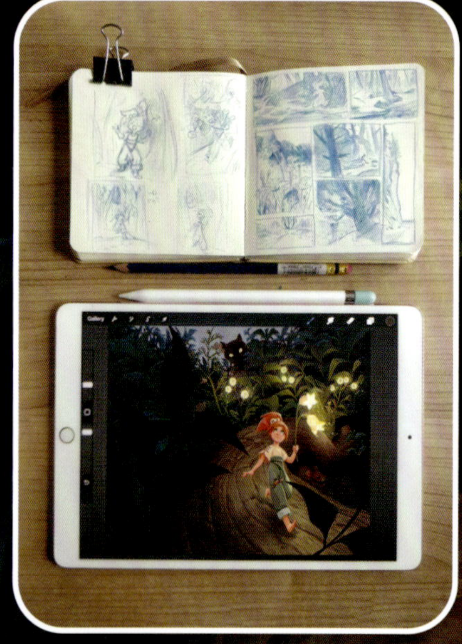

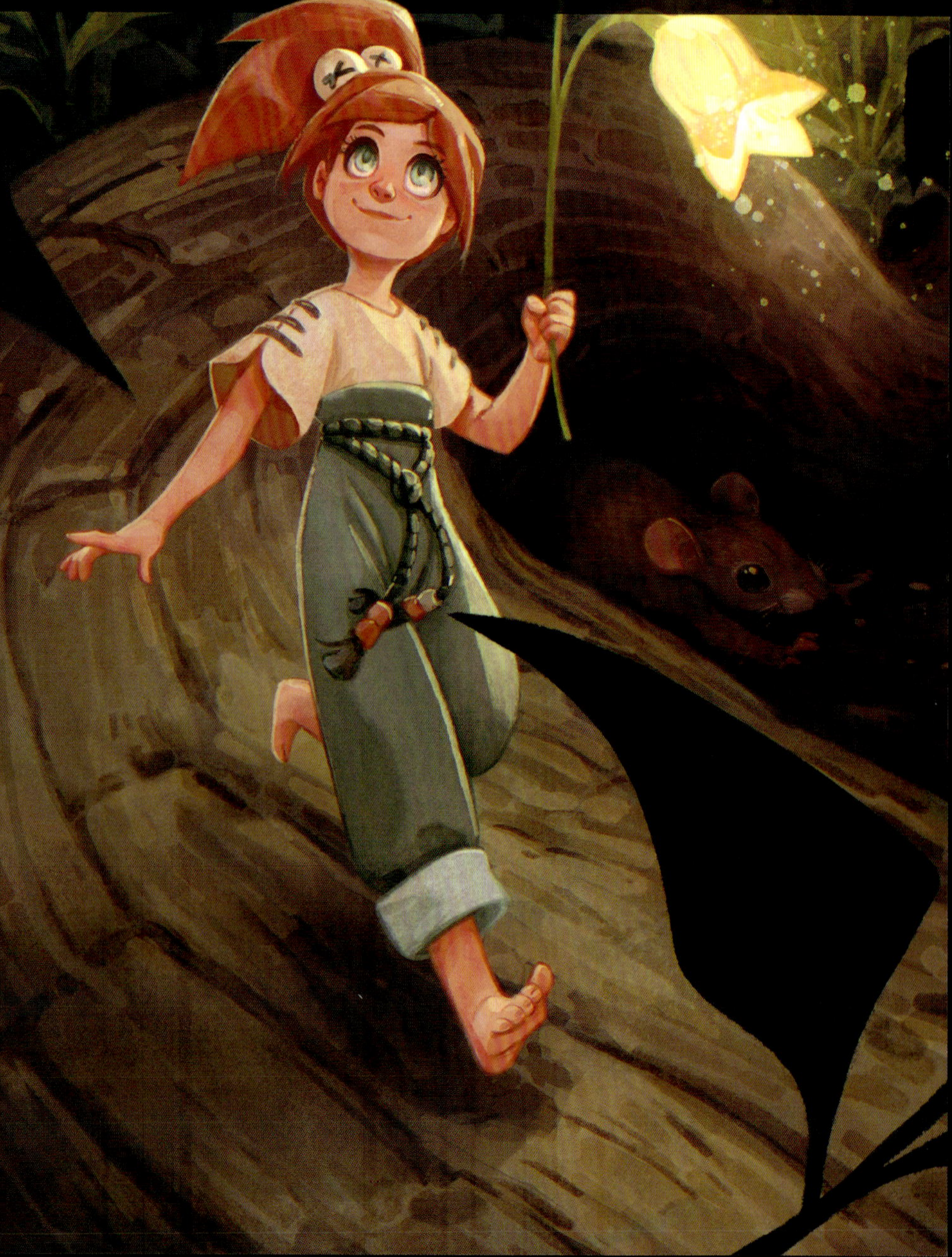

THE TOOLS OF
THE TUTORIAL

In this tutorial I would like to share with you a process that I use for many of my illustrations. I will explore ideas in my sketchbook on the topic of my little people and look for something that gives me an interesting lighting scenario and a bit of a story to captivate the audience.

When done with the sketches, I will take photos and iterate on them where necessary, creating the final illustration in Procreate.

I'll be using my current sketchbook, which is a Royal Talens 12 x 12 cm (which is perfectly fine but nothing special), a blue PRISMACOLOR Col-Erase, and my trusty old iPad Pro from 2017, with a first-generation Apple Pencil.

The first three thumbnails explore the idea of a small character running down a winding branch

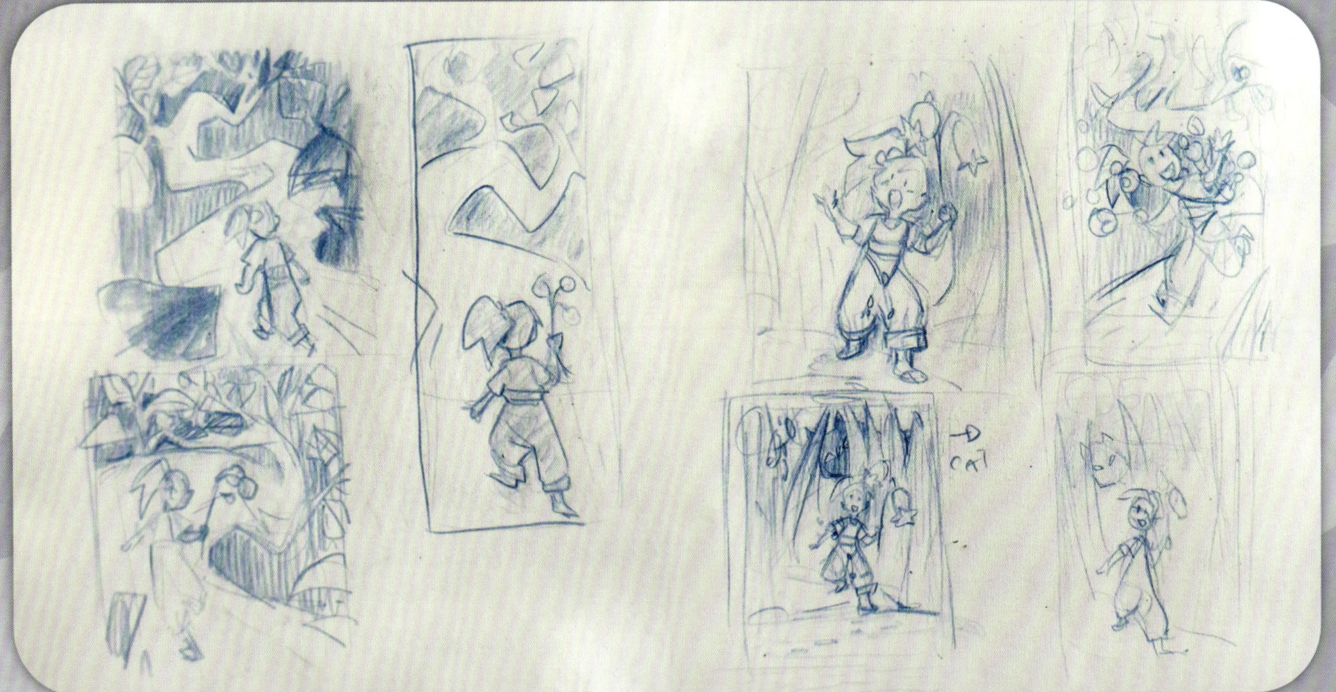

I add a threat of danger, of which the character may not be aware

SEARCHING FOR IDEAS

My first idea stems from an exercise for practising composition. I fill a page with panels using different formats and then add random lines to each panel, until my brain starts to see patterns and add meaning to what I'm drawing. My first bunch of thumbnails are very free, just playing with the shapes of a long branch. Gradually, ideas start to take hold, like the character holding a bunch of berries.

It would be nice to view the character from the front, so I create four more thumbnails and the first hints of a story start to appear. I explore the character's pose and add a potentially dangerous animal to the background.

TWO BECOME ONE

To further refine my ideas, I take photos of the thumbnails and drop them into the template for the magazine cover, paying attention to the composition, lighting, and values. To balance the logo at the top right, I want the character to be positioned diagonally at the bottom of the illustration, slightly left of centre. The glowing berries and flower will create an interesting lighting situation. To add more depth, I add a more pronounced foreground, with a glowing flower in the first sketch and leaf silhouettes in the second.

At this stage, it is nice to have some outside input. My editor comments that it might be nice to try a combination of both illustrations, which works really well. I combine the nice, winding composition of the second sketch with the drama of the cat from the first.

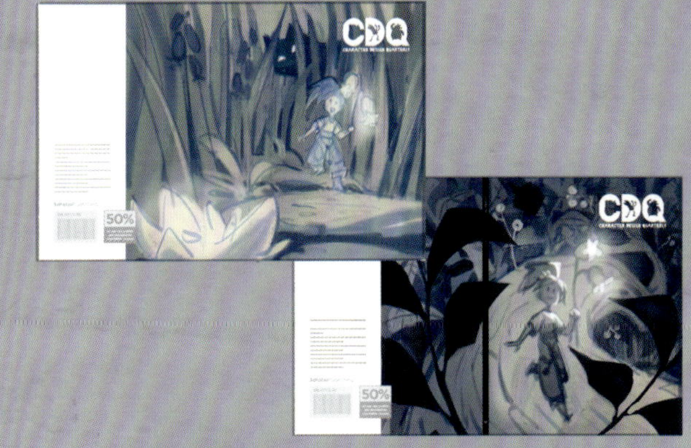

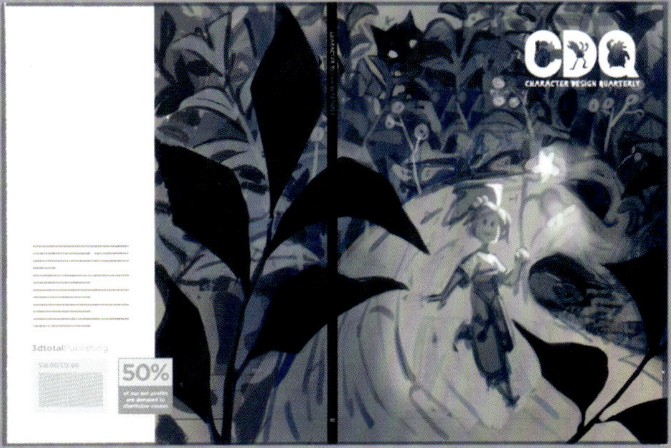

Digitally refining the two ideas from my sketchbook and then combining them into one drawing

I create separate layers for the foreground leaves, character line art, character 'block in', and background line art

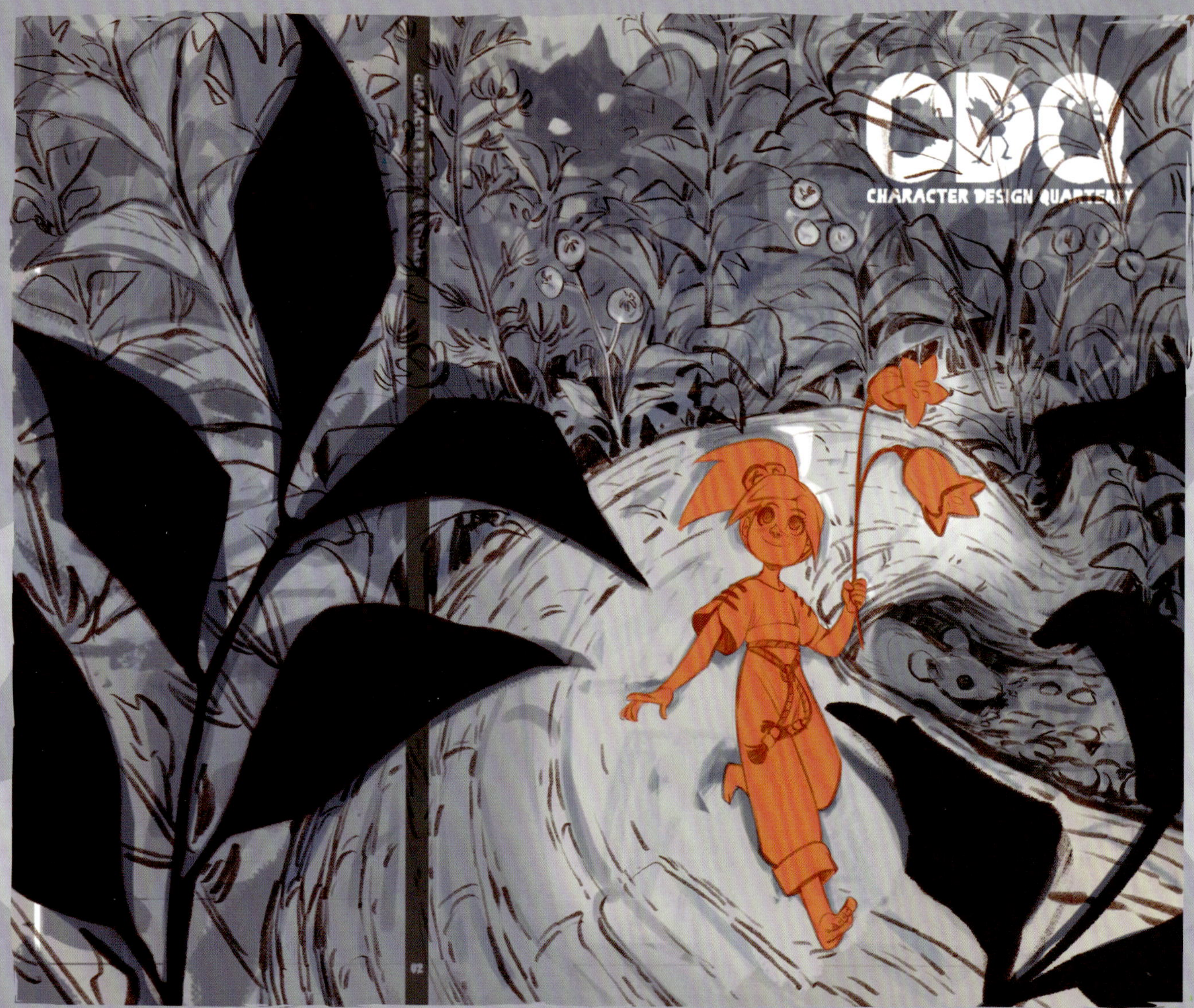

CLEANING UP THE SKETCH

With the composition approved, it's now time to clean up the sketch by drawing the line art. I use Procreate, but any painting program will work just as well.

To work on the sketch, it needs to be fairly light on the screen. I add a layer filled with white and lower the opacity a little so the sketch faintly shines through. If you make the sketch too visible when working on the line art you will probably end up with lines that only look good with the sketch showing. Having the sketch 10–20% visible prevents your brain from using the sketch to 'fill in the blanks'. I have found that this level of opacity is light enough for the brain to keep sketch and line art apart.

The brush I use is a favourite of mine: 'Charcoal Pencil – The General', from Lane Brown's Charcoal Master Pack. It has a nice texture and is responsive to pressure.

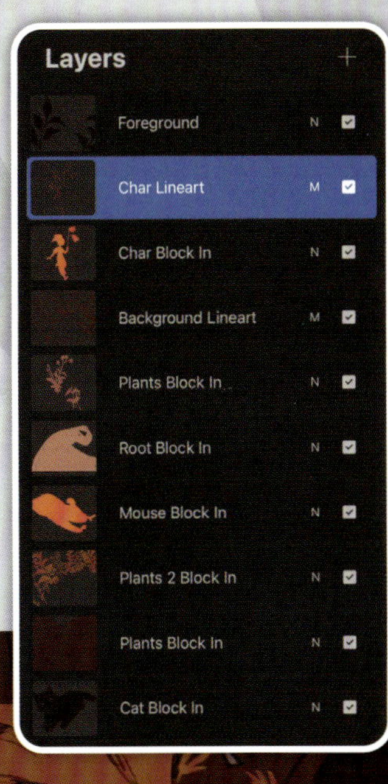

BETTER CONTROL THROUGH LAYERS

To make painting easier later in the process, I tend to block in all my major elements and shapes on separate layers. This gives me a hierarchy to show what is on top of what. The line-art layers go on top of the flat, blocked-in shapes. This ensures that when I start painting, I can retain clear edges where I want them from the start, by clipping my paint layers onto these shapes with clipping masks.

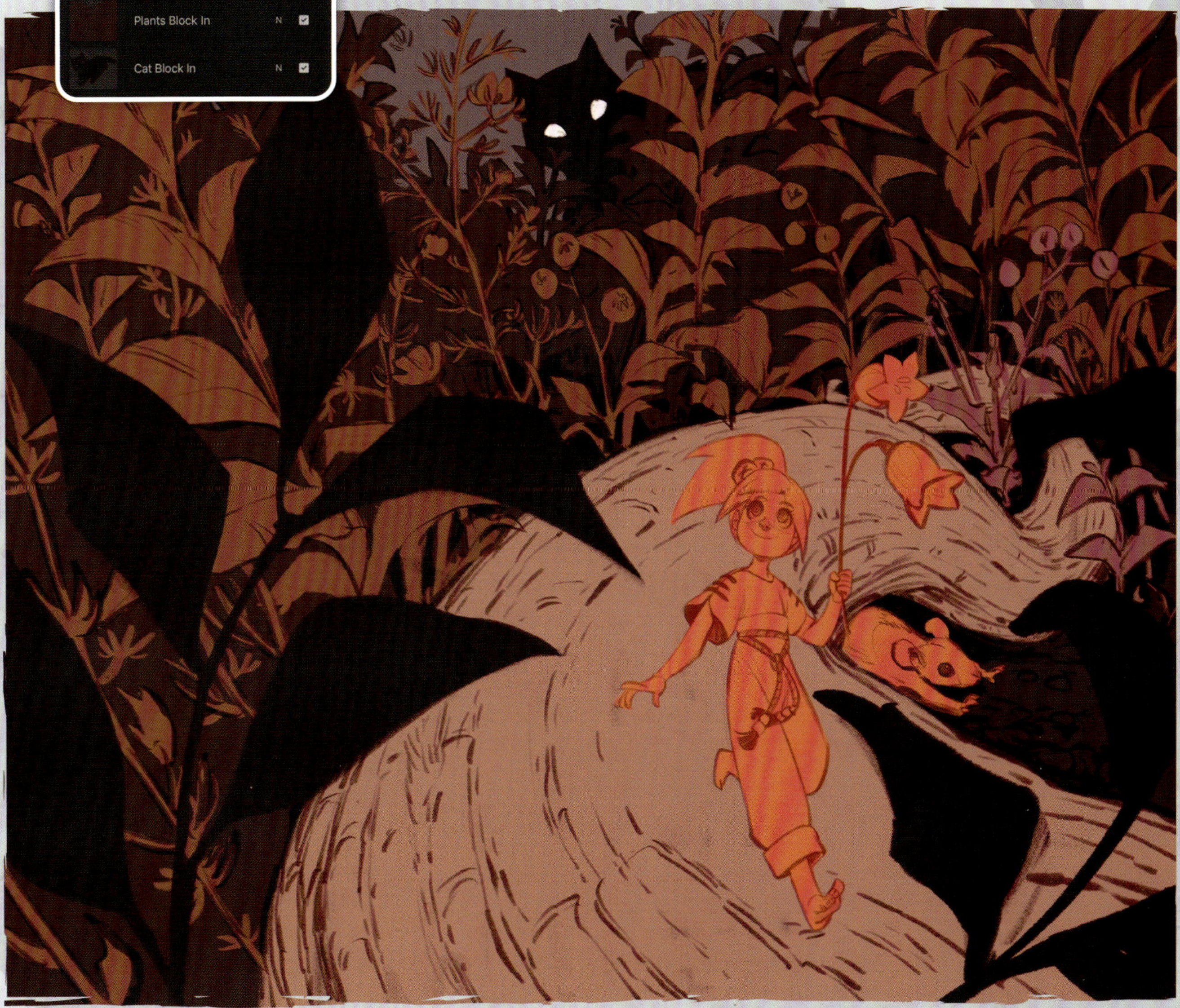

Refining your work on separate layers leads to less work further down the line

COLOUR DISTRIBUTION

Next, I start to add colour to the drawing. I consult my thumbnail with my planned values and then go to Pinterest to look for similar lighting scenarios. I imagine this scene to look a little murky, but not quite night, with illumination coming from the glowing berries.

I begin to distribute my background colours, working from back to front, and continuously consulting my references. The temperature of the leaves closest to the light berries should be warmer – with the plant shapes already on separate layers, I only have to 'colour' them in. I use clipping masks here – the flat shape will be the only areas that are coloured when you clip a layer onto it. The character's colours are predetermined, since I designed her a while ago.

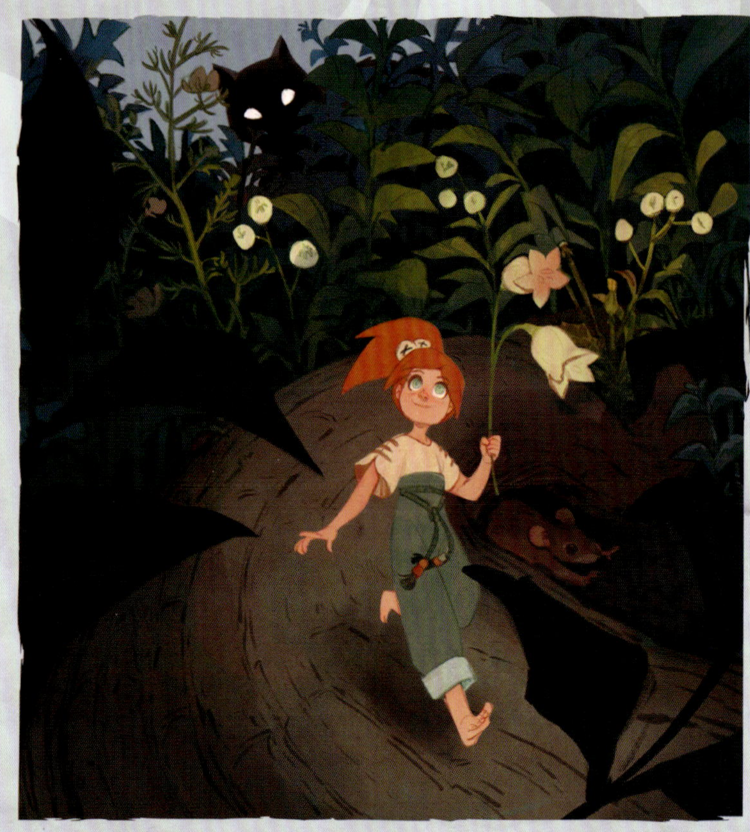

The initial stage of adding colour to the drawing

Keep your textures intact by using layer effects like Multiply when shading

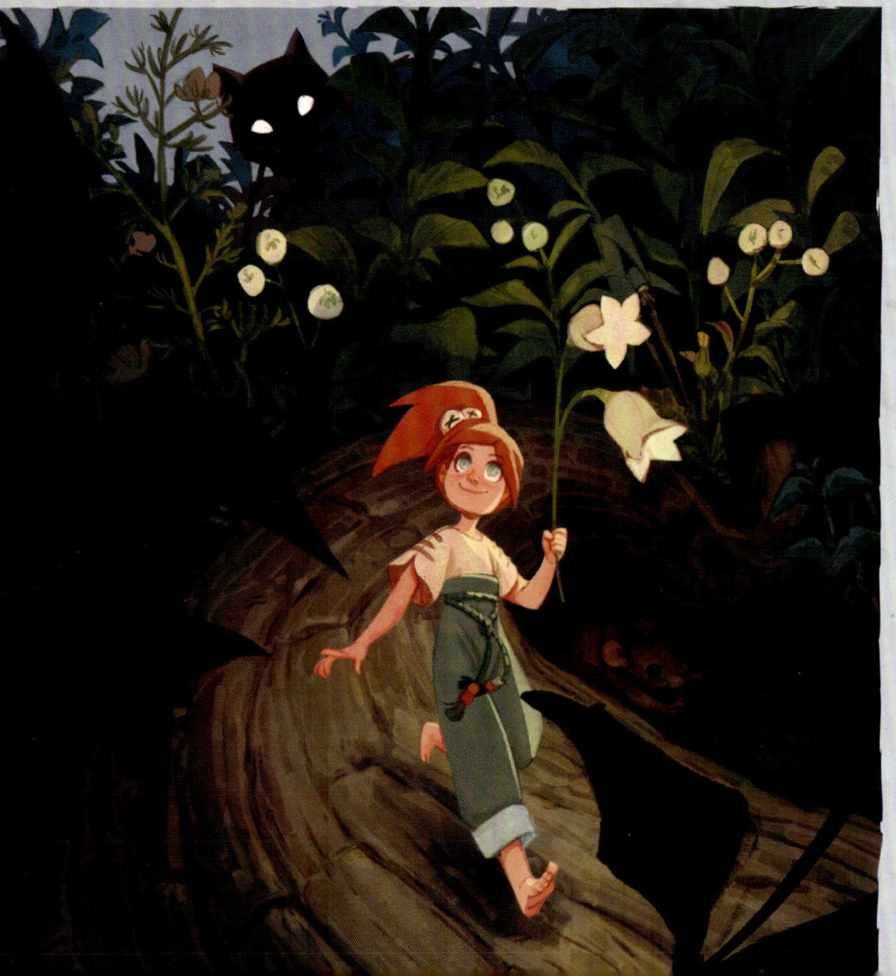

SHADING ALL THE ELEMENTS

My colours have a grainy texture to them, thanks to the watercolour brushes by Max Ulichney that I use – I want to keep this effect mostly intact as I add shading. I add shadows to my character and the background by painting them onto layers set to Multiply, clipped onto my block-in layers from earlier. I usually pick the shadow colours directly from the object I'm shading and the Multiply layer then ensures I am painting with a darker version. If the shade looks too dark, I either adjust the shadow colour or reduce the layer's opacity.

I use a soft yellow colour to paint light onto new layers as well. These layers are set to Normal, with the opacity slightly reduced, and clipped to the block-in layers. With this done, all that's left is to add extra little details and glowing effects, and the cover artwork is finished.

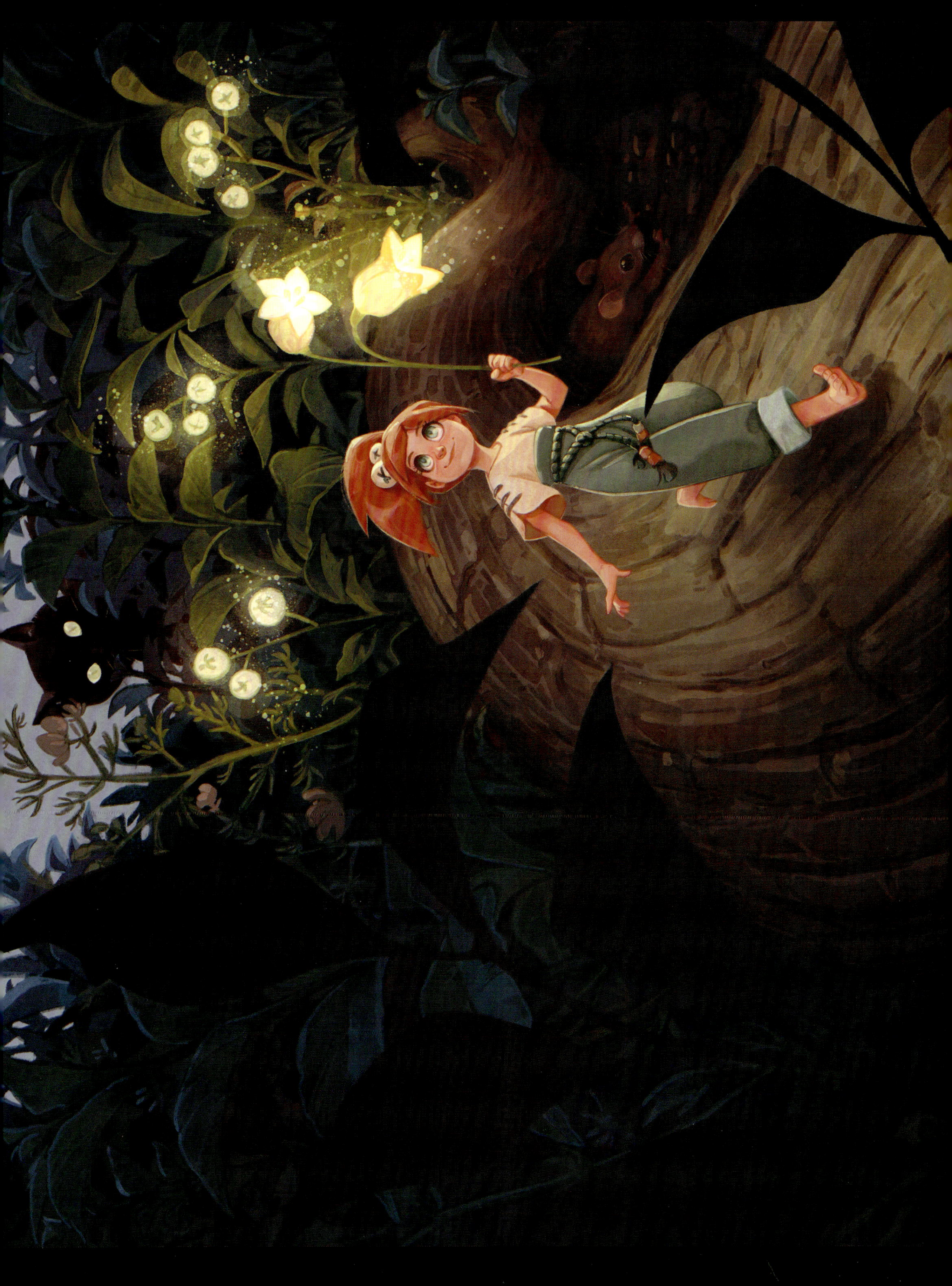

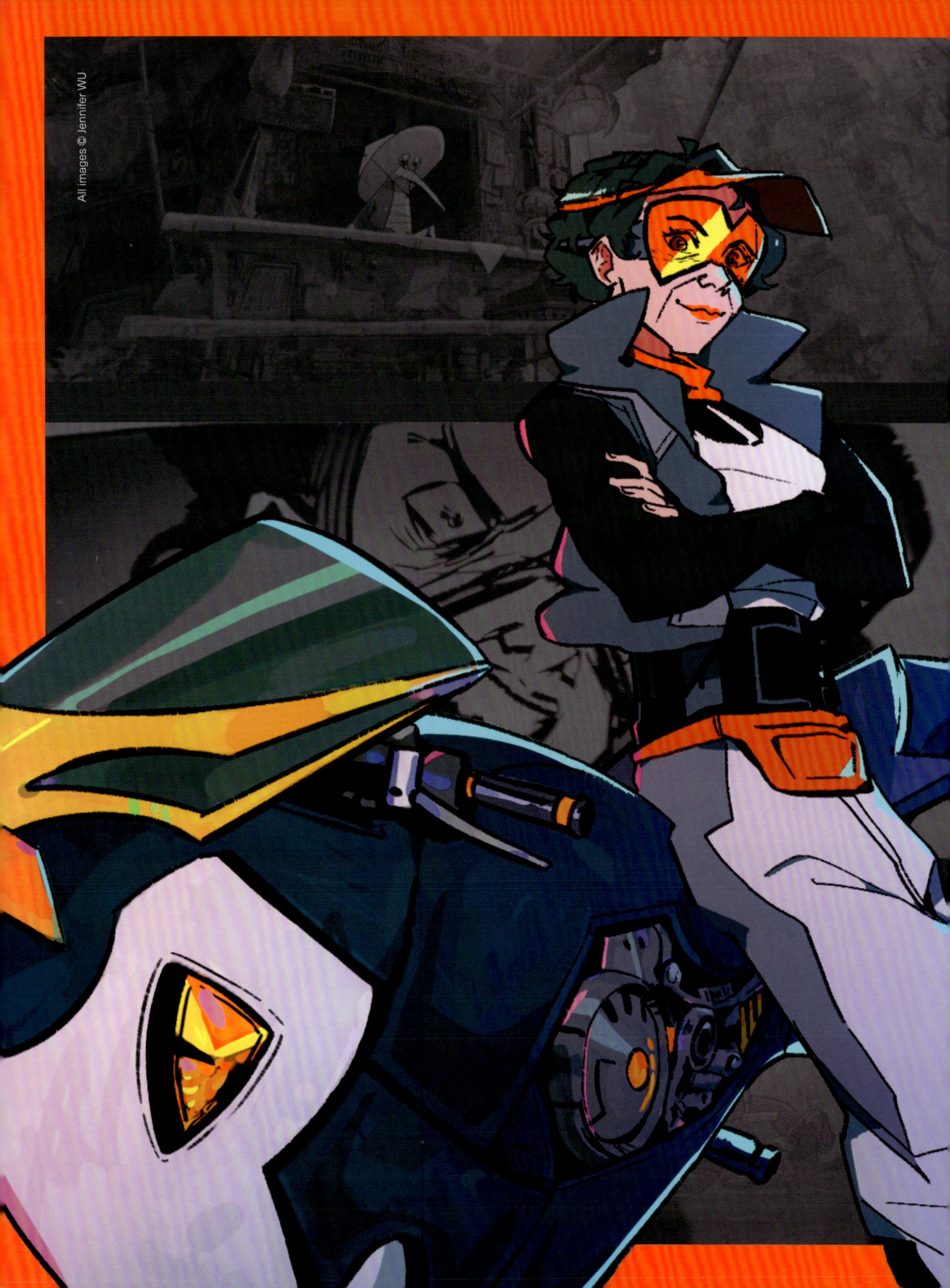

JENNIFER WU

MISSION POPO

Jennifer Wu shows us how her grandmother and macaroni penguins served as unlikely inspiration for her short-film, *Mission Popo*.

SCAN THE QR CODE TO WATCH MISSION POPO NOW!

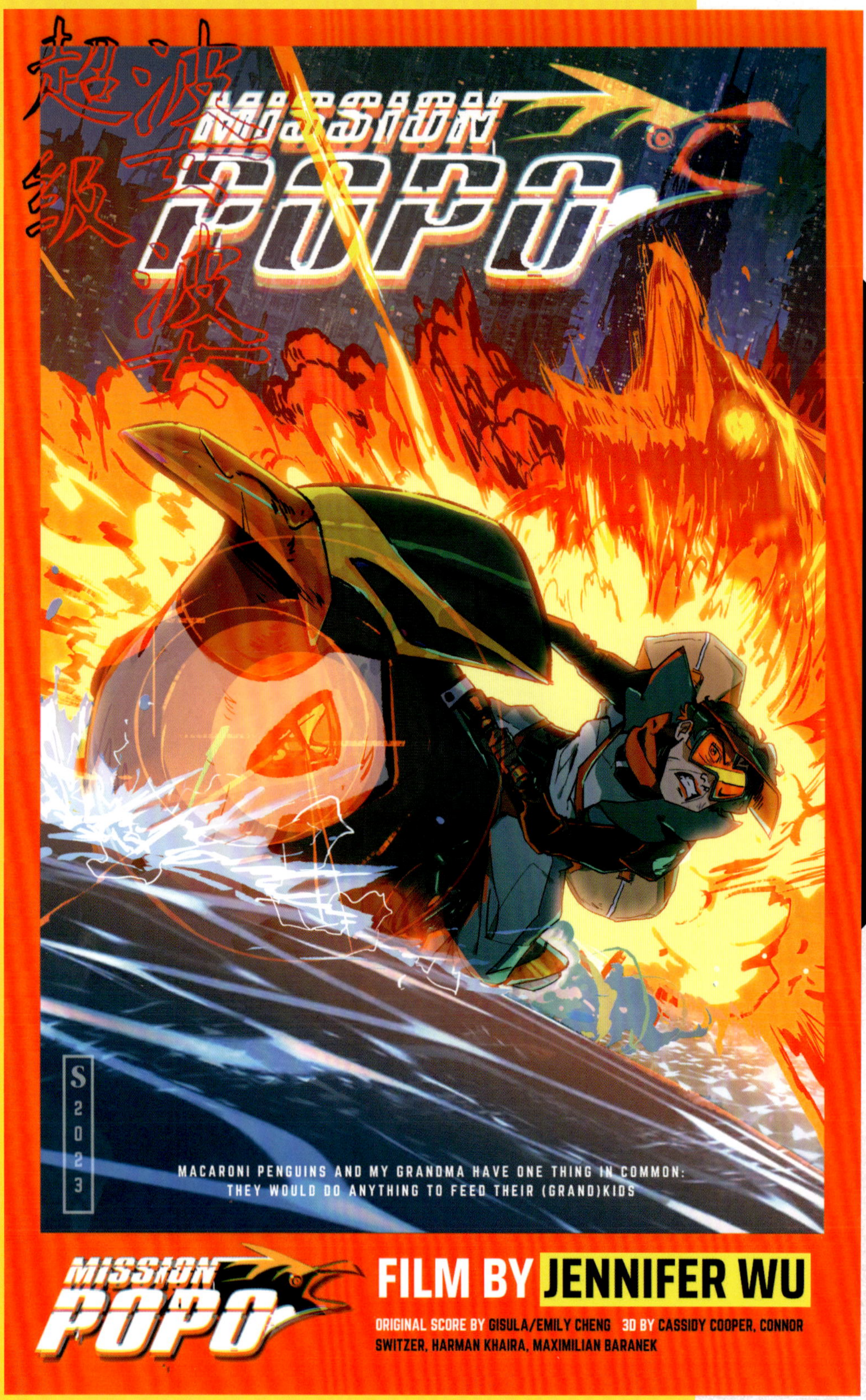

STARTING FROM SCRATCH

A memorable film needs great characters, with unique designs, and meaningful development throughout the story. The process of creating characters for your own animation can be daunting, especially when it comes to balancing appeal and practicality. In the following steps, I'll break down what went into creating the characters in my thesis film, *Mission Popo*. From not knowing what to even make my film about, to creating the final model sheets, this is a helpful guide if you find yourself struggling to make a unique story and character on a tight deadline.

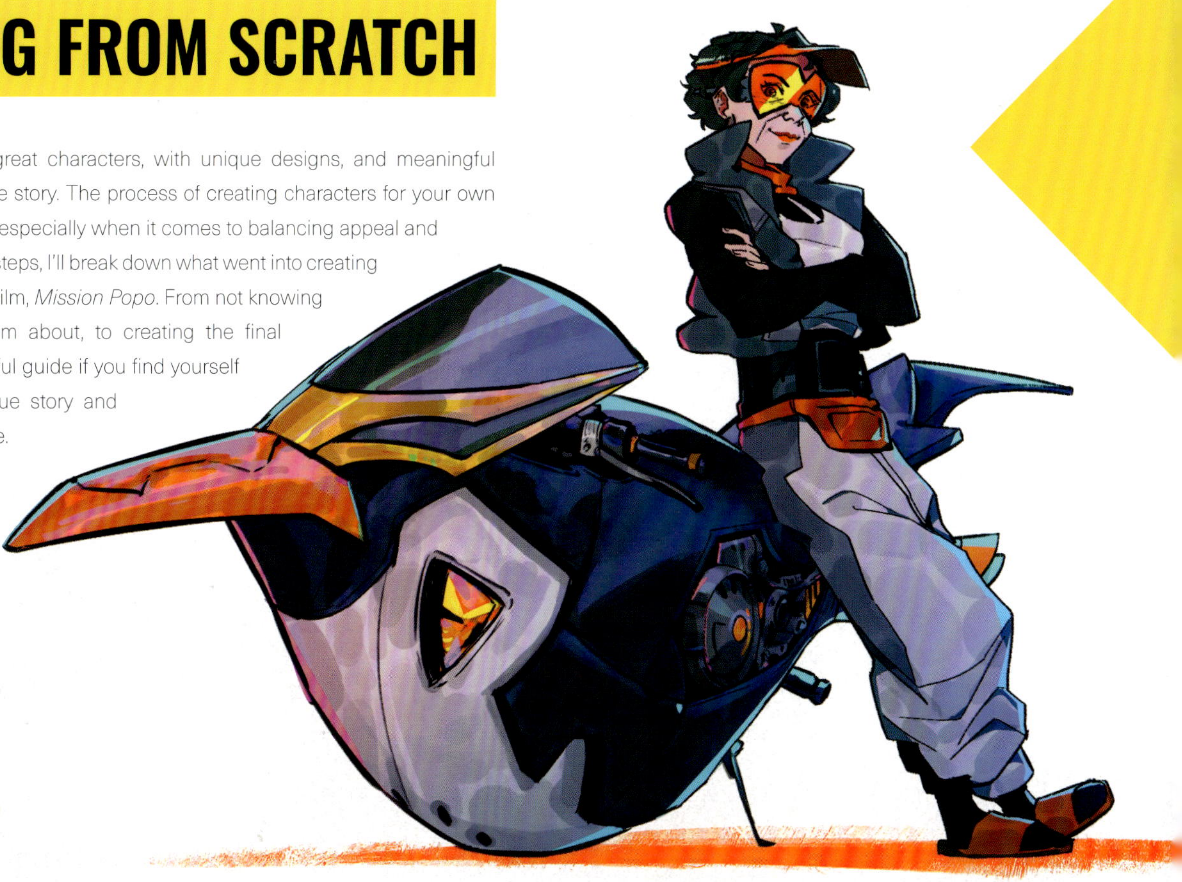

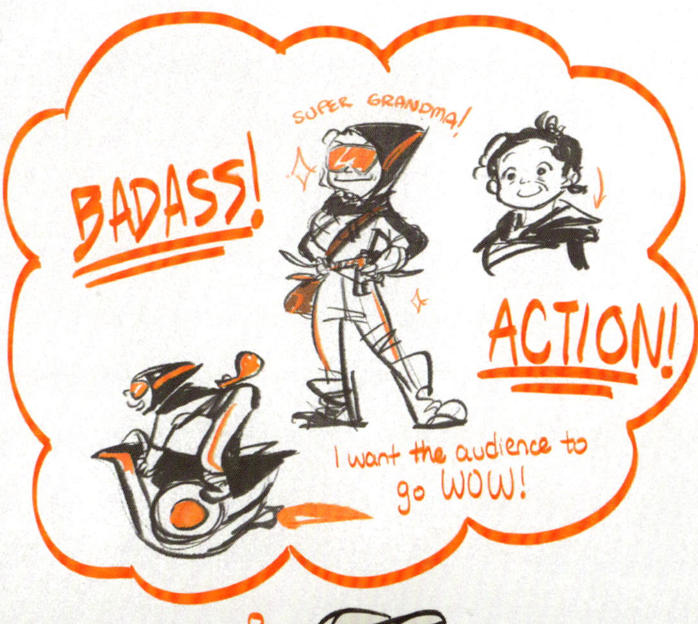

FINDING THE STORY

If you could make a film about anything, what would you choose? If there's no particular story you want to tell, it helps to narrow down what genre you want to work in, and what you want the audience to feel at the end of your film. For *Mission Popo*, I decide on action because all I really want is to make a badass film. Your reason for making a film or character doesn't have to be complex, it just has to be clear to you so it can guide your decision making.

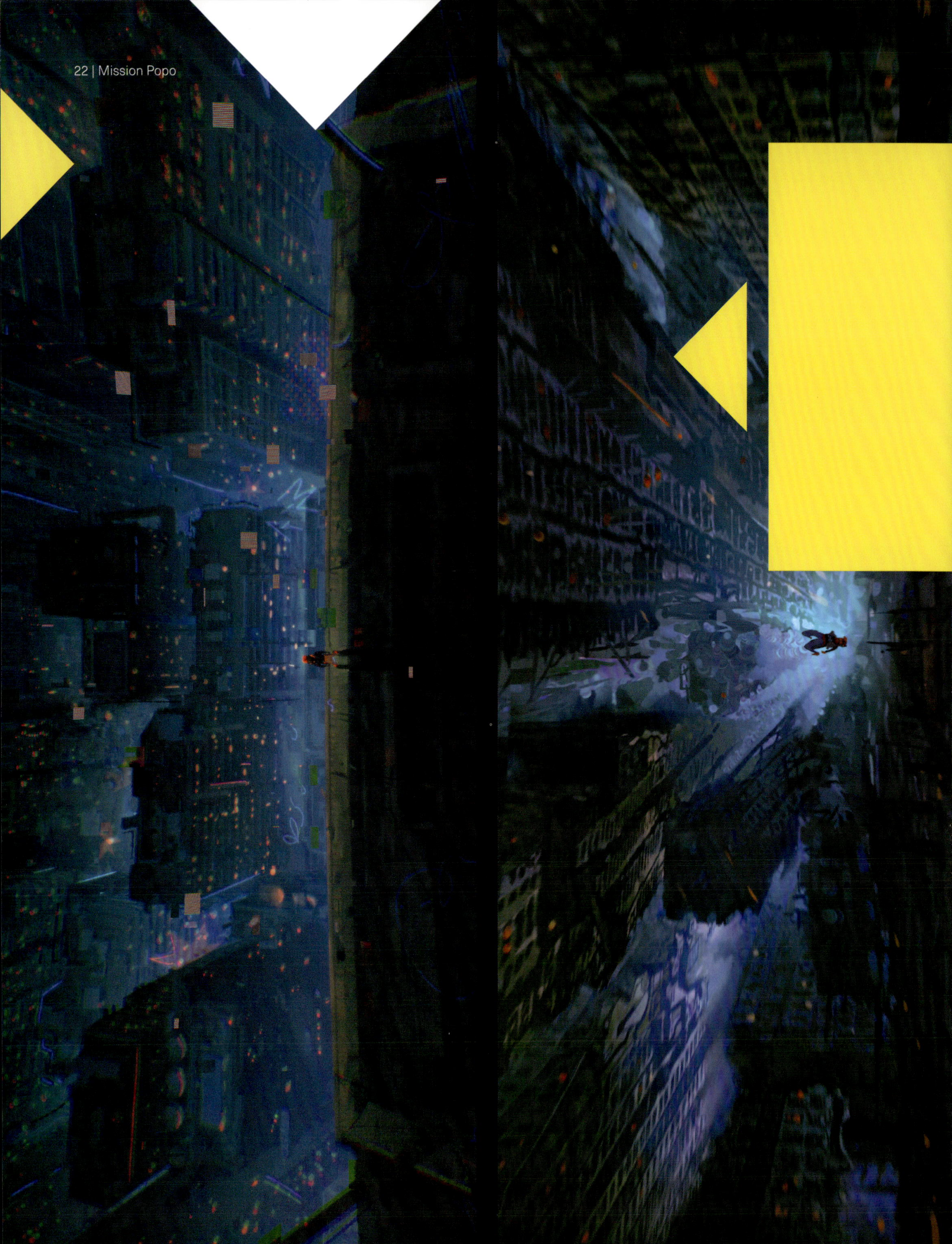

INSPIRED BY NATURE

If you're on a time crunch but want to make a unique world from scratch, then nature is a great place to look for inspiration – everything is already intricately designed to work together in perfect balance. For me, it was the epic journeys of macaroni penguins that caught my attention while I was watching nature documentaries, because the way they jumped off the cliff edge reminded me of the 'leap of faith' scene from *Spider-Man: Into the Spider-Verse*. While others may see a funny looking penguin, I see one of the most awesome and dedicated parents in the natural world.

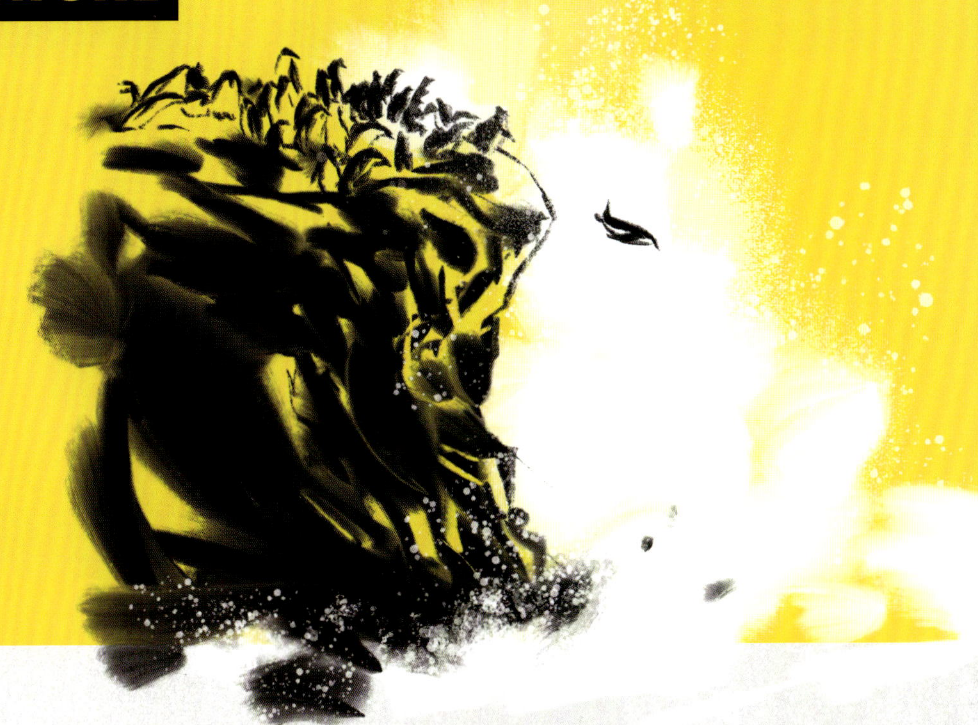

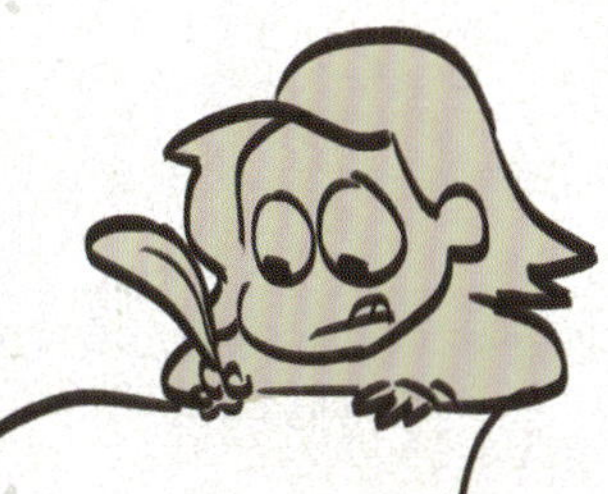

MEET YOUR CHARACTER

It's time to find out who your character is. The most important questions to keep in mind are: what is their goal, their motivation, and their conflict? Great stories with great characters make these answers clear and simple. I decide to make this film about my grandma, because she's just as badass as macaroni penguins, and they share the same goals and motivations.

REAMS OF RESEARCH

Now for the most fun and time-consuming part of the process: research. There are three categories of research I collect: story, literal, and stylistic. Story research is the journey macaroni penguins go through; their habitats, quirks, and hunting grounds. I want my film to be a sci-fi retelling of the trip macaroni penguin parents make, so I spend lots of time watching nature documentaries. For literal research, I look at pictures of cyberpunk streetwear, my grandma, and anything else that I will be drawing. Stylistic research involves consuming art that contains cinematography, line quality, or styles that I like and want to feature in the film. By the end of this process, I have hundreds of images to use for reference.

STORY

- live at top of rocky cliffs
  └> sharp claws to help them climb up
- red nictitating membrane eyes to help see underwater
- territorial & sassy
- mate for life
- torpedo body shape
- predators : leopard seals, giant petrels
- prey : krill
- parents take turns hunting

LITERAL

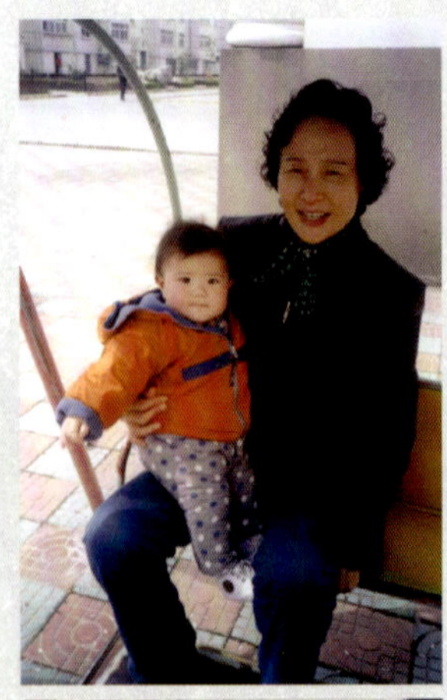

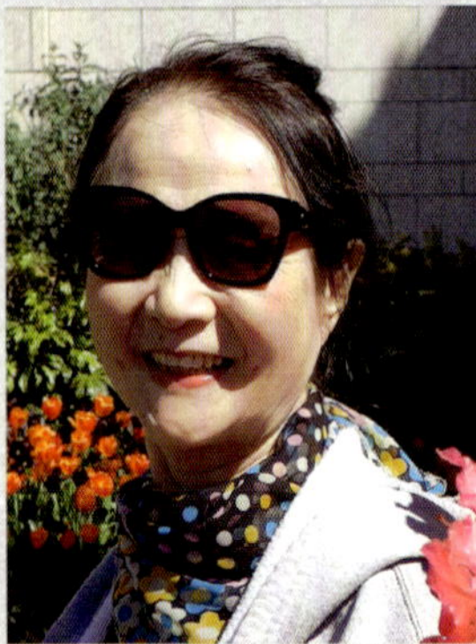

- curly or straight hair?
- cares a lot about looking young (make-up)
- sunglasses?
- scarf

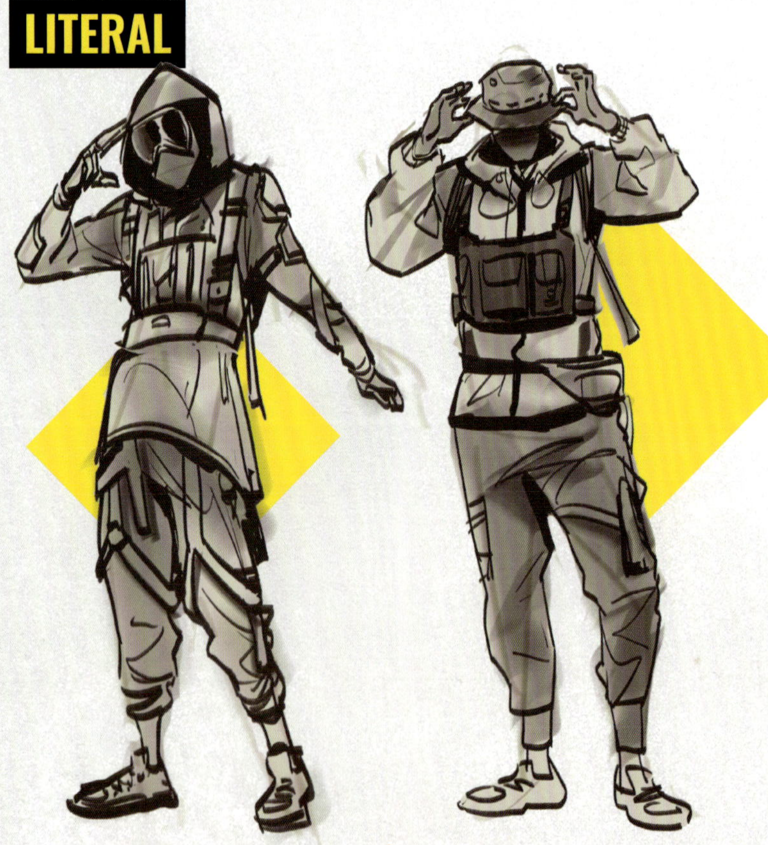

THINGS I LIKE:
- belts + straps
- goggles

- fanny pack
- gloves
- low pants (mimics penguins)
- baggy clothing

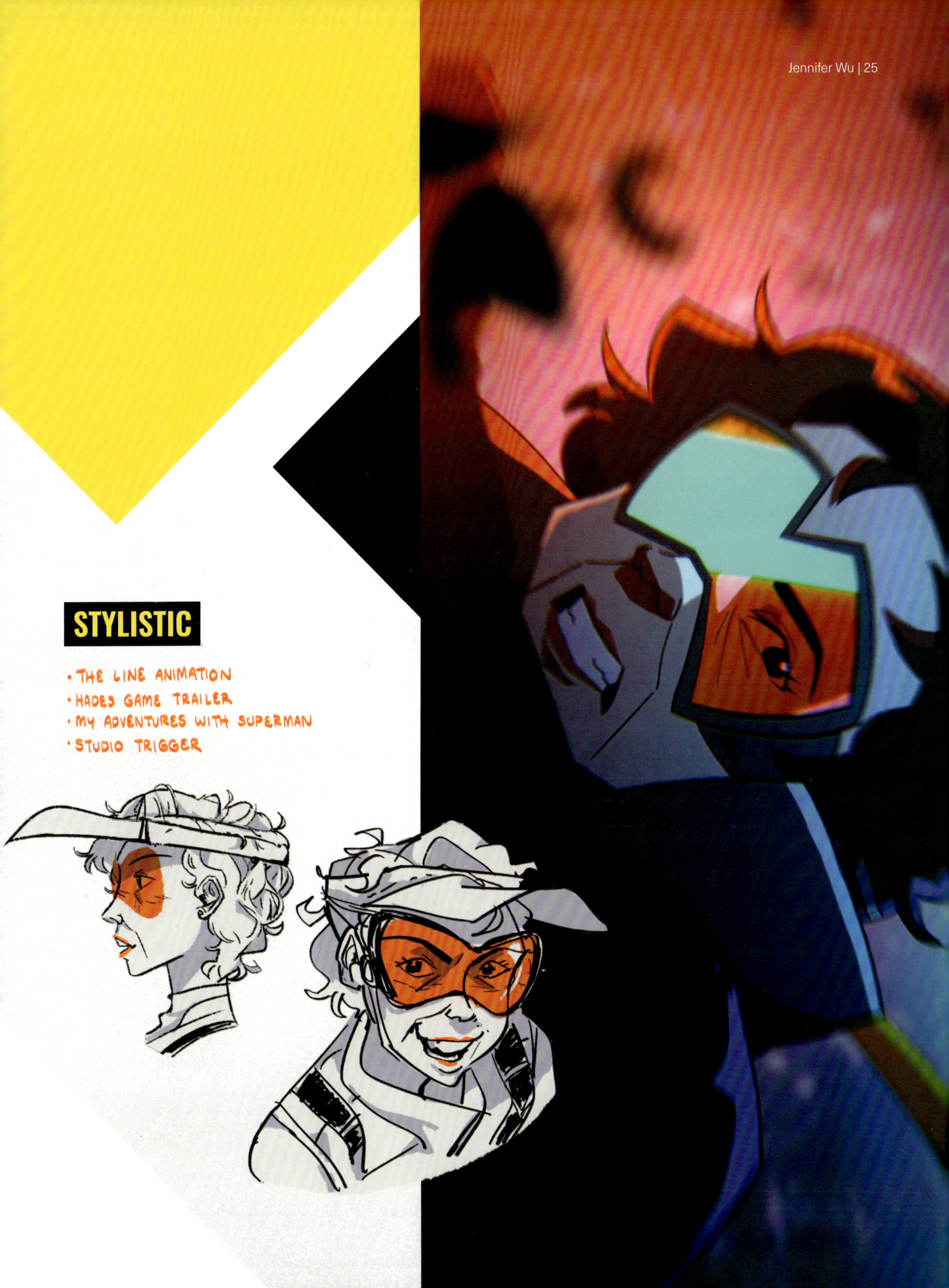

STYLISTIC

- THE LINE ANIMATION
- HADES GAME TRAILER
- MY ADVENTURES WITH SUPERMAN
- STUDIO TRIGGER

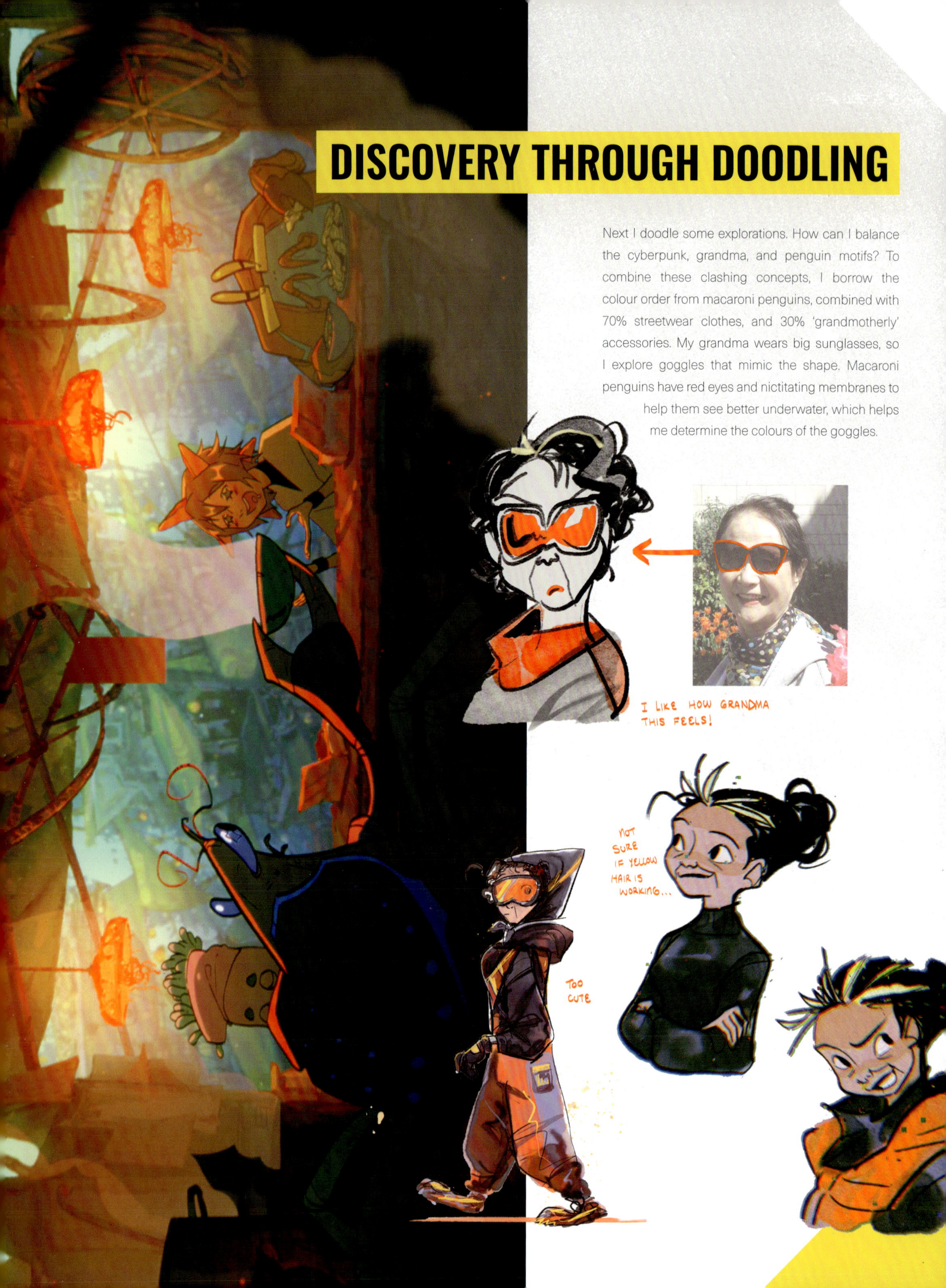

DISCOVERY THROUGH DOODLING

Next I doodle some explorations. How can I balance the cyberpunk, grandma, and penguin motifs? To combine these clashing concepts, I borrow the colour order from macaroni penguins, combined with 70% streetwear clothes, and 30% 'grandmotherly' accessories. My grandma wears big sunglasses, so I explore goggles that mimic the shape. Macaroni penguins have red eyes and nictitating membranes to help them see better underwater, which helps me determine the colours of the goggles.

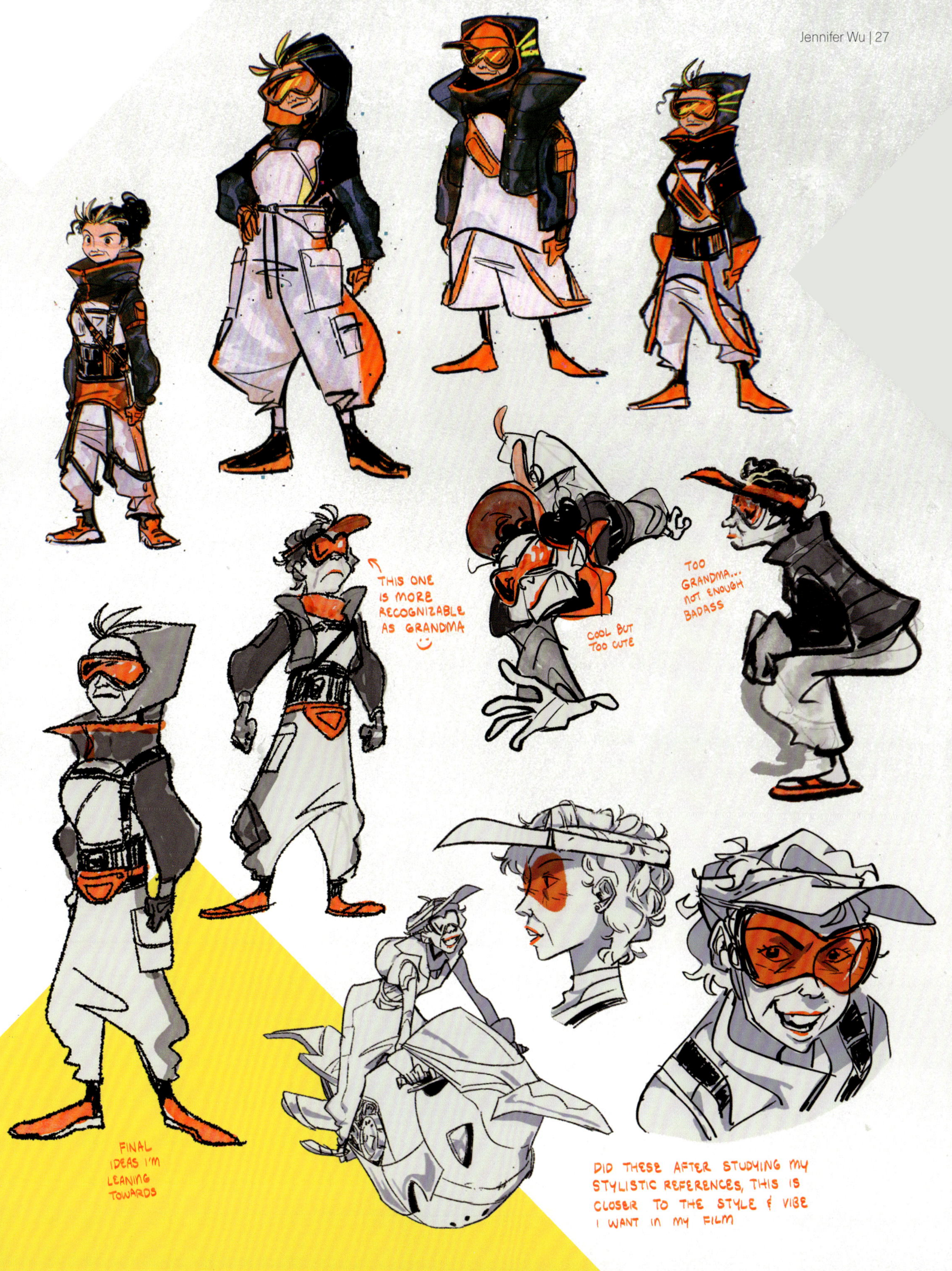
THIS ONE
IS MORE
RECOGNIZABLE
AS GRANDMA
COOL BUT
TOO CUTE
TOO
GRANDMA...
NOT ENOUGH
BADASS
FINAL
IDEAS I'M
LEANING
TOWARDS
DID THESE AFTER STUDYING MY
STYLISTIC REFERENCES, THIS IS
CLOSER TO THE STYLE & VIBE
I WANT IN MY FILM

STORYBOARD TESTS

Now I have a rough idea of what I want my character to look like, I put it to the test in the storyboard stage. I practise drawing simplified versions of each character to preview if the design functions and if it's feasible to draw a million times. If not, I'll need to change and simplify it.

I consider whether I can use any other elements of the character to enhance the story, like the reflection in the goggles, or the hat flying off. I check the silhouette is clear and distinguishable and make sure clothing isn't hindering the character's movement.

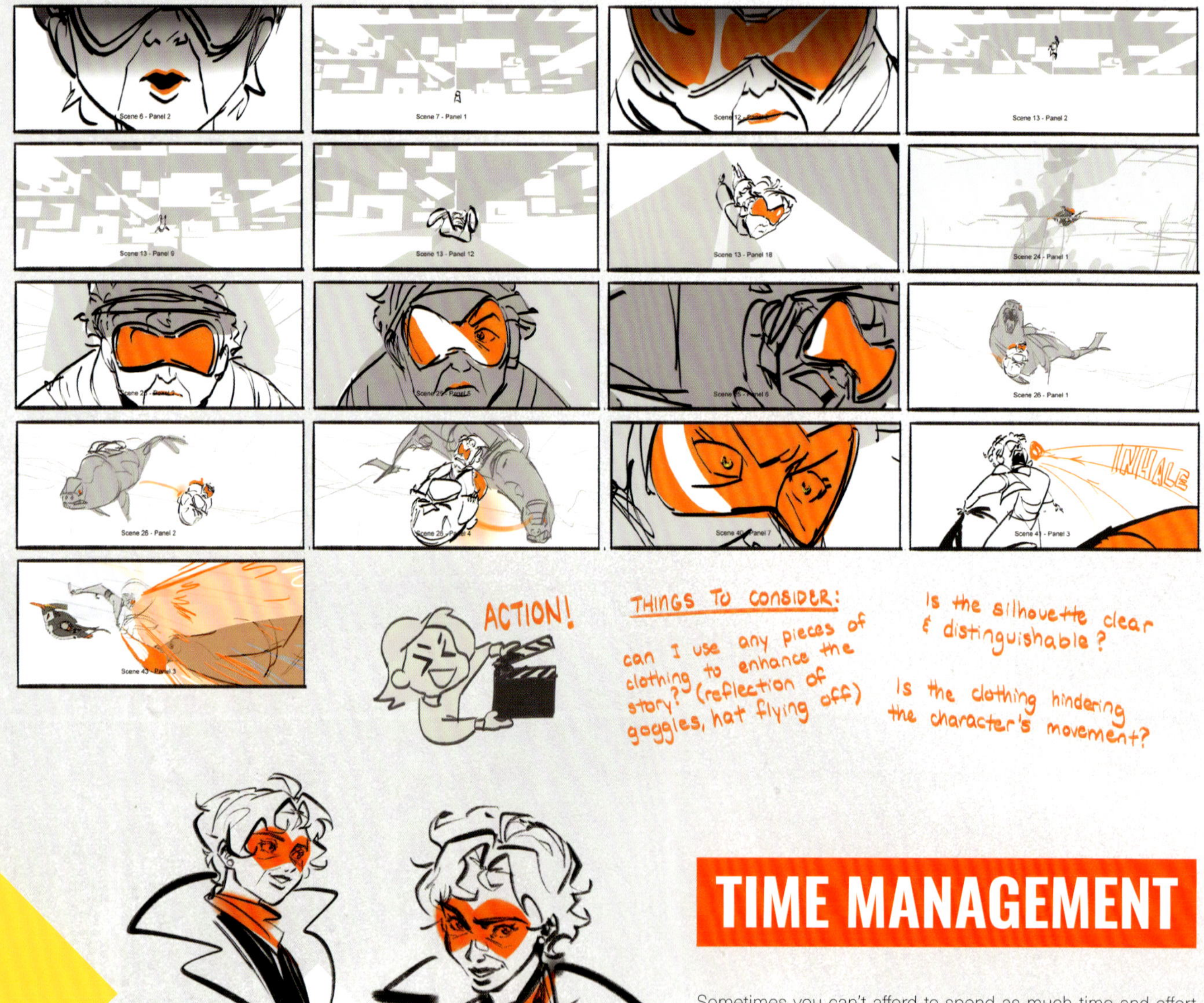

TIME MANAGEMENT

Sometimes you can't afford to spend as much time and effort on every character, and that's okay, because not all characters have the same screen time. Appealing characters can come from anywhere, like doodling krill in your sketchbook for a couple of hours, for instance. But no matter how rushed you are to design a character, always keep in mind your references, think about the function of your designs, and make sure you will be comfortable drawing them over and over again.

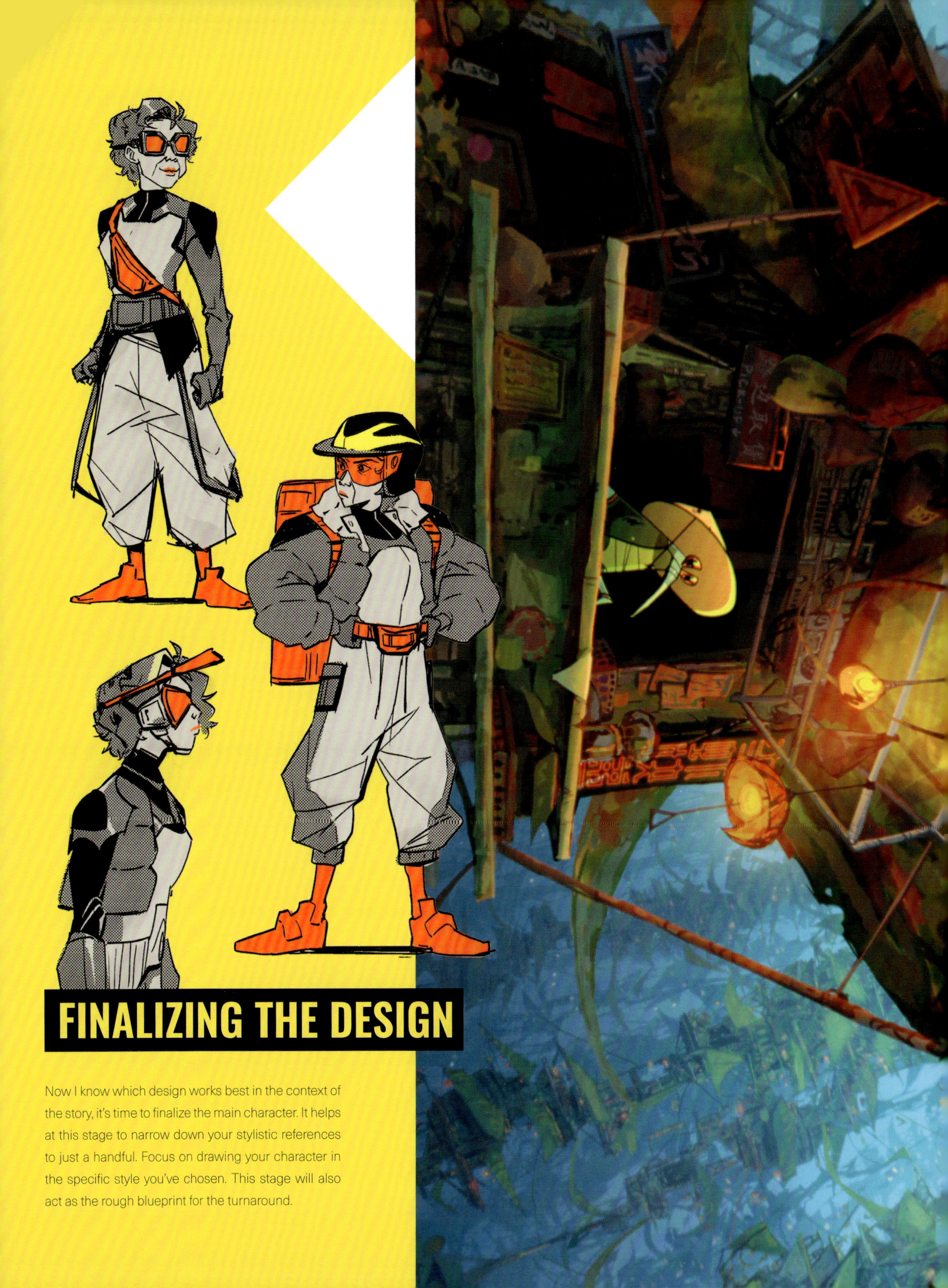

FINALIZING THE DESIGN

Now I know which design works best in the context of the story, it's time to finalize the main character. It helps at this stage to narrow down your stylistic references to just a handful. Focus on drawing your character in the specific style you've chosen. This stage will also act as the rough blueprint for the turnaround.

PICKING THE PERFECT POSE

It's important to compare your final designs with the poses that are most prominent in your film. My character is sitting on her bike for eighty percent of the short, so I focus on this pose and her silhouette. Having a cool outfit is nice, but what's the point if the silhouette isn't clear for most of the film? Don't be afraid to ask your friends for help if you are struggling to decide which version of your design works best.

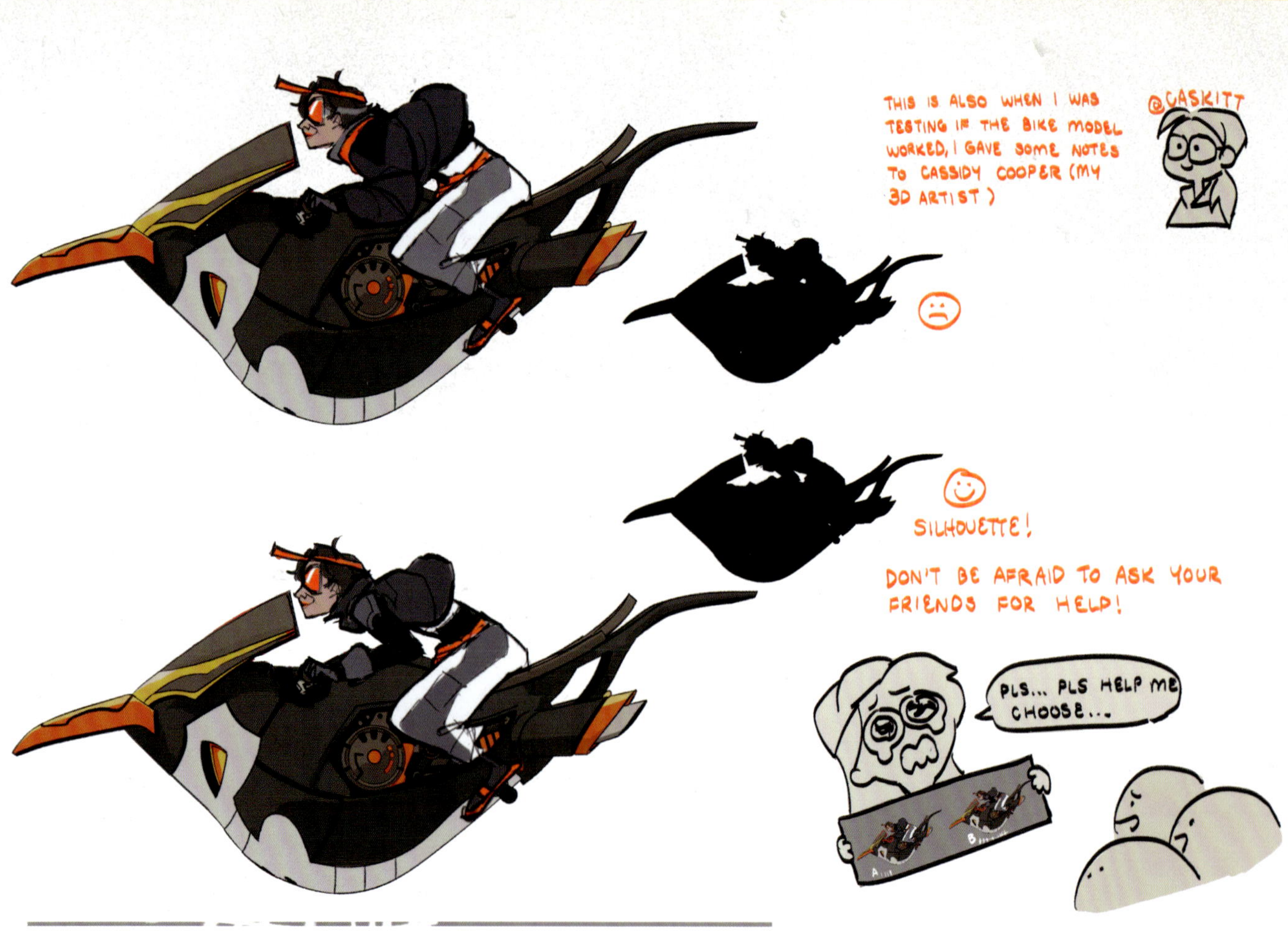

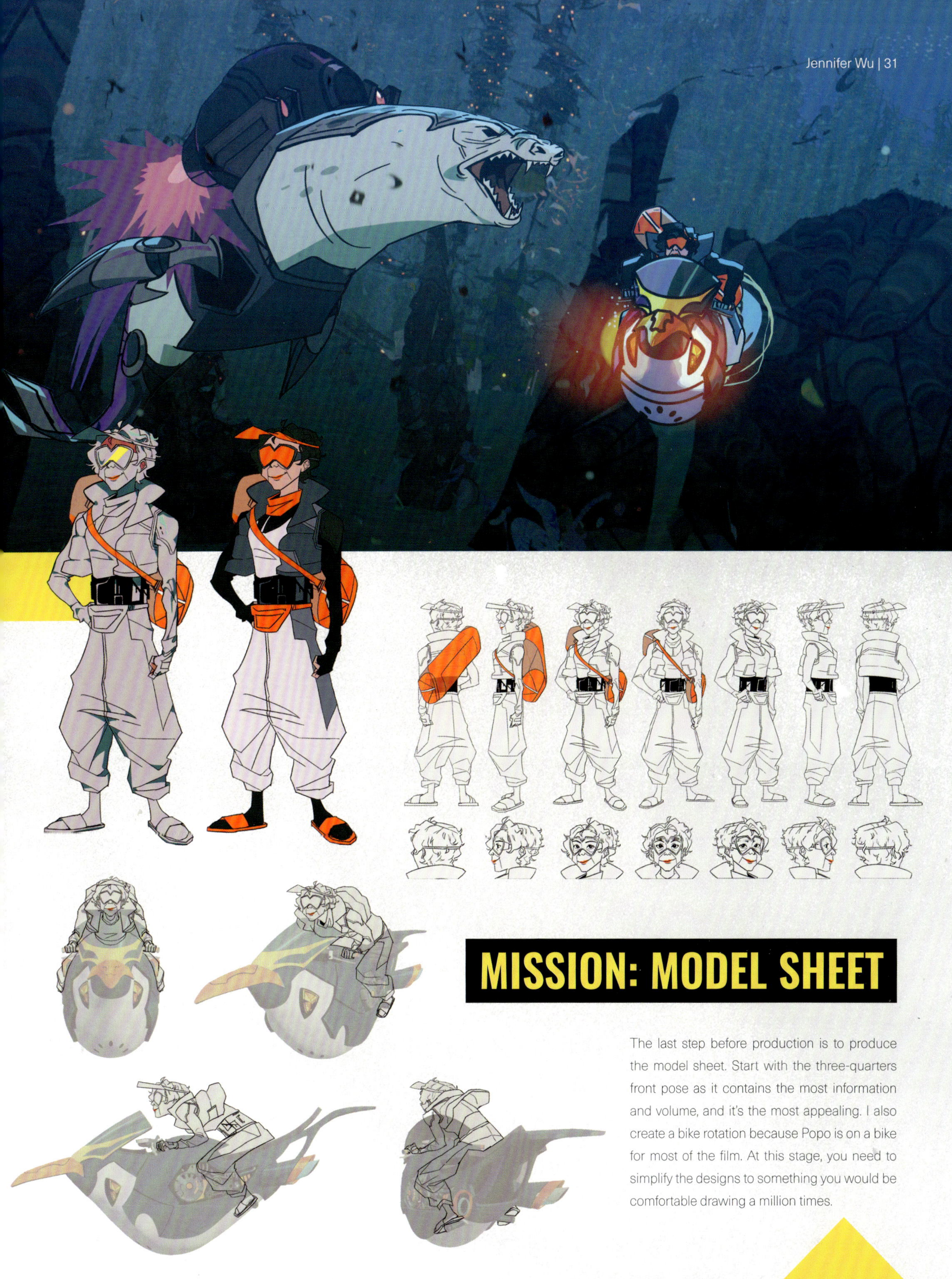

MISSION: MODEL SHEET

The last step before production is to produce the model sheet. Start with the three-quarters front pose as it contains the most information and volume, and it's the most appealing. I also create a bike rotation because Popo is on a bike for most of the film. At this stage, you need to simplify the designs to something you would be comfortable drawing a million times.

the magic of MerMay

We speak to the hosts of the social-media sensation #MerMay

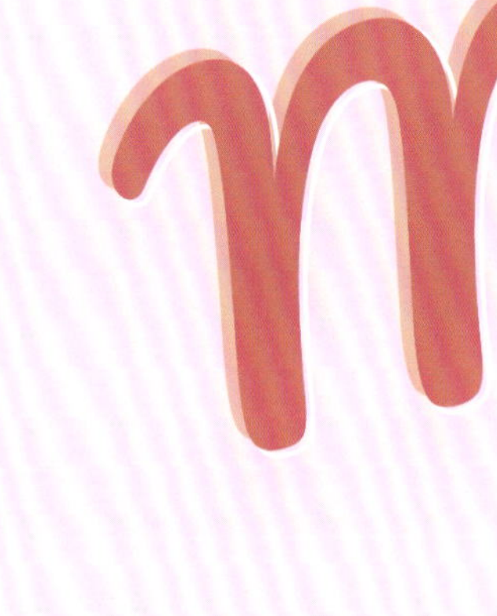

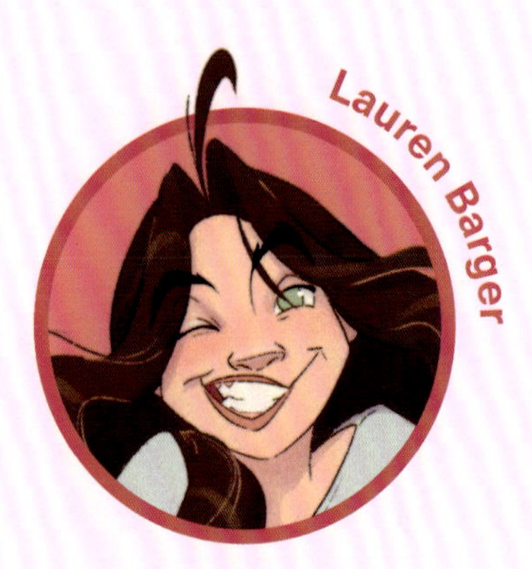

Lauren Barger

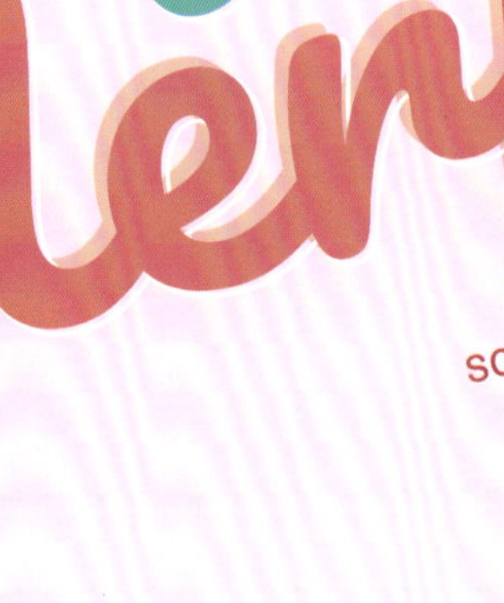

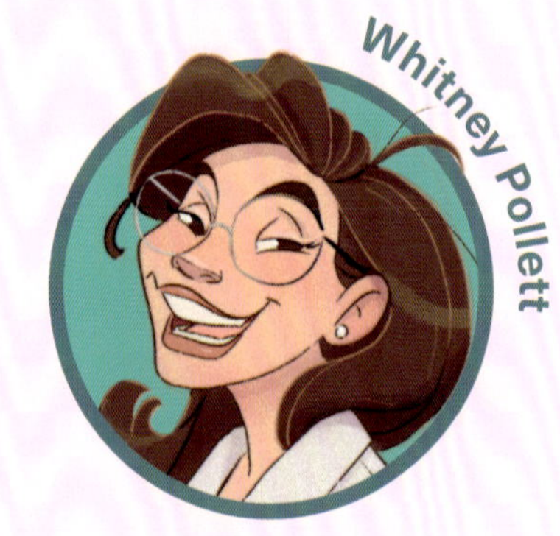

Whitney Pollett

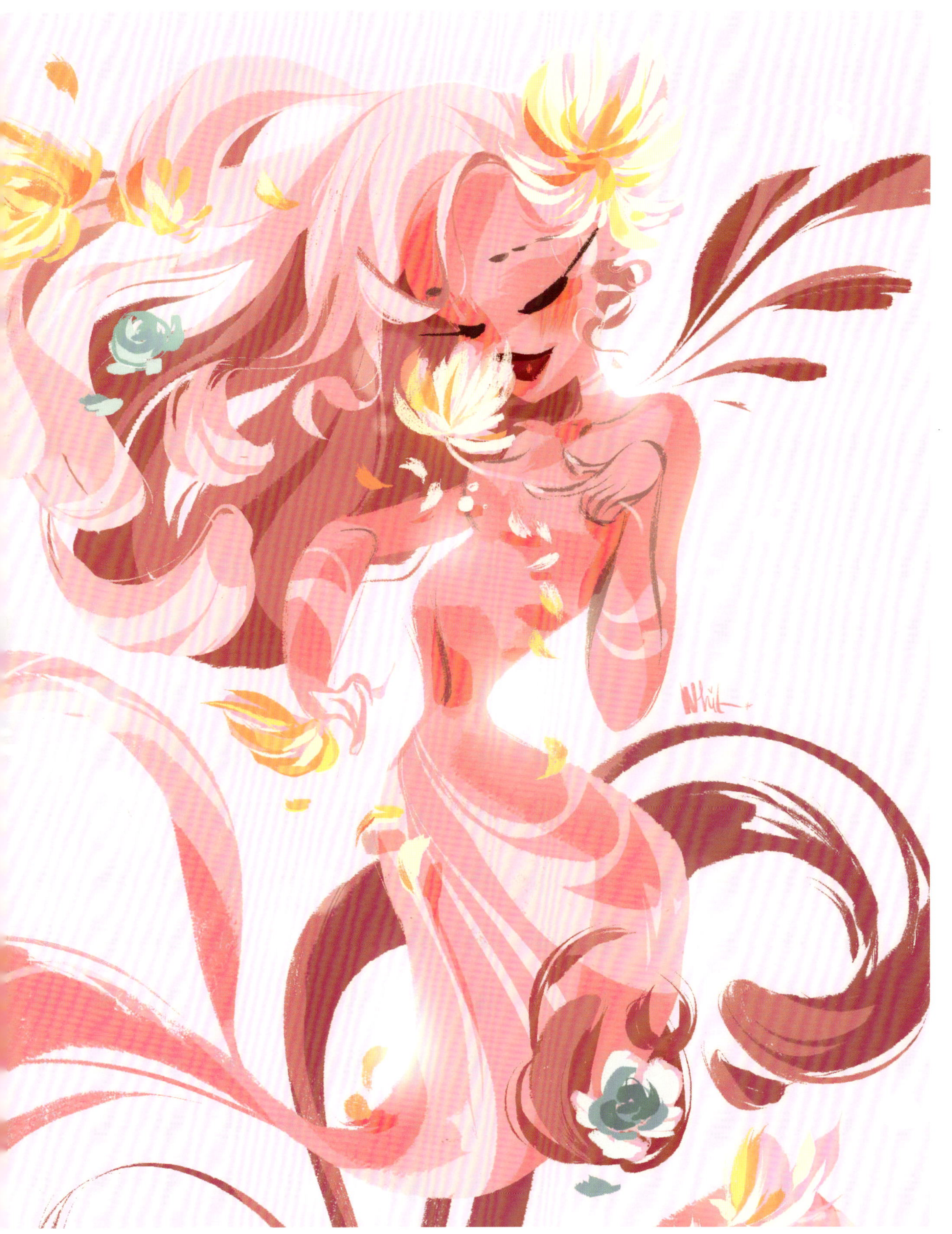

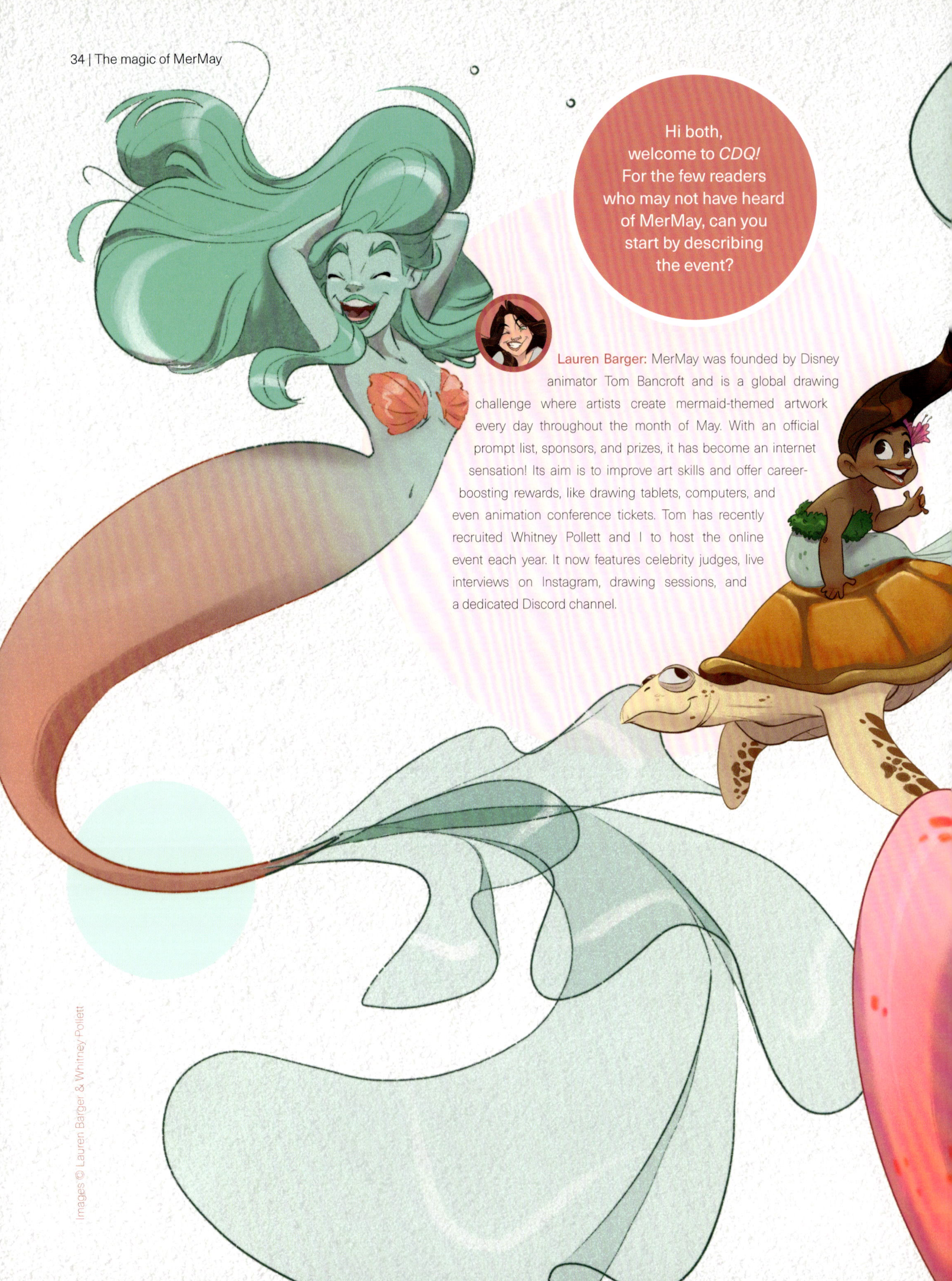

Lauren Barger: MerMay was founded by Disney animator Tom Bancroft and is a global drawing challenge where artists create mermaid-themed artwork every day throughout the month of May. With an official prompt list, sponsors, and prizes, it has become an internet sensation! Its aim is to improve art skills and offer career-boosting rewards, like drawing tablets, computers, and even animation conference tickets. Tom has recently recruited Whitney Pollett and I to host the online event each year. It now features celebrity judges, live interviews on Instagram, drawing sessions, and a dedicated Discord channel.

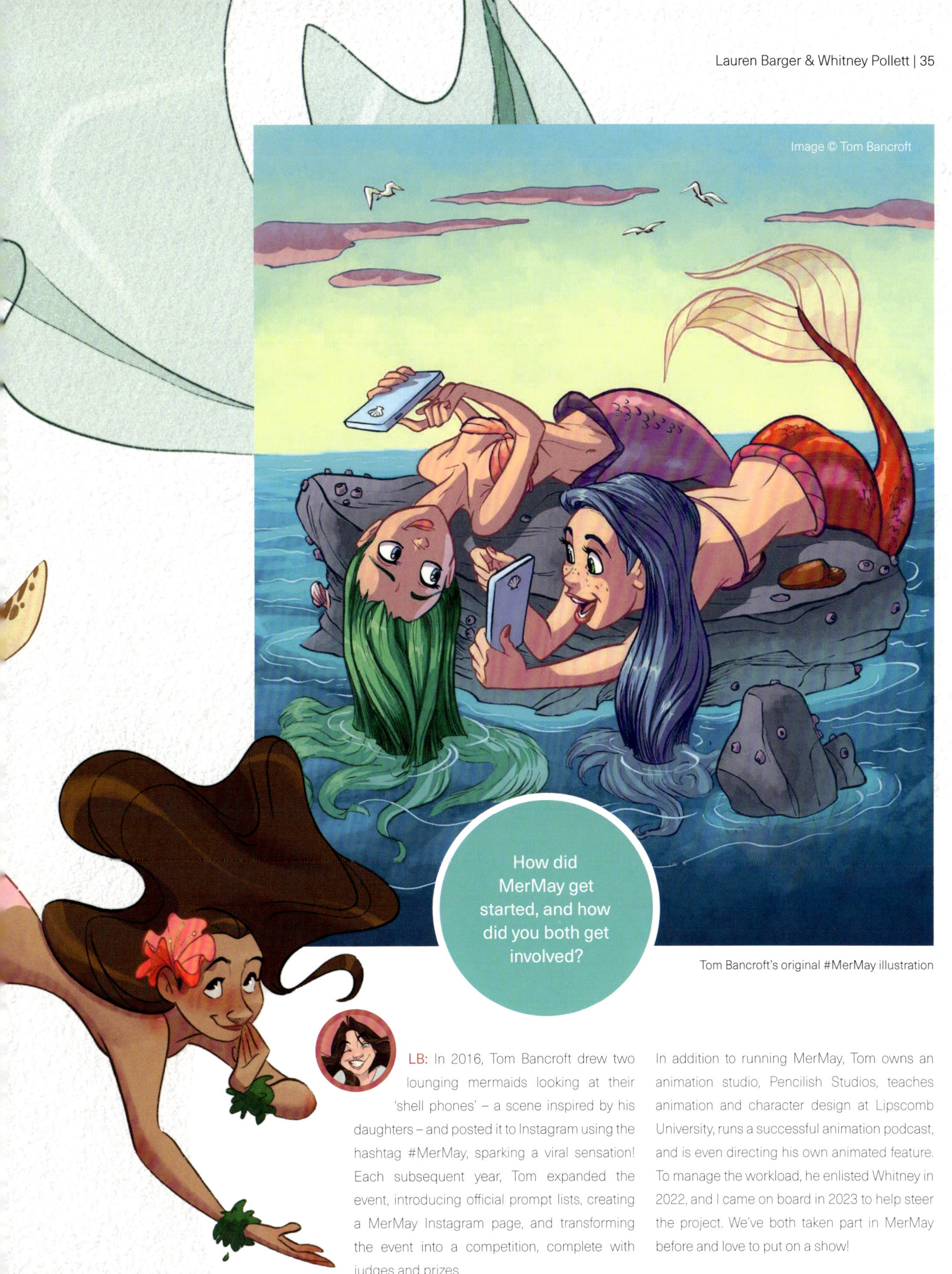

Tom Bancroft's original #MerMay illustration

LB: In 2016, Tom Bancroft drew two lounging mermaids looking at their 'shell phones' – a scene inspired by his daughters – and posted it to Instagram using the hashtag #MerMay, sparking a viral sensation! Each subsequent year, Tom expanded the event, introducing official prompt lists, creating a MerMay Instagram page, and transforming the event into a competition, complete with judges and prizes.

In addition to running MerMay, Tom owns an animation studio, Pencilish Studios, teaches animation and character design at Lipscomb University, runs a successful animation podcast, and is even directing his own animated feature. To manage the workload, he enlisted Whitney in 2022, and I came on board in 2023 to help steer the project. We've both taken part in MerMay before and love to put on a show!

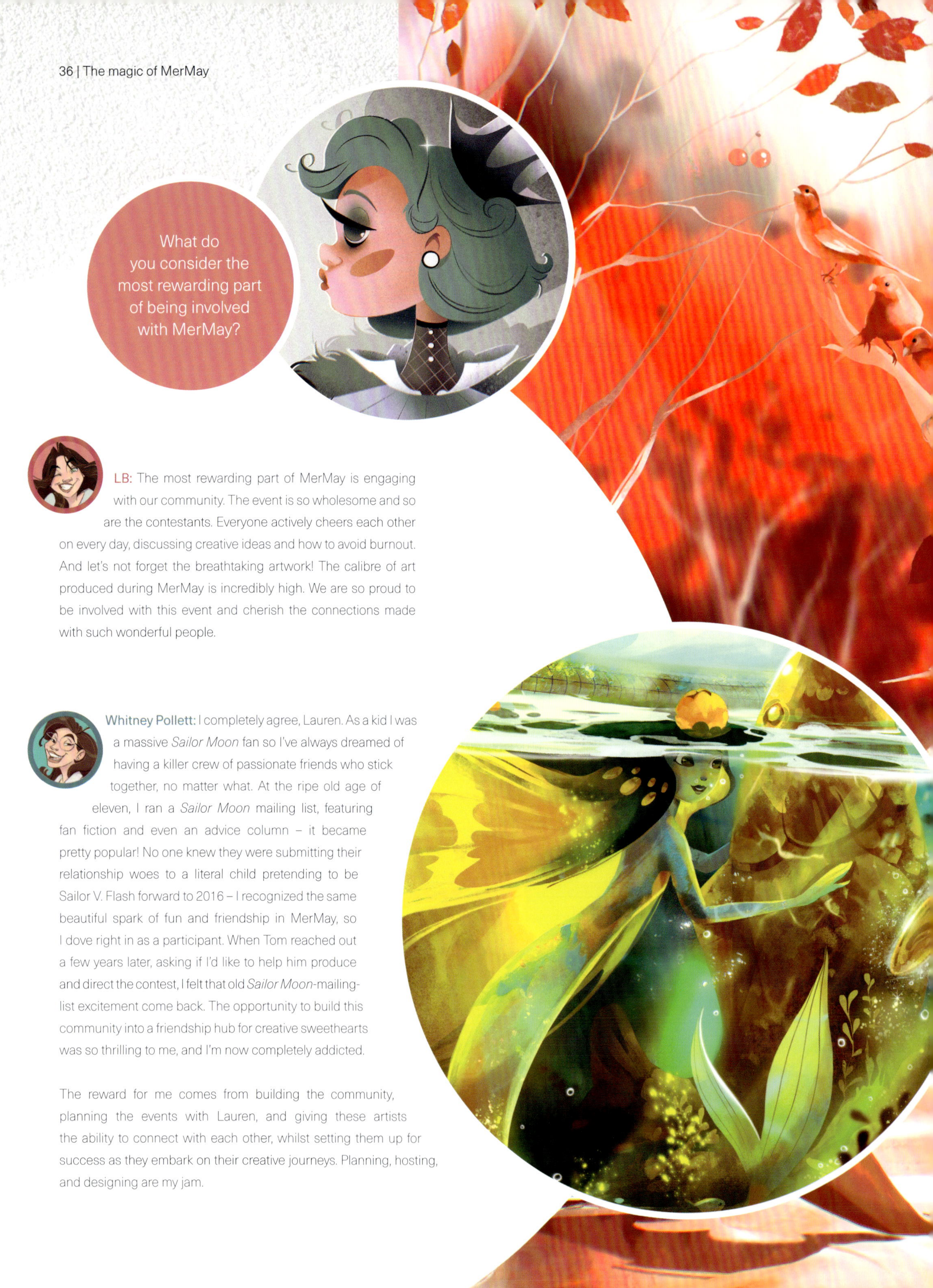

What do you consider the most rewarding part of being involved with MerMay?

LB: The most rewarding part of MerMay is engaging with our community. The event is so wholesome and so are the contestants. Everyone actively cheers each other on every day, discussing creative ideas and how to avoid burnout. And let's not forget the breathtaking artwork! The calibre of art produced during MerMay is incredibly high. We are so proud to be involved with this event and cherish the connections made with such wonderful people.

Whitney Pollett: I completely agree, Lauren. As a kid I was a massive *Sailor Moon* fan so I've always dreamed of having a killer crew of passionate friends who stick together, no matter what. At the ripe old age of eleven, I ran a *Sailor Moon* mailing list, featuring fan fiction and even an advice column – it became pretty popular! No one knew they were submitting their relationship woes to a literal child pretending to be Sailor V. Flash forward to 2016 – I recognized the same beautiful spark of fun and friendship in MerMay, so I dove right in as a participant. When Tom reached out a few years later, asking if I'd like to help him produce and direct the contest, I felt that old *Sailor Moon*-mailing-list excitement come back. The opportunity to build this community into a friendship hub for creative sweethearts was so thrilling to me, and I'm now completely addicted.

The reward for me comes from building the community, planning the events with Lauren, and giving these artists the ability to connect with each other, whilst setting them up for success as they embark on their creative journeys. Planning, hosting, and designing are my jam.

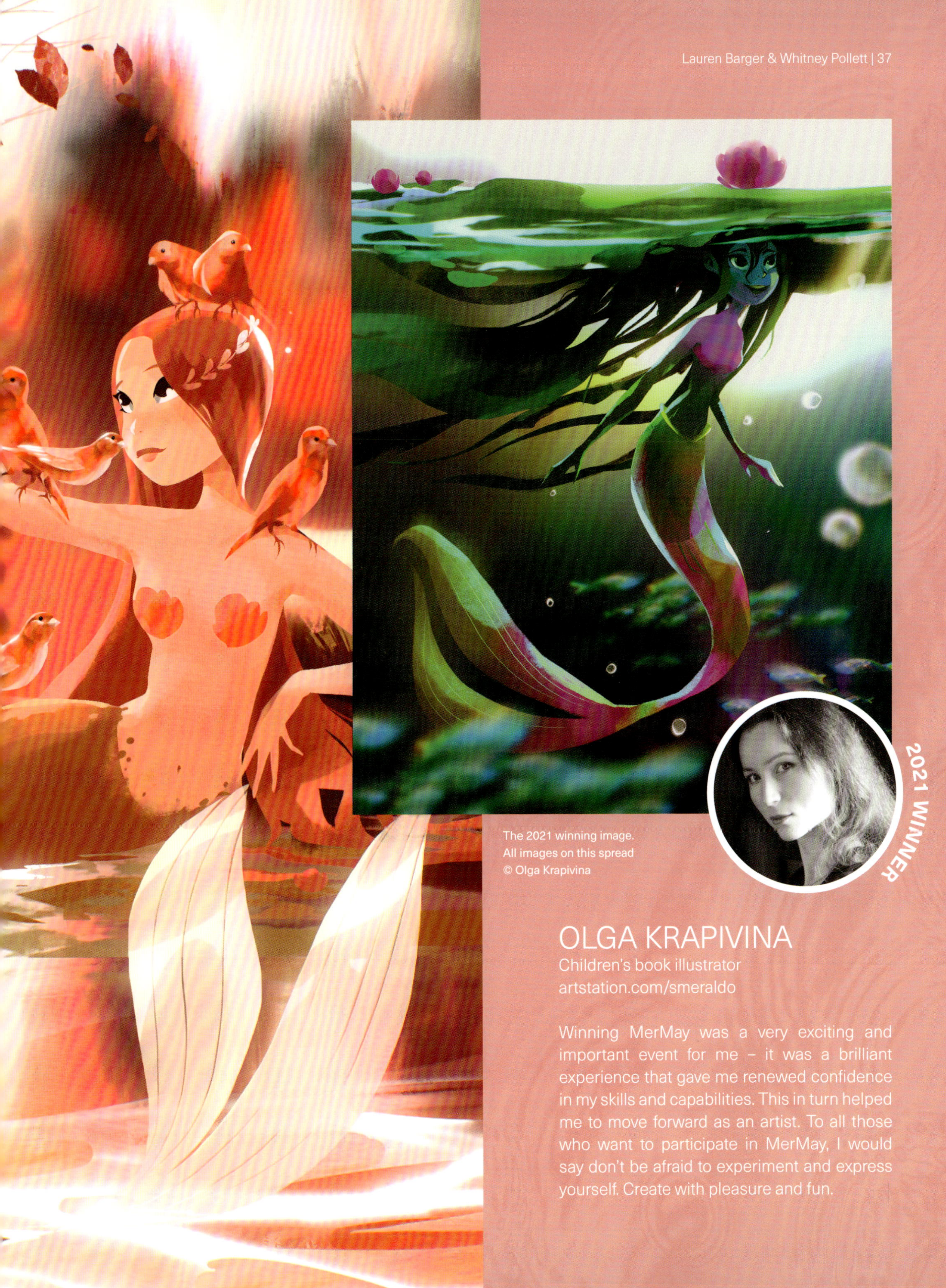

The 2021 winning image.
All images on this spread
© Olga Krapivina

OLGA KRAPIVINA

Children's book illustrator
artstation.com/smeraldo

Winning MerMay was a very exciting and important event for me – it was a brilliant experience that gave me renewed confidence in my skills and capabilities. This in turn helped me to move forward as an artist. To all those who want to participate in MerMay, I would say don't be afraid to experiment and express yourself. Create with pleasure and fun.

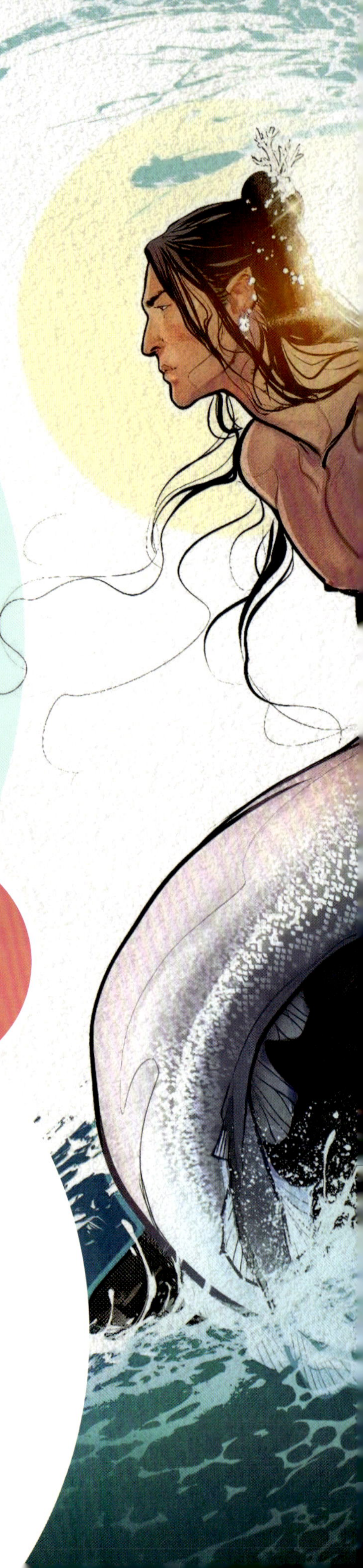

What challenges do you face running an online event like this?

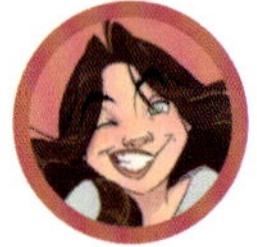

LB: Ensuring participant satisfaction is a challenge. We put a lot of effort into understanding artists' needs and sources of inspiration to craft prompts that resonate. We want the prompts to be enjoyable and maybe reflect elements of pop culture, broadening the appeal beyond just artists. Our aim is to amplify participants' visibility by reaching a wide audience.

Inclusivity is also paramount. We welcome artists from beyond the illustration and animation sphere, offering prizes that support business owners and freelancers, and we have even offered job opportunities! Our panel of judges is curated to represent as many creative professions as possible, from toy design, to children's literature, comic art, and animation. We aim to have a well-rounded evaluation process.

WP: Having a diverse selection of judges not only keeps our taste varied, it also gives budding creators a broader idea of what kind of commercial artist they could become. Animators get a lot of love, but not a lot of people know or think about being a toy designer, for example. Showcasing and interviewing these judges is so much fun, because we know they're inspiring artists to think outside of their own creative bubble.

What do you think is the key to MerMay's success?

LB: The key to MerMay's success lies in its participants! MerMay thrives because of the community of artists who come together to celebrate each year.

WP: Also, I think the general fascination with mermaids plays a role. Mermaids can be very cute and wholesome characters, but they can also be seductive sirens, ruthless man-eaters, and so many mysteriously unsavoury things in between – that's what makes them so much fun to design. The lore and mythology that's out there is global, timeless, and ever-evolving. What resonates with some folks may be a total surprise to others. We love that about MerMay. The stories people tell through the lens of their own MerMay experiences are fabulous, heartfelt, and so interesting.

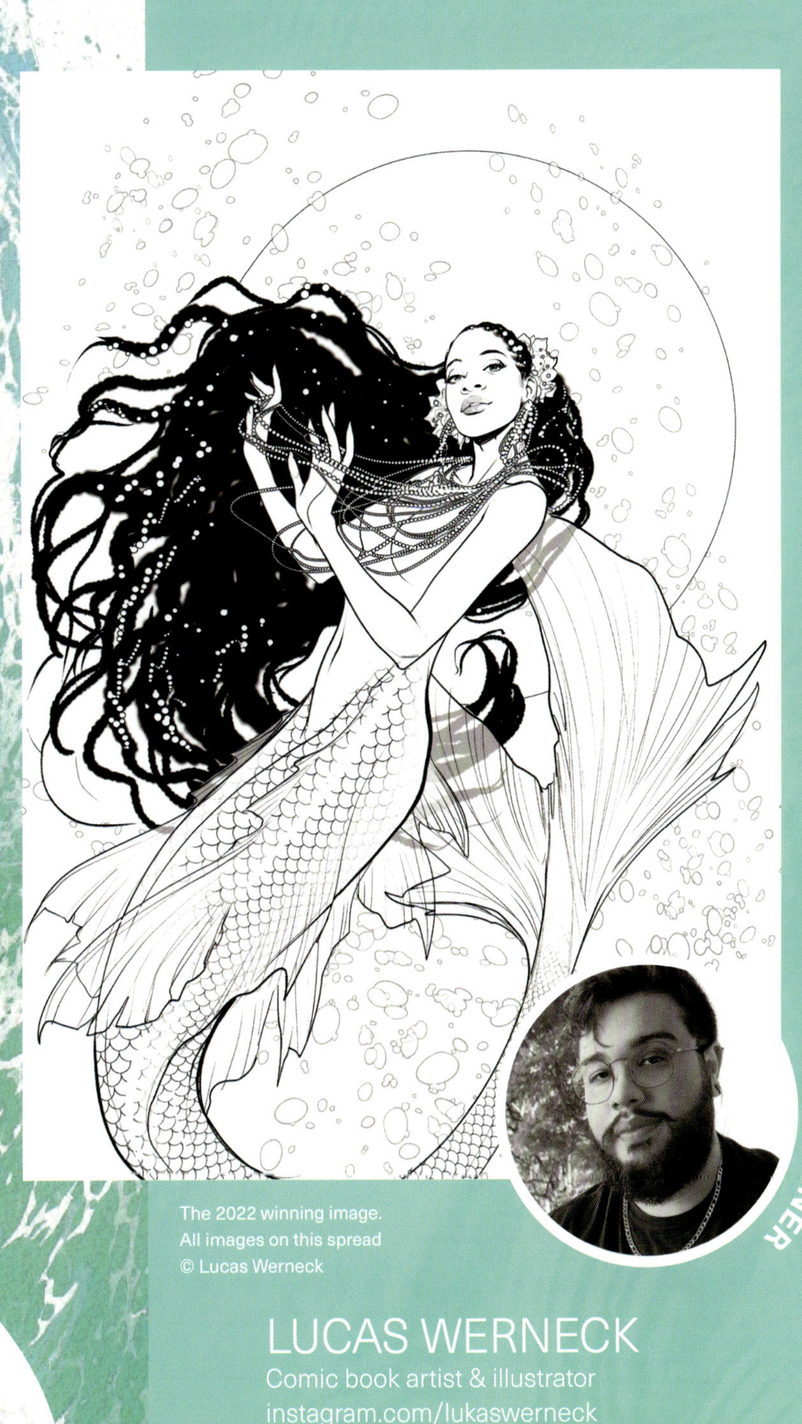

The 2022 winning image.
All images on this spread
© Lucas Werneck

LUCAS WERNECK

Comic book artist & illustrator
instagram.com/lukaswerneck

It meant a lot to me to win. I remember when I discovered MerMay, it was like finding a community that I had been looking for all my life. I have always loved mermaids and drawing them has been part of my routine since childhood, so you can imagine how I felt when I won the contest – it was a huge, wonderful surprise!

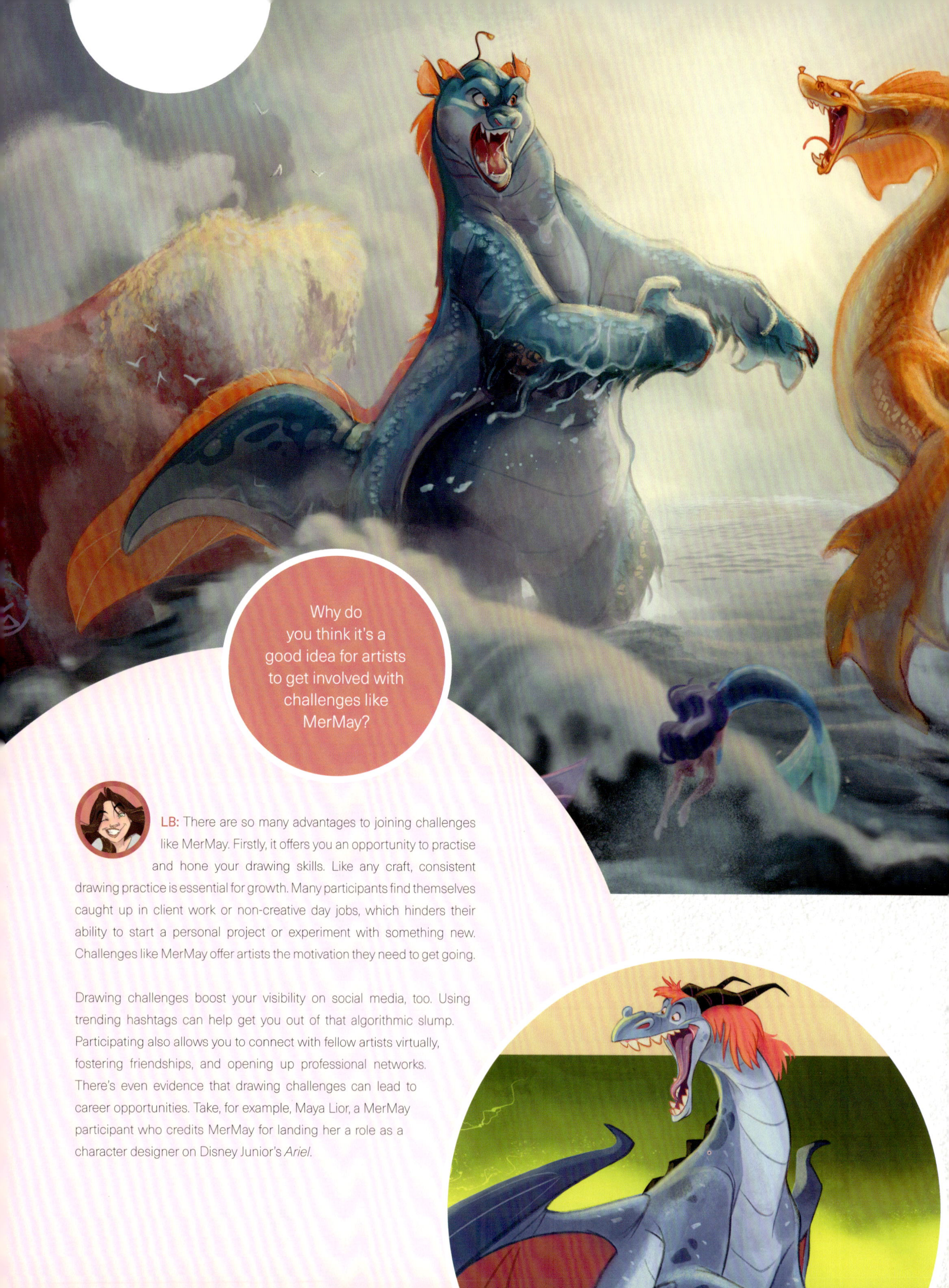

LB: There are so many advantages to joining challenges like MerMay. Firstly, it offers you an opportunity to practise and hone your drawing skills. Like any craft, consistent drawing practice is essential for growth. Many participants find themselves caught up in client work or non-creative day jobs, which hinders their ability to start a personal project or experiment with something new. Challenges like MerMay offer artists the motivation they need to get going.

Drawing challenges boost your visibility on social media, too. Using trending hashtags can help get you out of that algorithmic slump. Participating also allows you to connect with fellow artists virtually, fostering friendships, and opening up professional networks. There's even evidence that drawing challenges can lead to career opportunities. Take, for example, Maya Lior, a MerMay participant who credits MerMay for landing her a role as a character designer on Disney Junior's *Ariel*.

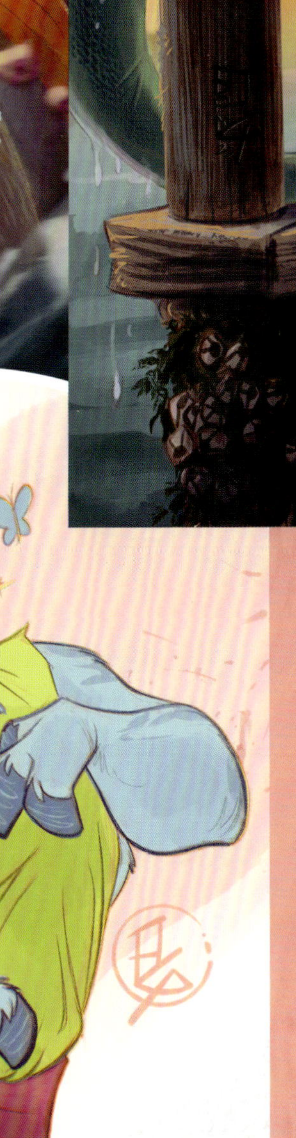

The 2023 winning image.
All images on this spread
© Adam Bunch

2023 WINNER

ADAM BUNCH
Comic-book artist & illustrator
adamisarting.com

I love the supportive and positive community of artists who participate in MerMay. Tom Bancroft, and the other judges and hosts for the challenge, have invested so much time and effort into building the community and seeing that it continues to grow. Everyone encourages each other to keep doing what they love and to share their creations.

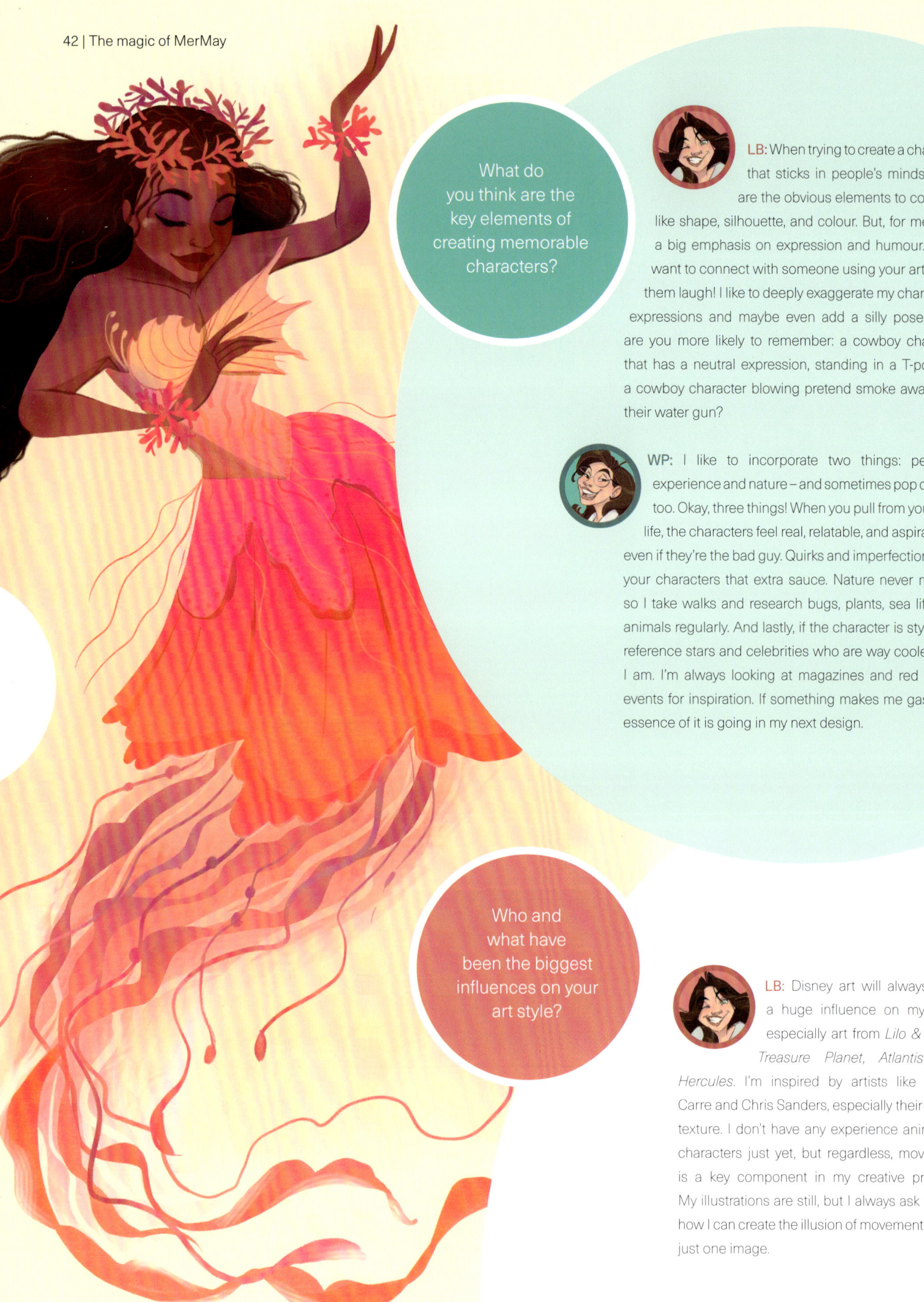

What do you think are the key elements of creating memorable characters?

LB: When trying to create a character that sticks in people's minds, there are the obvious elements to consider, like shape, silhouette, and colour. But, for me, I put a big emphasis on expression and humour. If you want to connect with someone using your art, make them laugh! I like to deeply exaggerate my character's expressions and maybe even add a silly pose. What are you more likely to remember: a cowboy character that has a neutral expression, standing in a T-pose, or a cowboy character blowing pretend smoke away from their water gun?

WP: I like to incorporate two things: personal experience and nature – and sometimes pop culture, too. Okay, three things! When you pull from your own life, the characters feel real, relatable, and aspirational, even if they're the bad guy. Quirks and imperfections give your characters that extra sauce. Nature never misses, so I take walks and research bugs, plants, sea life, and animals regularly. And lastly, if the character is stylish, I'll reference stars and celebrities who are way cooler than I am. I'm always looking at magazines and red carpet events for inspiration. If something makes me gasp, the essence of it is going in my next design.

Who and what have been the biggest influences on your art style?

LB: Disney art will always have a huge influence on my style, especially art from *Lilo & Stitch*, *Treasure Planet*, *Atlantis*, and *Hercules*. I'm inspired by artists like Cécile Carre and Chris Sanders, especially their use of texture. I don't have any experience animating characters just yet, but regardless, movement is a key component in my creative process. My illustrations are still, but I always ask myself how I can create the illusion of movement within just one image.

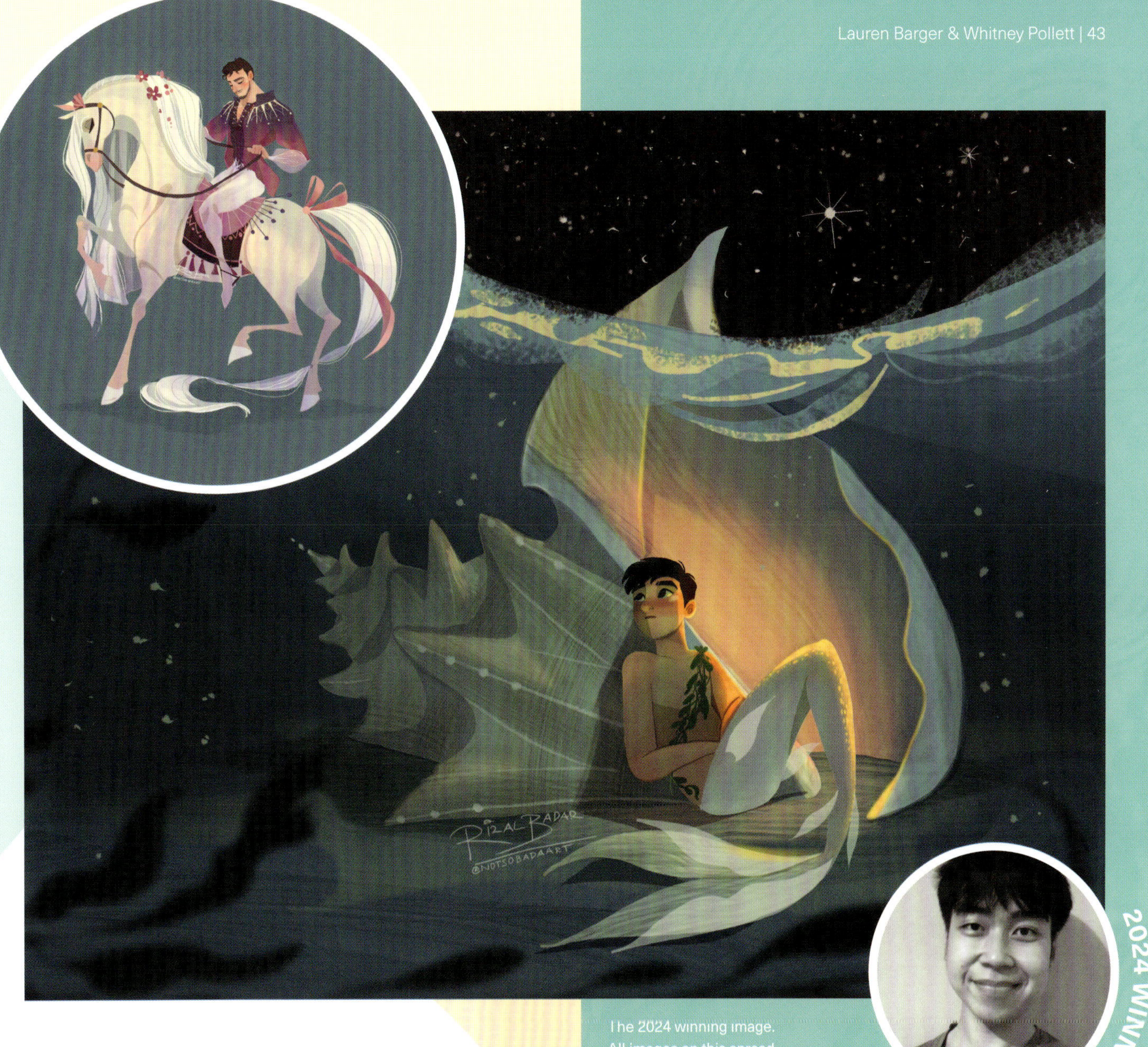

The 2024 winning image.
All images on this spread
© Rizal Badar

2024 WINNER

WP: Lauren could teach a master class on conveying weight, energy, and motion in a still – you'll have to ask her about her cheerleading days! She's also the go-to artist for humour. As a person, she's so hilarious and clever, and it shines through in everything that she does.

For my influences? Al Hirschfeld and Da Vinci are my knee-jerk reactions. I also adored my grandpa, who was an artist and inventor – he invented the mood ring! I find any genius artist with a lyrical line sensibility and a curiosity for how things work to be soul quenching.

RIZAL BADAR
Character designer & illustrator
Instagram.com/notsobadaart

Winning MerMay meant so much to me! Being recognized by such an amazing community, built by talented, genuine, and supportive artists was a big honour. The fact that MerMay is judged by a lot of major artists that I look up to is just amazing.

Whitney and Lauren share a selection of MerMay artists that have impressed them over the years

CECILIA EDWARDS
@ceciliaedwards.art

'Cecilia drew inspiration from the history of mermaids for her MerMay 2024 artwork. With each post, she created a video to accompany her art, sharing the historical elements that inspired her piece.'

Image © Cecilia Edwards

CELIA BEAUDUC
@linu_art_

'Celia is one of our favourite artists that work with traditional media. In the sea of digital art, traditional work can sometimes get lost, but her artwork definitely stands out.'

Image © Celia Beauduc

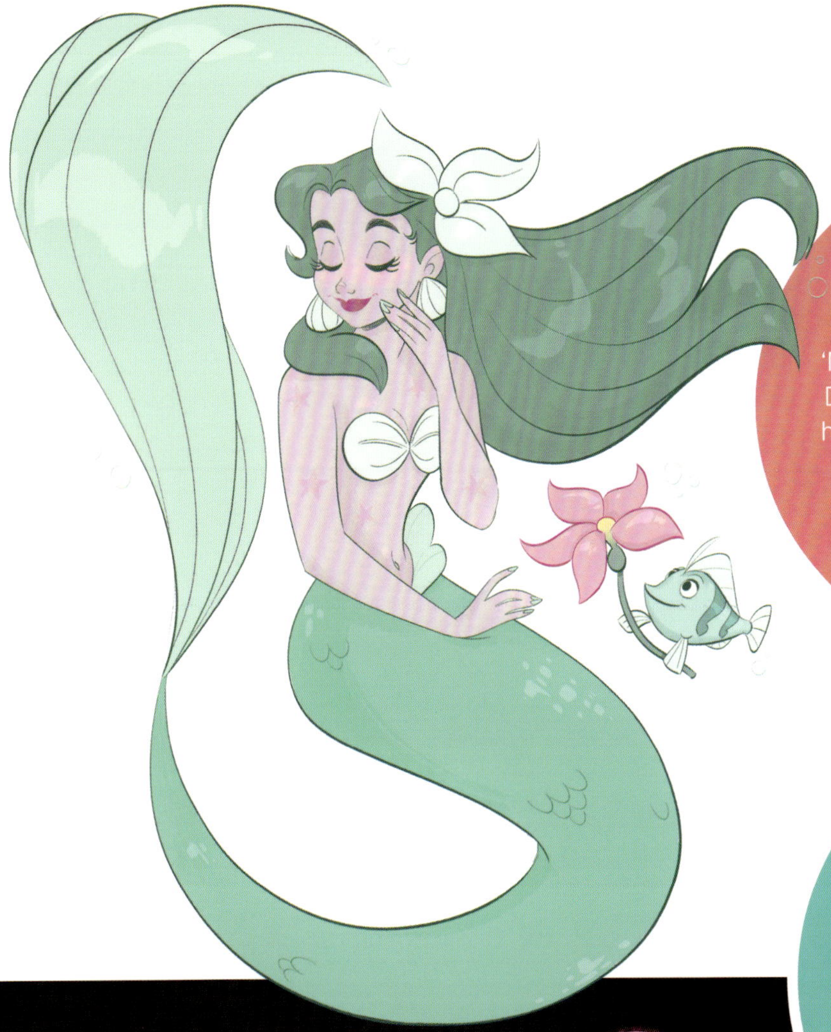

MAYA LIOR
@mdlior
'Maya is a character designer for Disney Junior's *Ariel* and credits her participation in MerMay over the years for helping her land this position. Her use of colour is particularly fantastic.'

RODRIGO RAPOSO
@raposodraws
'Winner of the December mermaid drawing challenge, Rodrigo is a fin-tastic artist. His illustrations are always so characterful and vibrant. His work has a vintage glam and charm that we love'

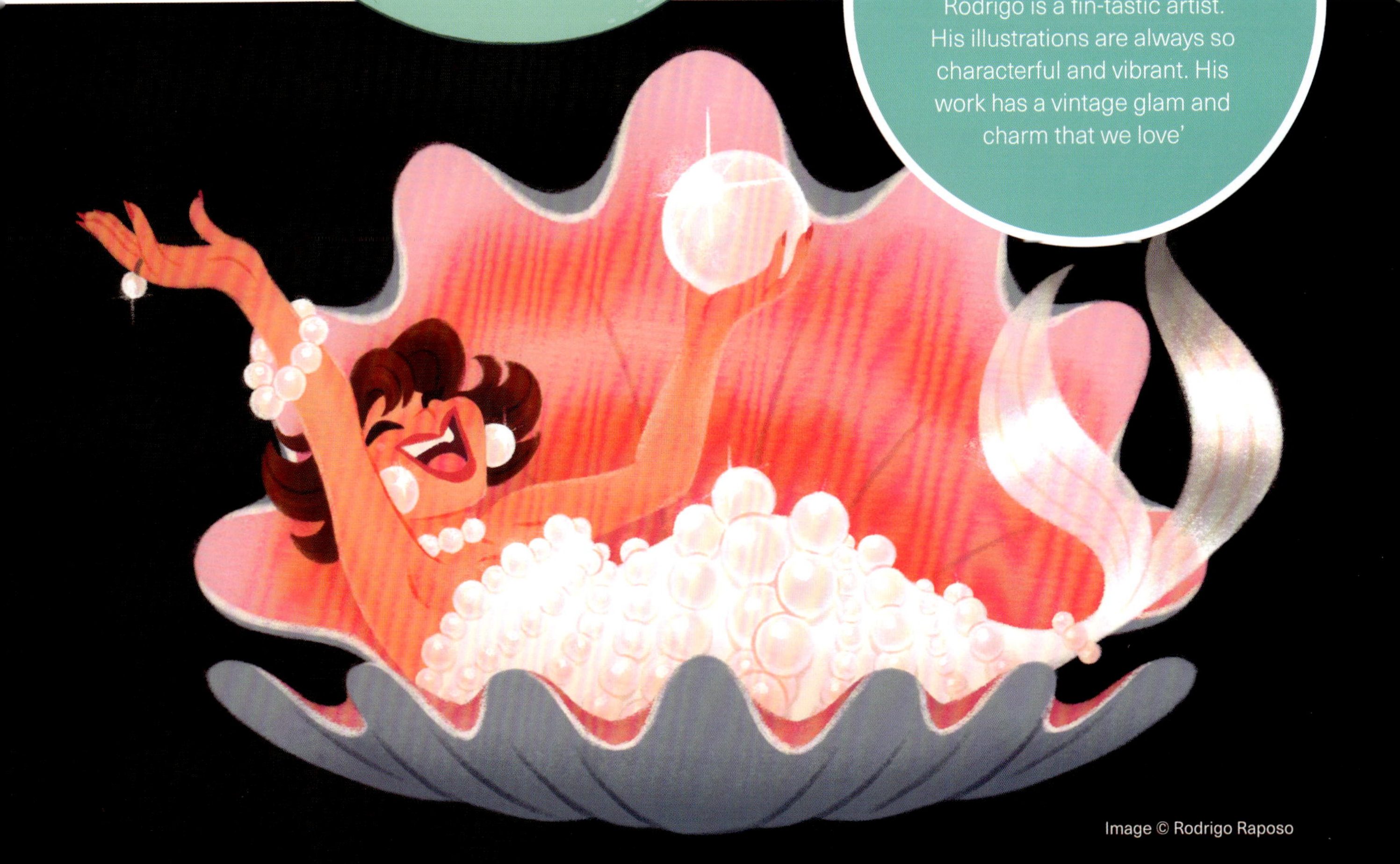

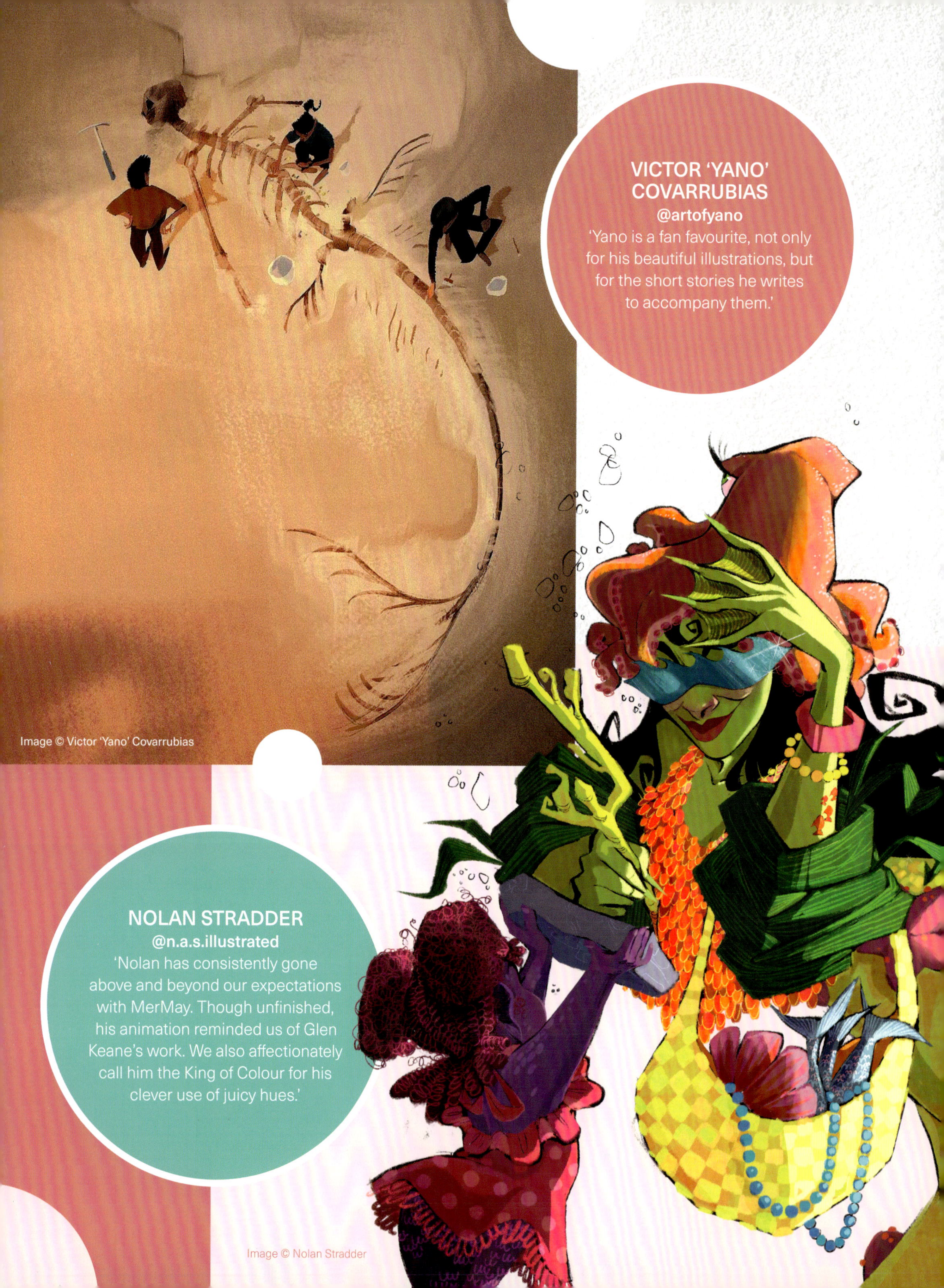

VICTOR 'YANO' COVARRUBIAS
@artofyano
'Yano is a fan favourite, not only for his beautiful illustrations, but for the short stories he writes to accompany them.'

NOLAN STRADDER
@n.a.s.illustrated
'Nolan has consistently gone above and beyond our expectations with MerMay. Though unfinished, his animation reminded us of Glen Keane's work. We also affectionately call him the King of Colour for his clever use of juicy hues.'

JOCHEM VAN GOOL
@jochemvangool
'Jochem placed second in 2023 and is a very successful freelancer. He has worked on *Klaus*, *Space Jam 2*, *Disney Lorcana*, and more. His characters are so full of emotion and movement.'

Thank you both for your time, we look forward to seeing all the fantastic MerMay art later in the year!

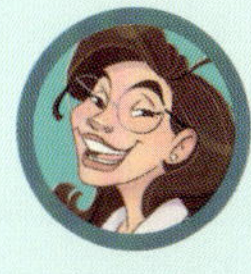

WP: Thank you so much for having us, *CDQ*! Mwah!

GRACE TRAN

I'm a digital illustrator who focuses on fantasy illustrations and concepts. Creating characters that are able to tell stories has always been a fascinating process for me. I hope these step-by-step breakdowns will show you a different approach to character design, especially if you like fantasy world-building!

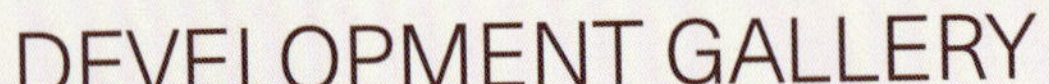

01. During sketching and thumbnail sessions, I usually create a lot of scribbles while looking for the best shapes and ideas. You always find more ideas when your brain is loosened up.

01

02. Refining the line work can be really stressful, since you need to focus more and try to make sure to deliver the feeling from your sketch. I focus on the line weight and fix some construction as I move forward.

02

03. To choose base colours I look at the character's archetype and the overall feeling that I wanted to deliver while picking the palette. In this case, a yellow helm should highlight his fun and easy-going personality.

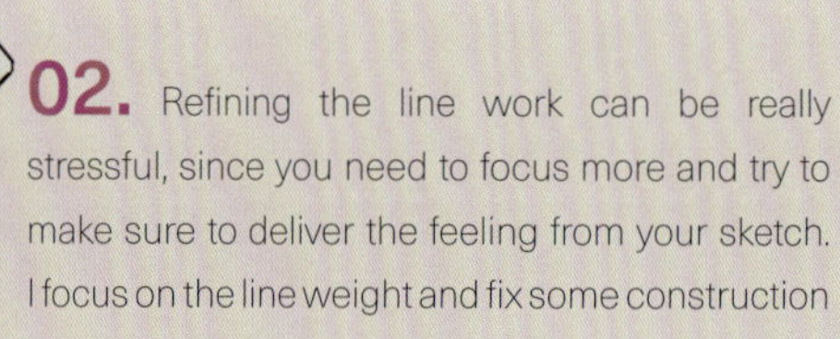

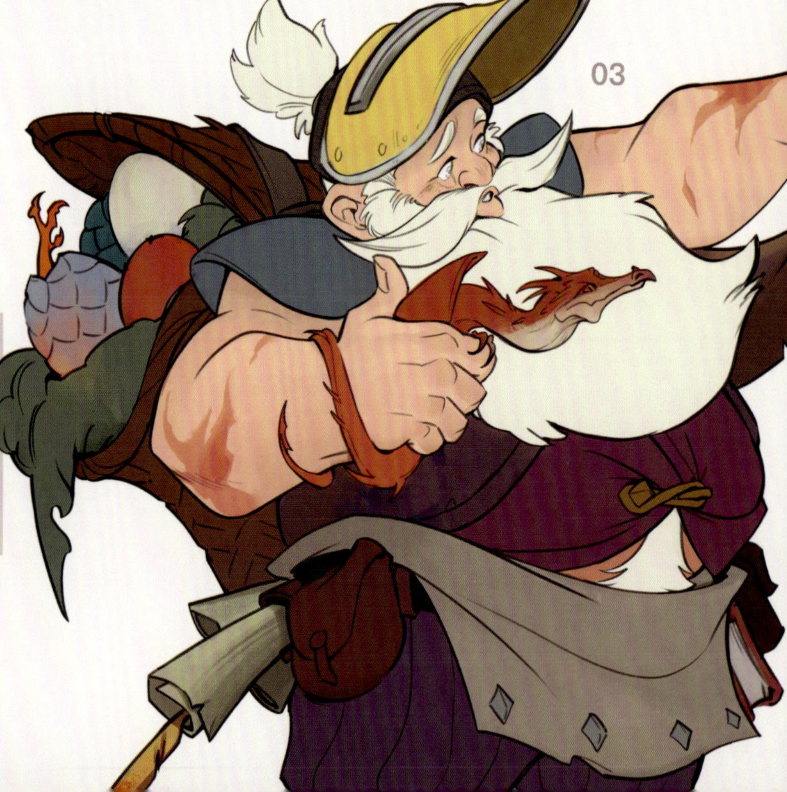
03

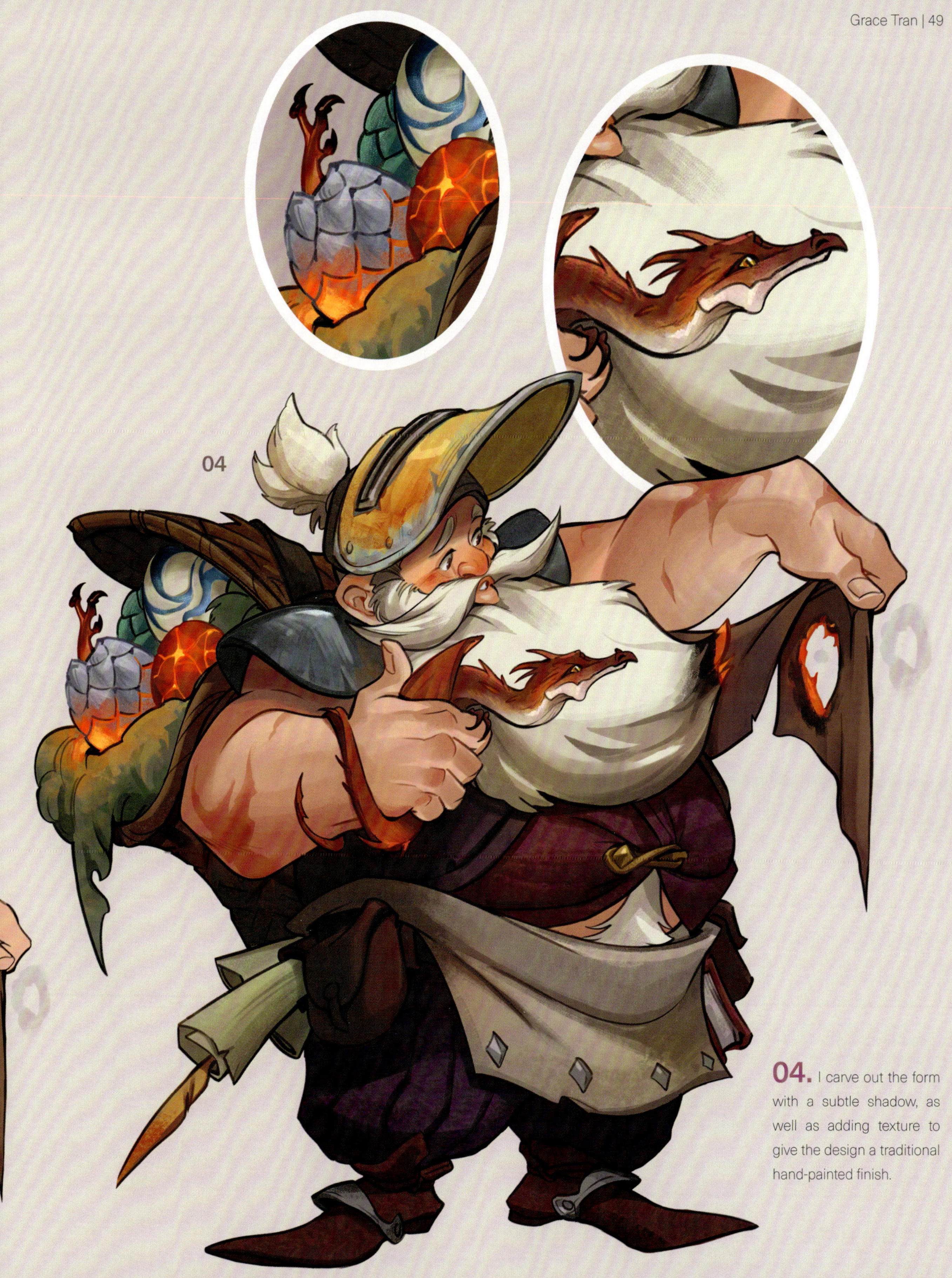

04. I carve out the form with a subtle shadow, as well as adding texture to give the design a traditional hand-painted finish.

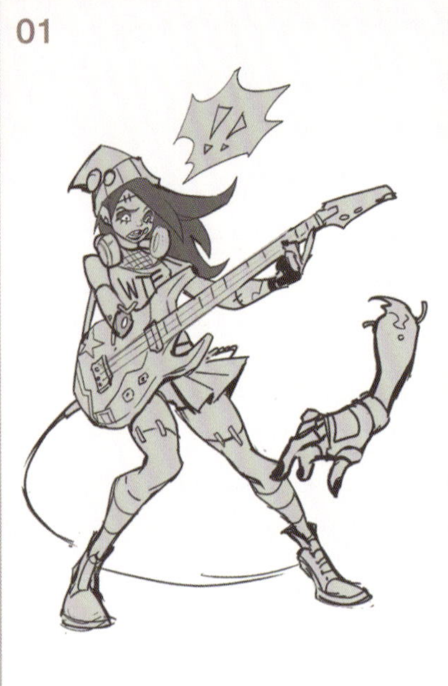

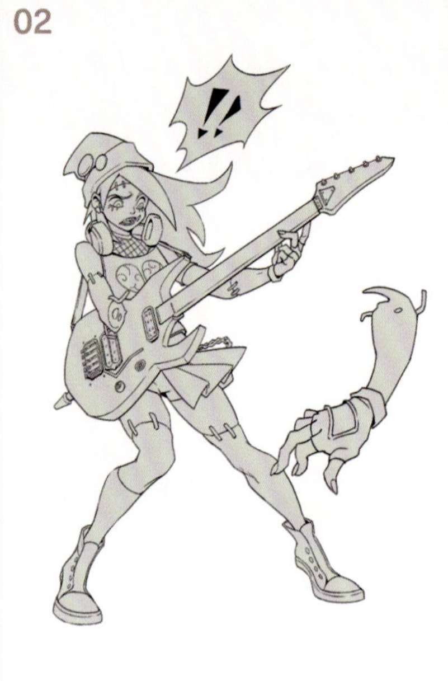

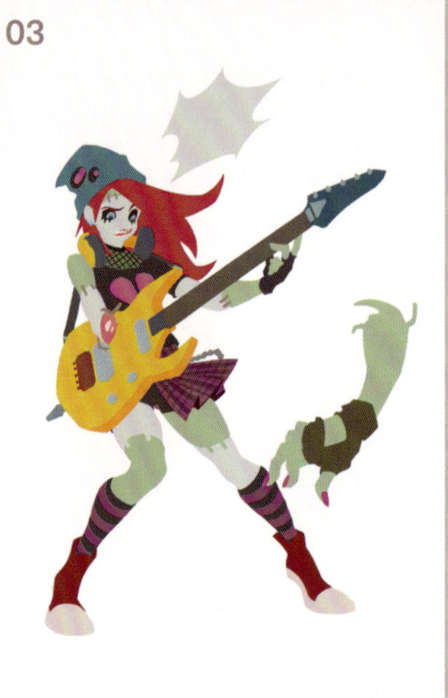

01. While sketching, I don't care too much about line weight, I'm just trying to push for a clean silhouette and a lively pose and expression.

02. For the inking I use a hard brush with no texture since I will be focusing more on the painting spectrum later. The lines are for marking and guidance only.

03. When choosing base colours, you should consider the overall feel of the piece, and also how you want to distribute your shapes. Learn about value grouping so your base doesn't appear shattered. If you squint your eyes when checking shapes and values, you'll find it easier to read what is and isn't working.

04. I lowered the opacity and coloured the line work, so it appears more blended in. As for shading, I designed shadow shapes that are crisp and stylized, on the thighs and hair.

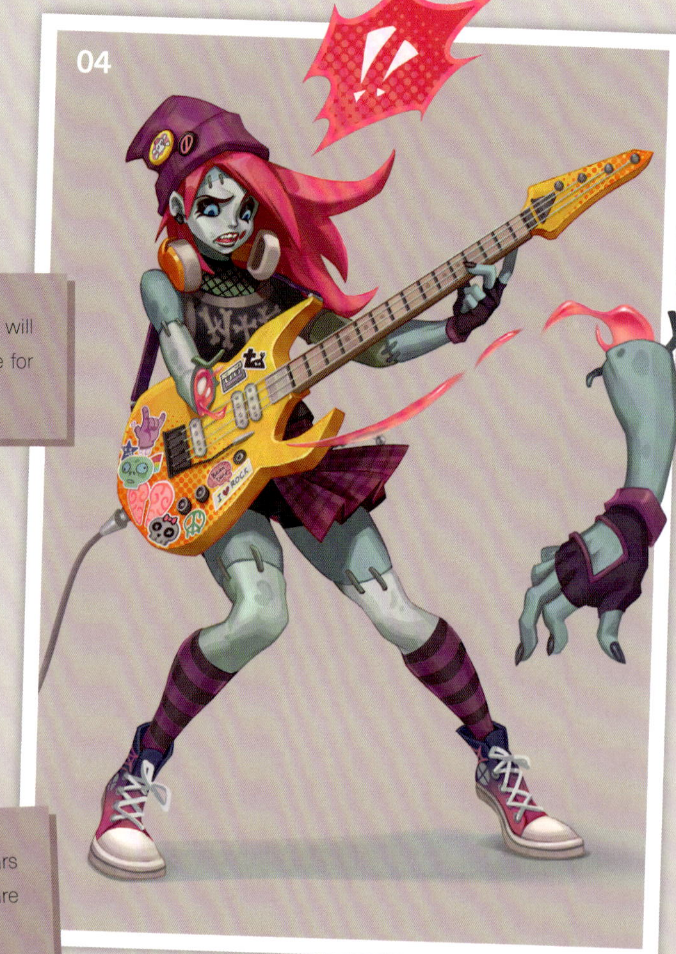

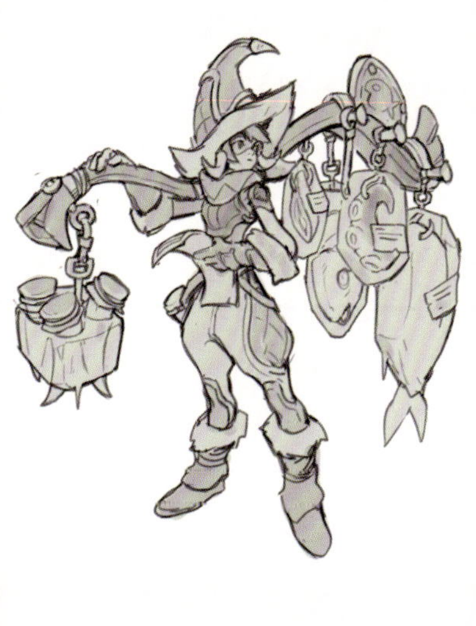

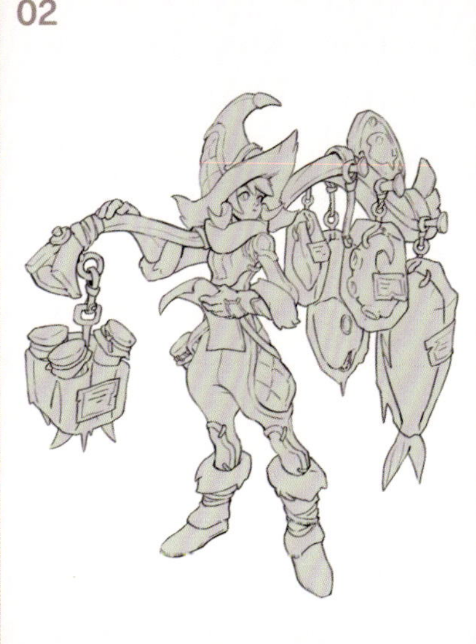

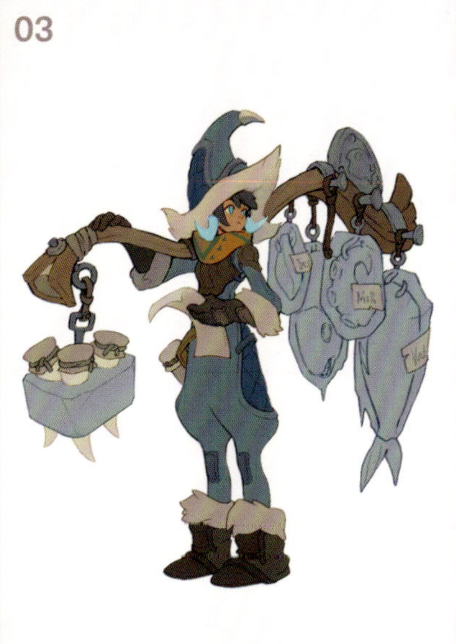

01. Sometimes I spend a lot of time on polishing and detailing the sketch in exchange for an easier inking process later. This can help to really nail down my ideas.

02. If the sketch is well established, then creating the line work is less effort, and you can almost complete this step on autopilot. For this piece, I decided to change her pose a bit at this stage.

03. Here are the base colours, with some minor changes to the character's legs. You may have noticed I use complementary palettes a lot. I personally think they are a simple, neat, and effective way of creating interesting designs.

04. Finally, I add a simple background for my character which emphasizes the concept. I'm going for a minimal render style to highlight the crisp line work.

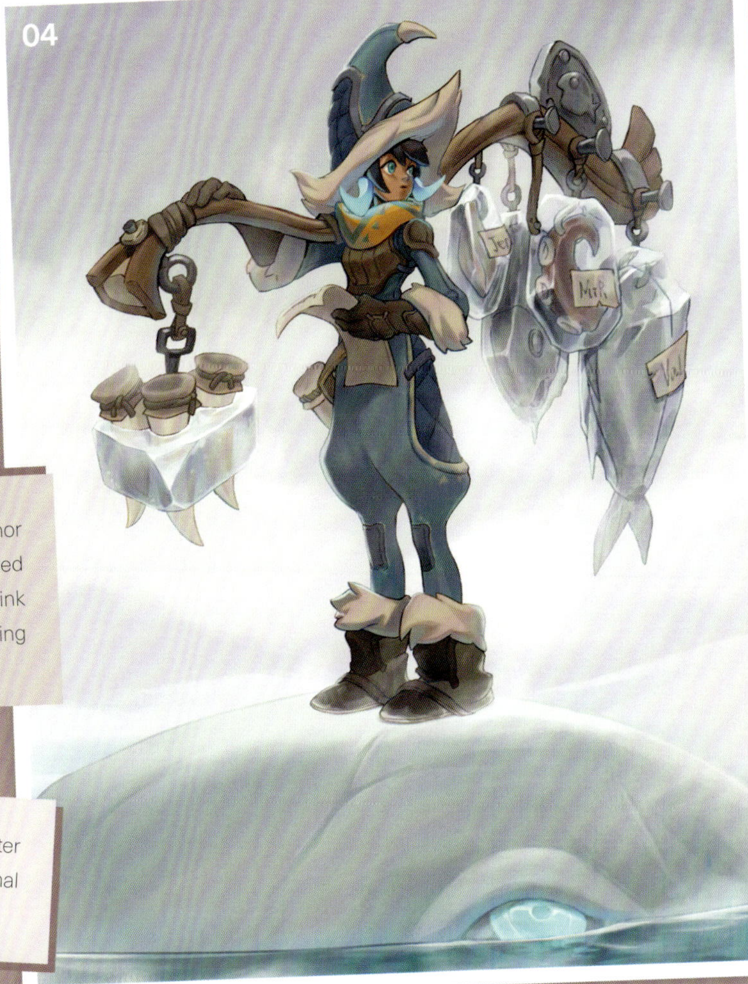

lighting
the way

Learn how to get the most from lighting your characters with Chelsea Blecha's illuminating tips

01

When beginning to light a character, start with the local colour. Local colour is the true colour of the character, without any influence from the lighting and the surroundings. Keep things flat with minimal textures. This sets the stage for the next steps.

USE COLOUR WITH PURPOSE

Using a limited colour palette can help your design look more unified. If you're unsure of where to start, try choosing a set of complementary colours first. Entirely saturating a piece may look prettier, but try to use colour with purpose. Pick and choose where you want to add saturation to convey the right mood.

02

After deciding on the local colour, add contact shadows to create form and ground the character. Contact shadows occur where two forms meet. This creates diffused lighting (or indirect filtered lighting) that helps create a neutral base for lighting your character.

03

To put your character in sunset lighting, use very warm, light, and cool shadows. In this example, the light is placed on the character's face. The forms remain soft, giving the hopeful and bright mood of the golden hour.

04

Light your character in the moonlight to create a dark, mysterious mood. Use cool colours to add moonlight from above. Light the top planes and let the shadows stay warm. You can also add a slight glow to the light to emphasize the mystical mood.

'IF YOUR LIGHT IS WARM, YOUR SHADOWS WILL BE COOL, AND VICE VERSA'

05

Use rim light to convey an intense or serious mood. Place a warm light source behind the character, but don't let the shadows get too dark, so we can still see the face. Remember to alternate the thickness of rim light throughout the form to ensure that things don't look too flat.

THE TEMPERATURE RULE

Don't just add white to the light or black to the shadows. Remember that if your light is warm, your shadows will be cool, and vice versa. Avoid muddy colours by sticking with this temperature rule. Another common mistake is to only show saturation in light, when in reality objects in shadow can often pick up a lot of saturation. Don't be afraid to use colour in your shadows.

Light coming from underneath will usually be from an artificial or unnatural source. Placing the light directly underneath the character's face can create a supernatural or magical mood. This directional cool light only touches the planes facing downward and the shadows are warm and dark. The cool light again conveys mystery, as opposed to a warm light that might evoke a more hopeful and familiar feeling. Cool lighting also adds to the drama of a scene.

06

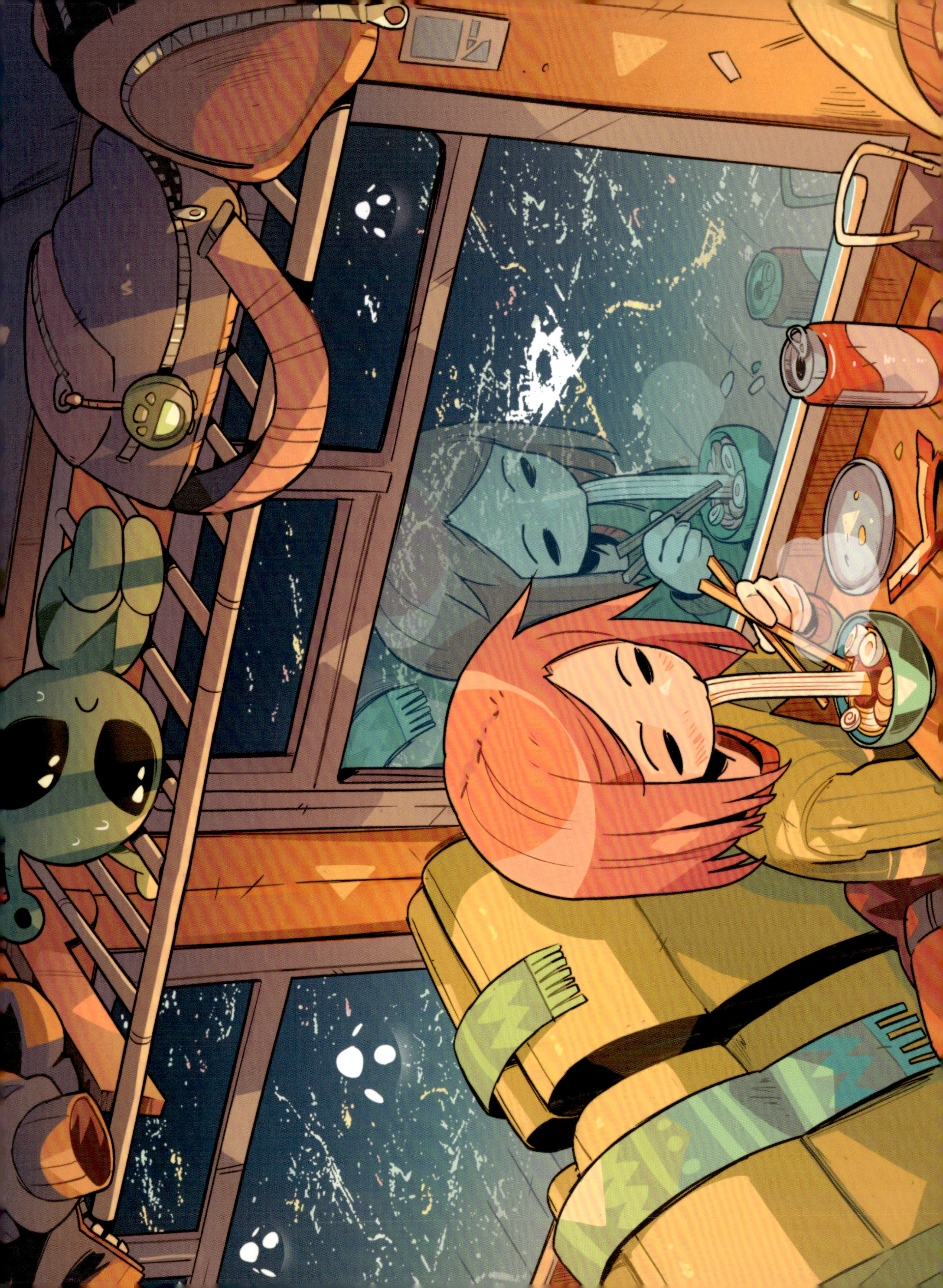

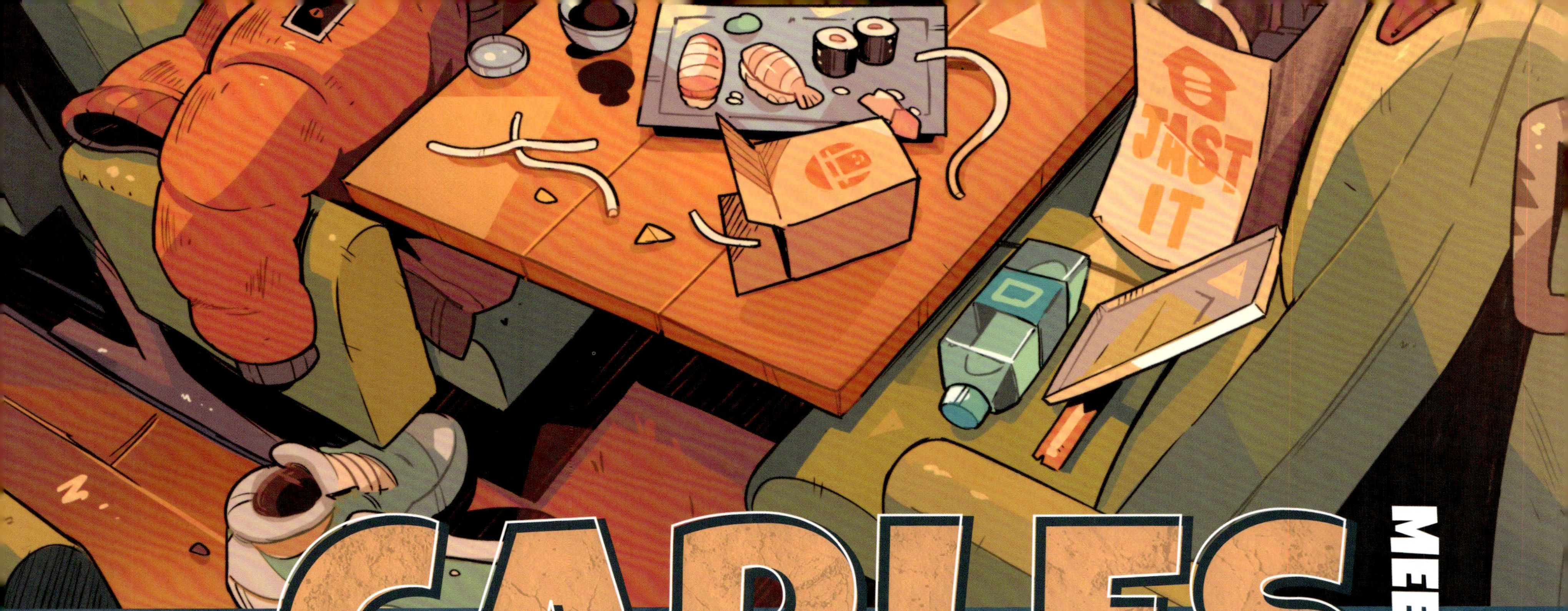

MEET THE ARTIST:

CARLES DALMAU

Comic and video-game artist Carles Dalmau talks about his career and art style.

I bought an alien plush from Ikea and wanted to use him in a drawing

All images © Carles Dalmau

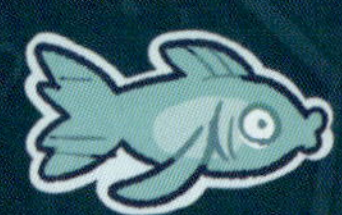

Mei is one of my first original characters – I would love to create a comic about her in the future

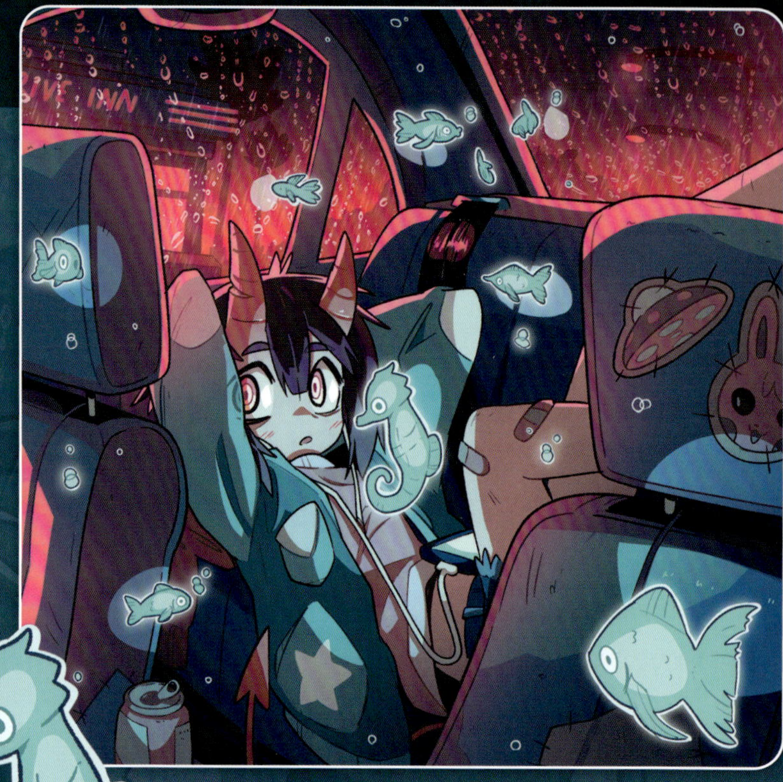

Hi Carles, welcome to *CDQ!* Can you tell our readers a little about your career so far?

Hello and thank you for having me! I'm an artist, based in Barcelona, and I have been drawing for almost seven years now. I started drawing back in university – I was studying audiovisual and multimedia communications, but I wasn't enjoying it at all. I started uploading my process on Instagram so my friends could see what I was doing at that time – this sort of 'pressured' me to keep drawing and improving as much as I could. With time, lots of people started to follow me on there. This gave me exposure I had never had before which led to people wanting to work with me. I started by doing portraits and commissions and with time this grew into bigger projects, freelancing for different companies as an illustrator or concept artist. I'm really lucky I've had the opportunity to learn so much from everything I have done so far.

Have you always wanted to be an artist?

Kind of, yes. It was more that I wanted to work on the stuff that I enjoyed the most, like video games or comic books. Every time I finished a comic or a game, I was thinking 'I want to do that!' I've always thought about fun ideas for projects. At first, I tried to express myself with my voice or by writing, but I found it hard to truly communicate this way. So, in the long run, I figured that if I wanted to get my ideas across, I would learn how to draw.

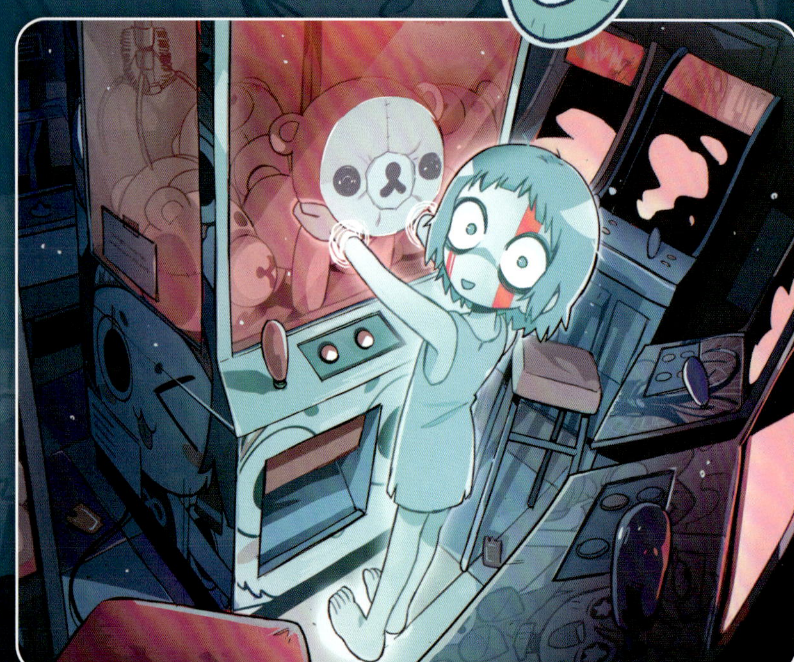

Little ghost in the arcade

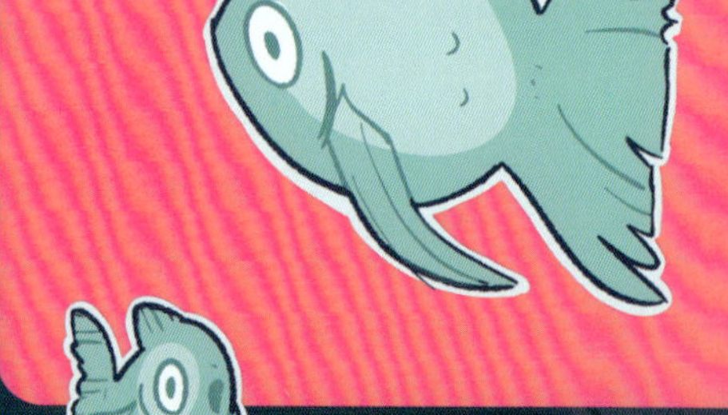

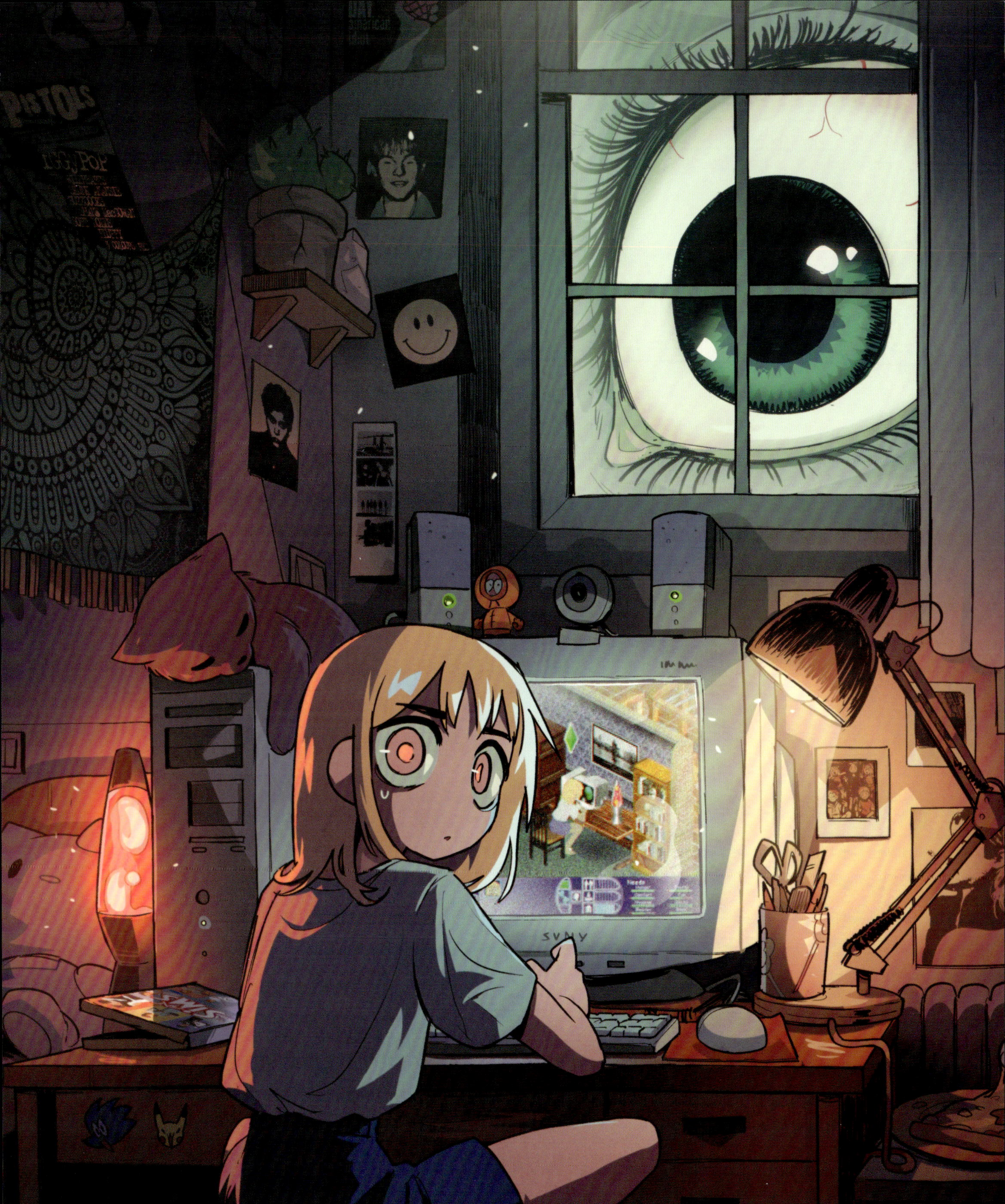

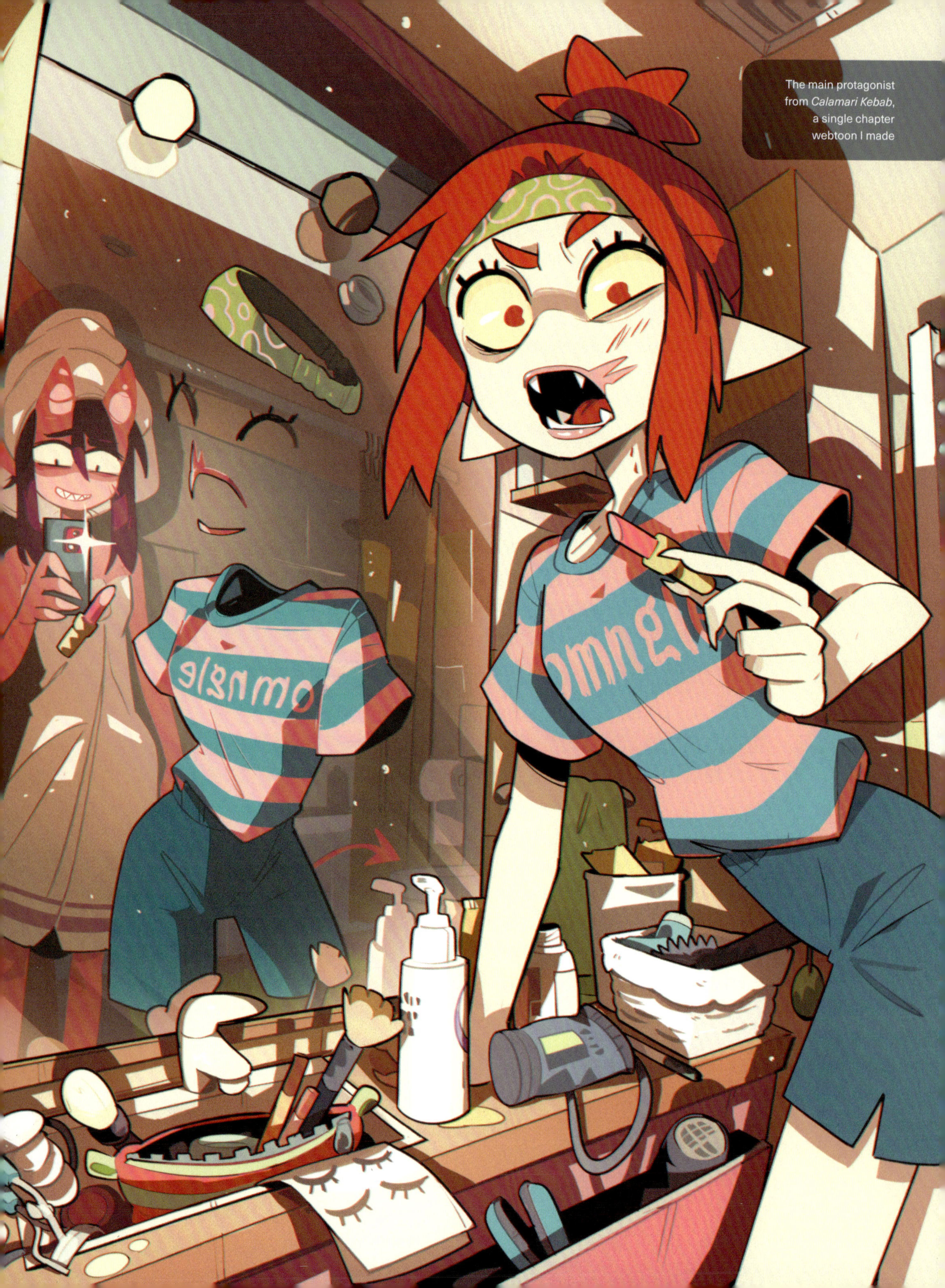

The main protagonist
from Calamari Kebab,
a single chapter
webtoon I made

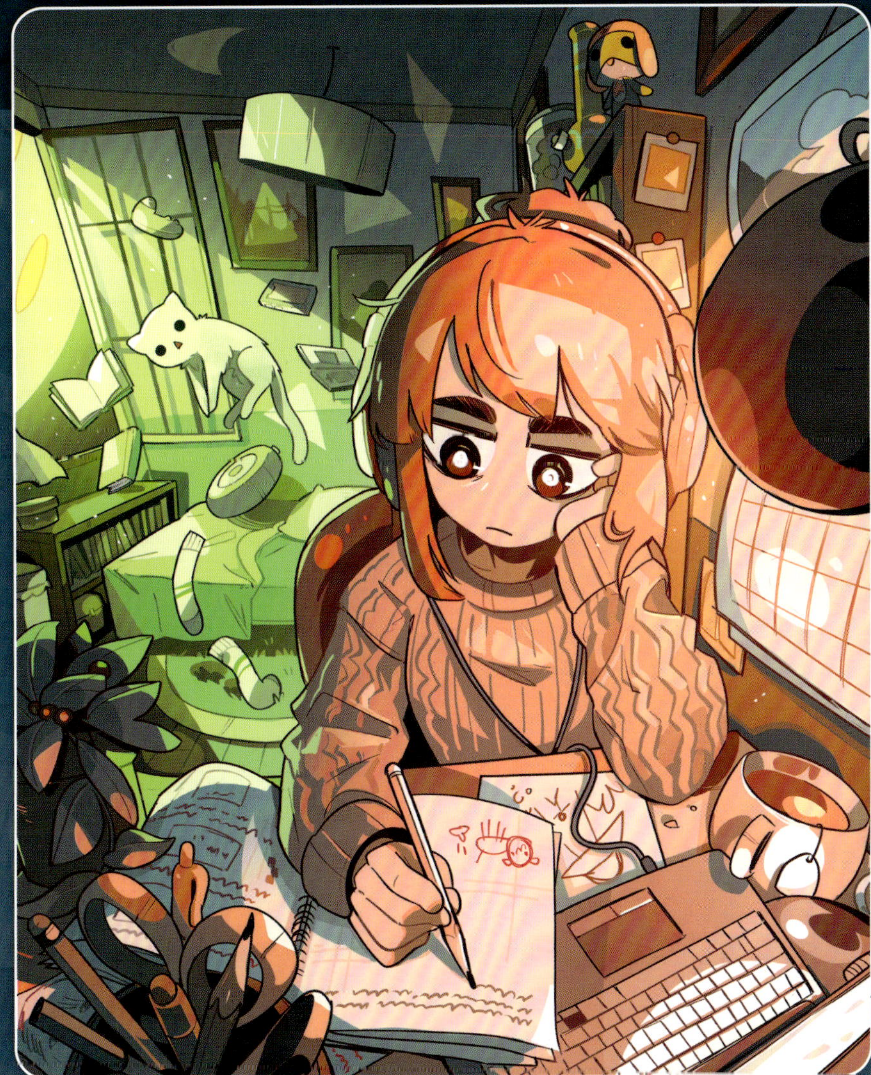

How did the opportunity to work on *Cult of the Lamb* come about, and what challenges did the project present?

Jimp, the Art Director at Massive Monster, reached out and asked me to work on the key art for a game about cults and cute animals that they were creating. I really loved the idea of the project because it was literally what I already enjoyed doing (mixing cute and creepy stuff), so I made the key art they asked me for and thought that was it. I really wanted to keep working on the game, but my impostor syndrome convinced me it wasn't a good idea to ask to create more. Luckily, the team seemed to love the work I did for them and asked me if I wanted to work more on *Cult of the Lamb*!

I think it was a year and a half before the initial release and they wanted someone who could work on pretty much anything they wanted in the art department. Since I've started working with them they seem to really love my ideas – they allow me to do pretty much anything I think of and I'm so grateful for that. This is the richest experience I've ever had, both personally and artistically, and since I'm working on so many different things at the moment I am learning and improving a lot.

Also, the team is great – all of them are amazing and it's a blast being able to work with so many wonderful and talented people.

Do you have any advice for artists who would like to work on character design for video games?

Speaking from my personal experience – knowing that each artist's journey is different – I believe it's super important to have the ability to draw pretty much anything. I notice that many artists tend to specialize in one particular area (which isn't a bad thing), but I've seen that many companies value the ability to draw a wide variety of subjects, from characters and monsters, to animals and environments. The experience I gained doing illustrations and comics really helped with that, so this may also work for you.

It's always better to know how to draw in a lot of different art styles, too, but I managed to work in this field only knowing how to work on stylized cartoon illustrations, so that's also possible. I did try learning realism, but I'm really bad at it!

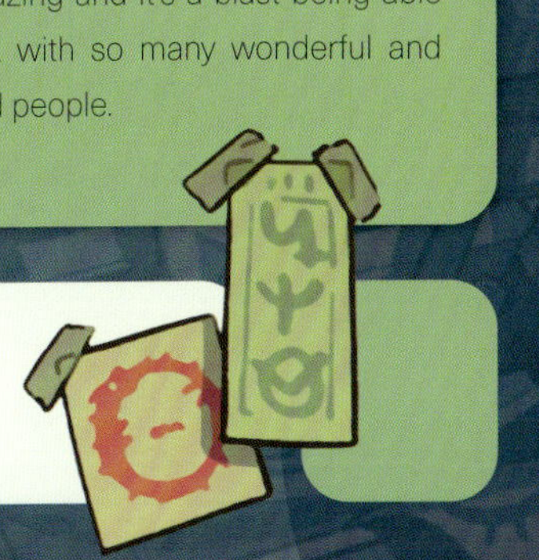

Who and what have been the big inspirations behind your art style?

Many of my thematic inspirations come from horror movies from the 80s and 90s that I rented from video stores when I was in elementary school. Artistically, I think I've blended a lot of things I enjoyed as a kid, including animes like *Sergeant Keroro* and *Magical DoReMi*, numerous Cartoon Network shows, and a variety of comics and video games I read and played, such as *Scott Pilgrim* and *Katamari Damacy*.

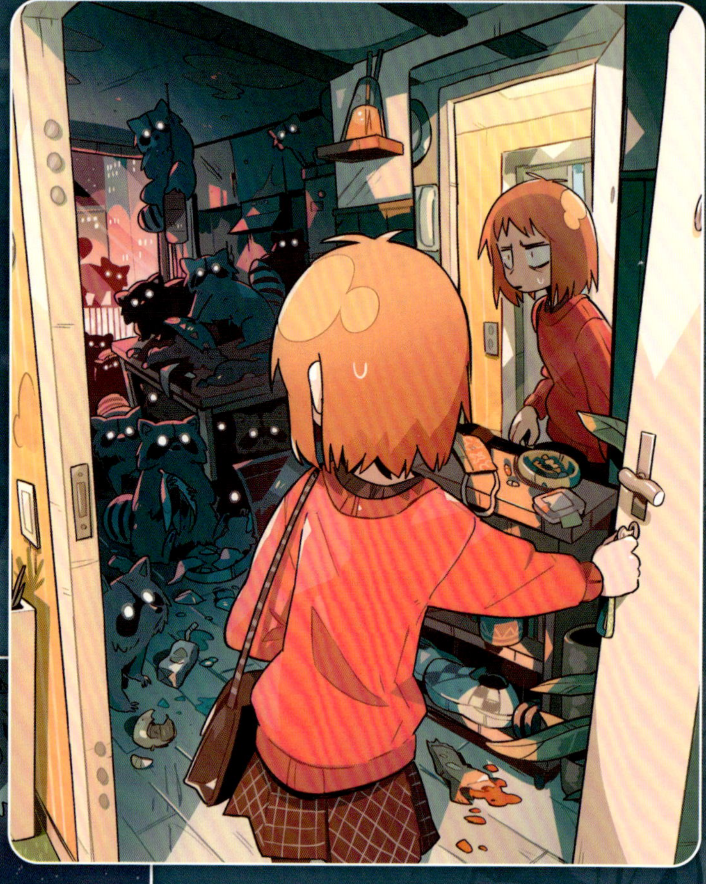
I had just watched a lot of racoon videos

How has your style evolved over time?

A lot! At first, I knew nothing about anatomy, perspective, composition, or anything art related, so my style was what it was because I didn't have the abilities to do much more than that. It was always a weird mix between European and American cartoons, and Japanese anime. Over time, my skills have improved (though I still have a lot of room to grow) but I think the core essence of my style has remained the same.

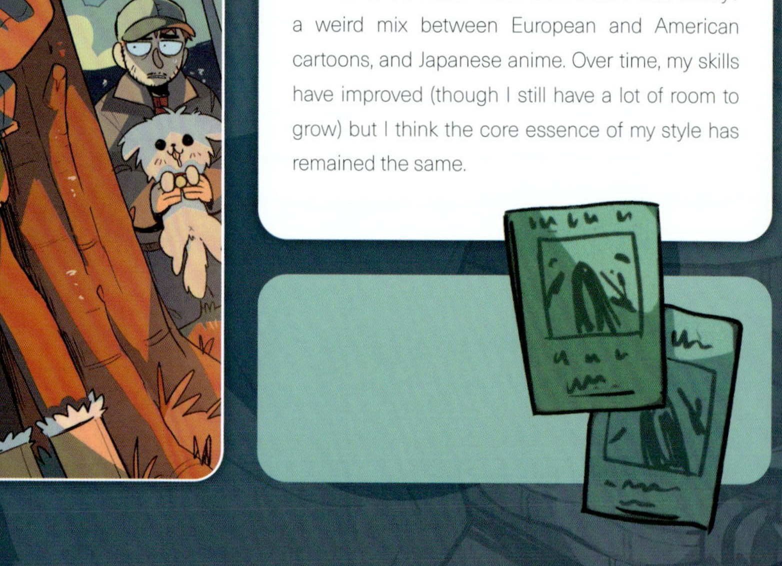
I'm a bit obsessed with giant lizard monsters

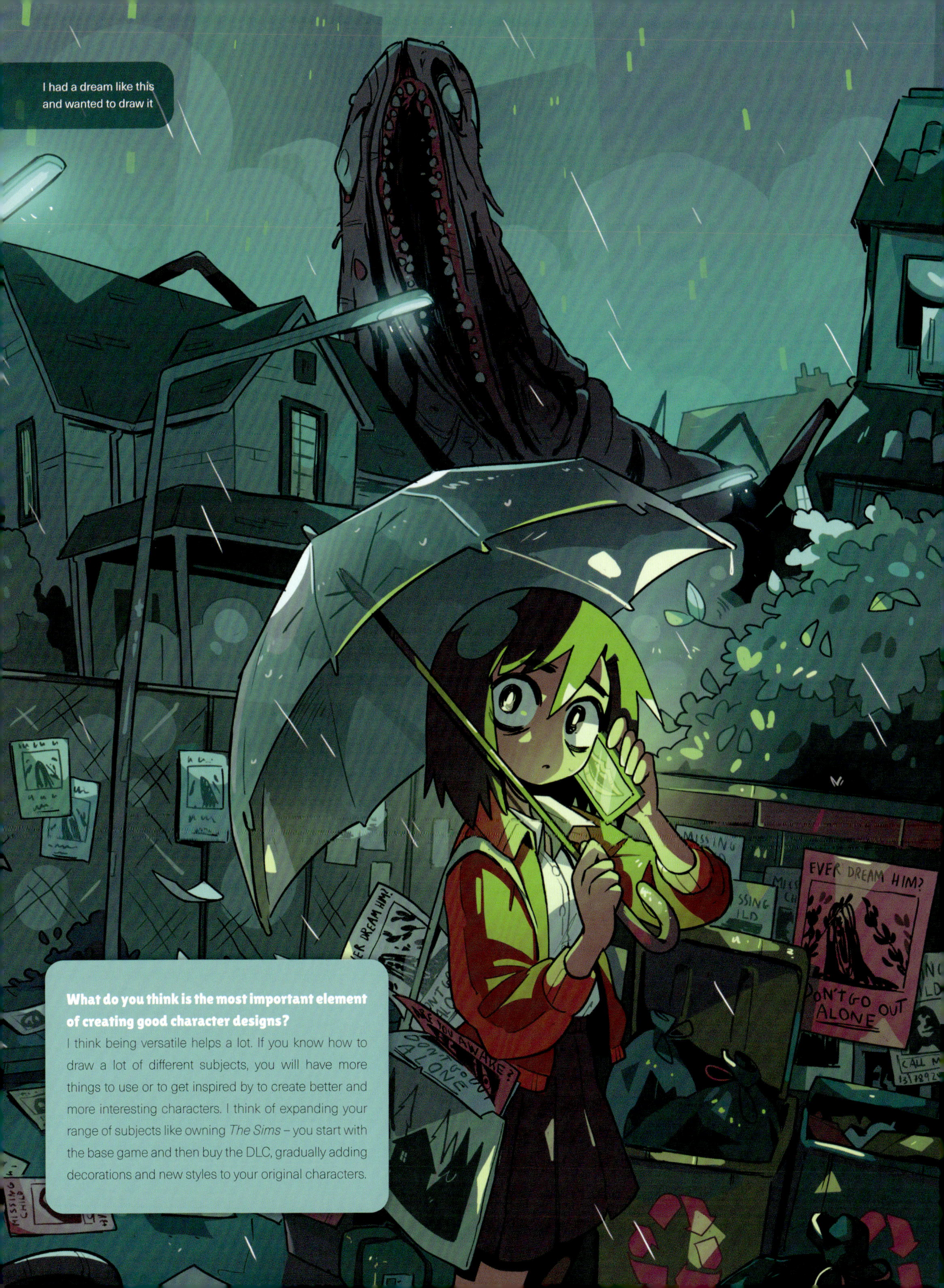

I had a dream like this and wanted to draw it

What do you think is the most important element of creating good character designs?

I think being versatile helps a lot. If you know how to draw a lot of different subjects, you will have more things to use or to get inspired by to create better and more interesting characters. I think of expanding your range of subjects like owning *The Sims* – you start with the base game and then buy the DLC, gradually adding decorations and new styles to your original characters.

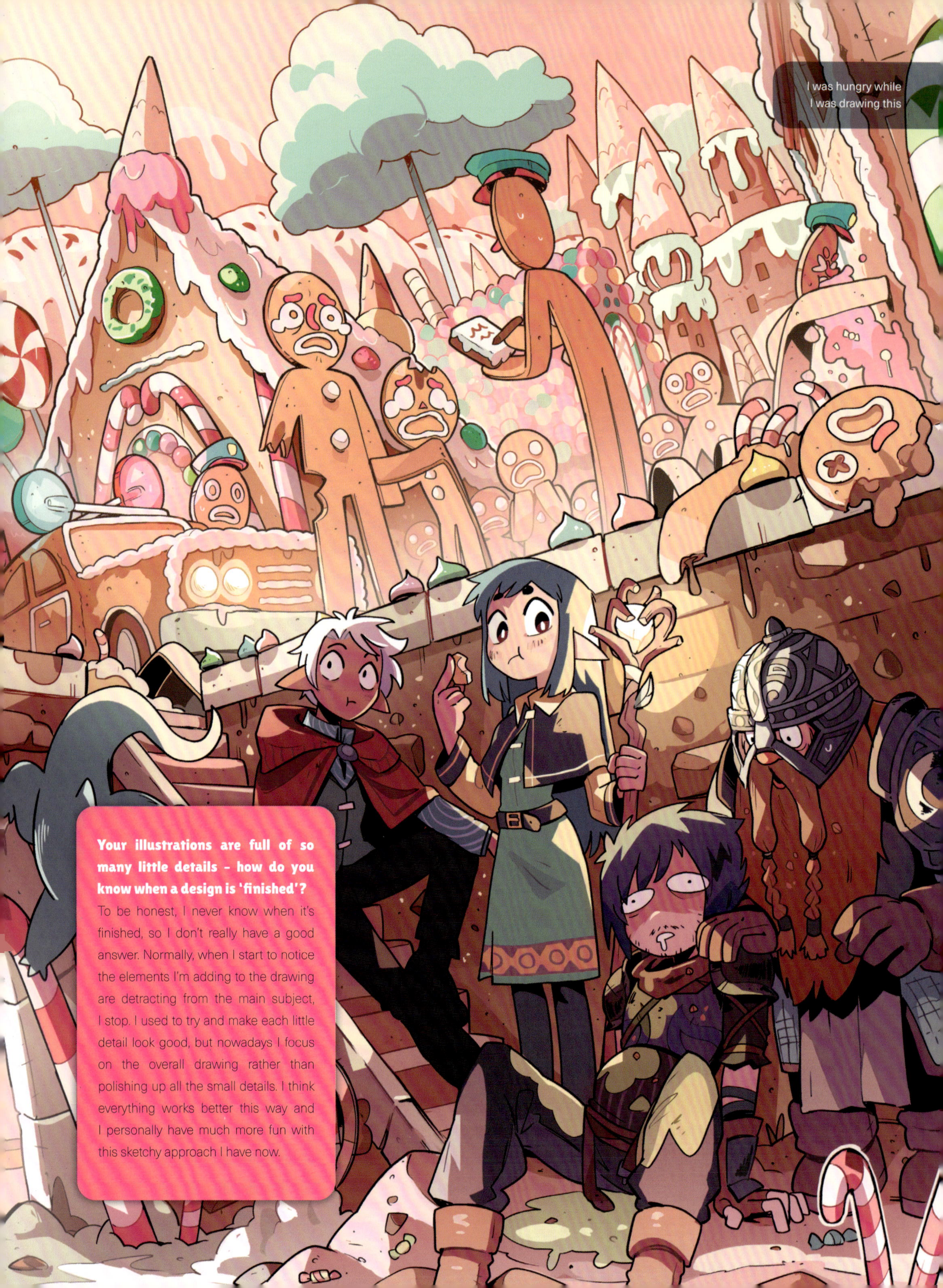

Your illustrations are full of so many little details - how do you know when a design is 'finished'?

To be honest, I never know when it's finished, so I don't really have a good answer. Normally, when I start to notice the elements I'm adding to the drawing are detracting from the main subject, I stop. I used to try and make each little detail look good, but nowadays I focus on the overall drawing rather than polishing up all the small details. I think everything works better this way and I personally have much more fun with this sketchy approach I have now.

Key art for the latest *Cult of the Lamb* DLC

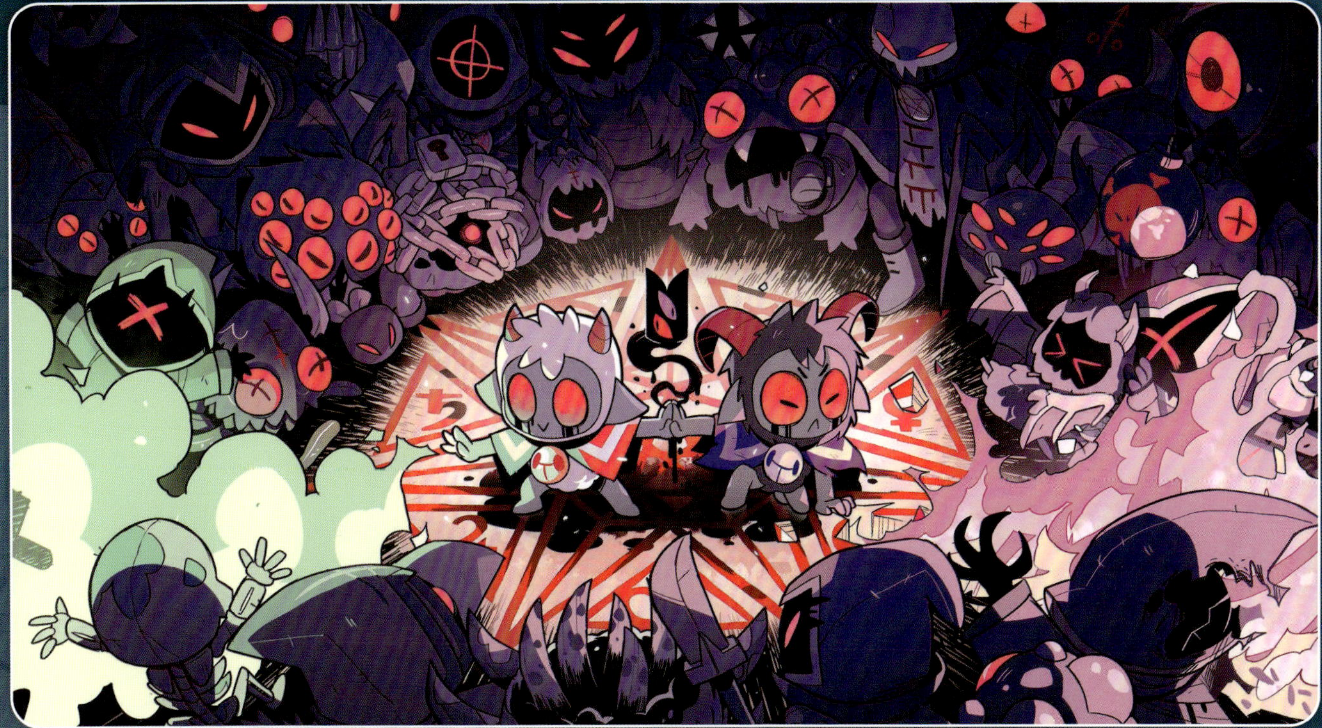

And how about colour? How do you make sure all these elements harmonize?

I'm not great at explaining this either, because I rely heavily on intuition, rather than being super technical about it. However, I do try to stay very organized with my drawing files. Keeping everything separated into different layers helps me focus on each part of the drawing without getting overwhelmed. Additionally, having a clear light source in mind helps a lot.

Thanks for chatting with us Carles! Are there any projects coming up we should be looking out for?

Thank you so much! Next year, Oni Press will publish *Soma*, a comic I worked on a few years ago which is finally getting translated into English. Also, if you are a *Cult of the Lamb* fan, I think you should be excited for some cool things to be announced in the future. I can't say any more right now, but I'm having a blast working on it!

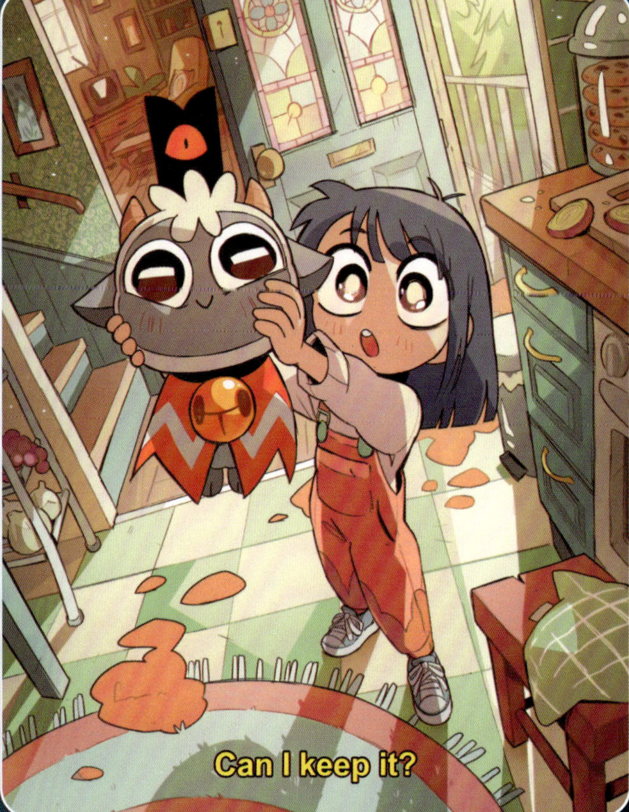

All praise the lamb!

SEASON OF THE WITCH

Learn how Carles Dalmau creates a fresh new character from scratch

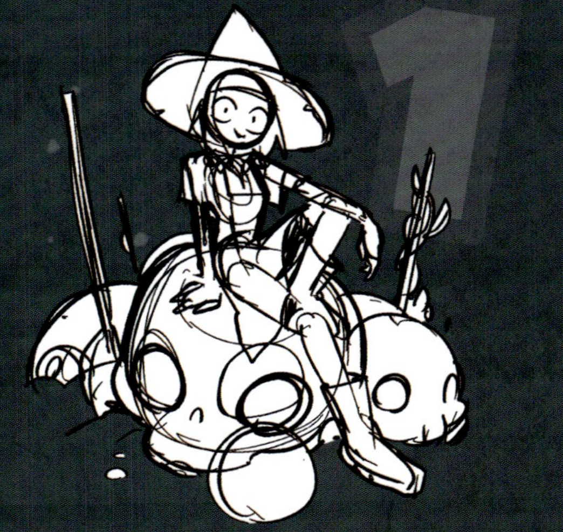

1 I start by loosely defining how the pose and overall composition will look. My sketches are very rough, but despite this, I will define how every key element of the character will look at this early stage.

2 I clean up the sketch so I understand how most of the details work. This will make the line-art process much easier for me. At this point the sketch is still looking quite loose – I'll have more fun improvising the fine details when I get to the line art.

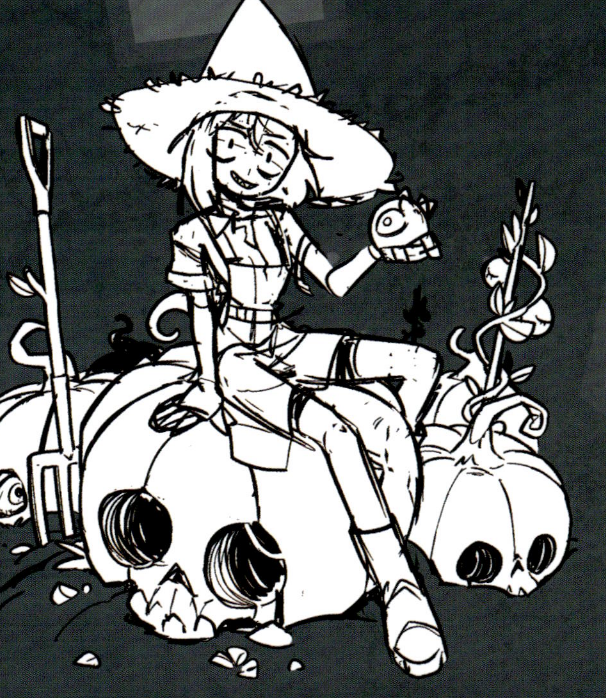

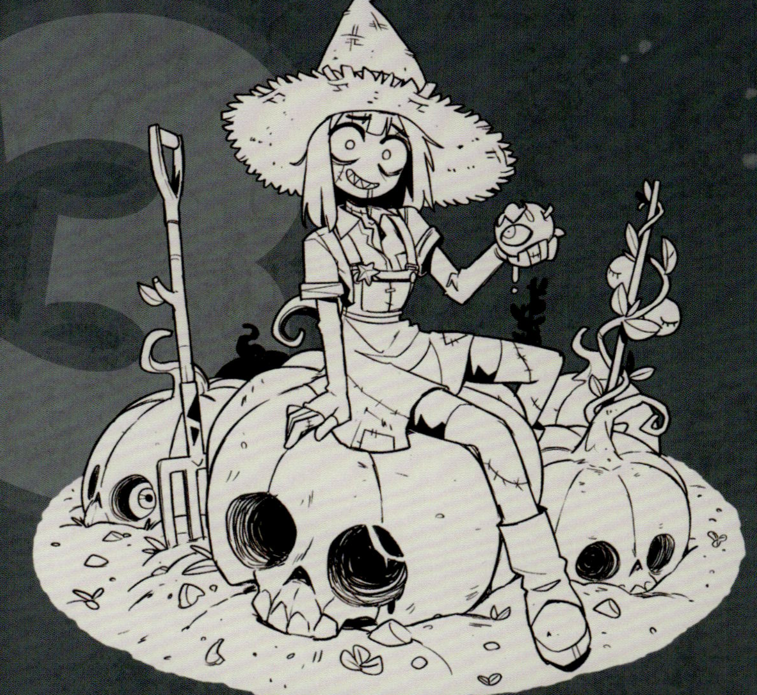

3 I draw all the line art on a layer on top of the sketch. The line art may look clean when looking at the full piece, but if you were to zoom in on the details, they are still a bit loose. I used to make everything look super clean, but now I prefer how this sketchy line art looks. I find it helps to focus on the overall piece rather than small, isolated elements.

4 I separate each main part on to a different layer (the witch, the pumpkins, and so on), so everything is more organized for the rendering stage. I try to use colours without too much contrast, since they will look better together.

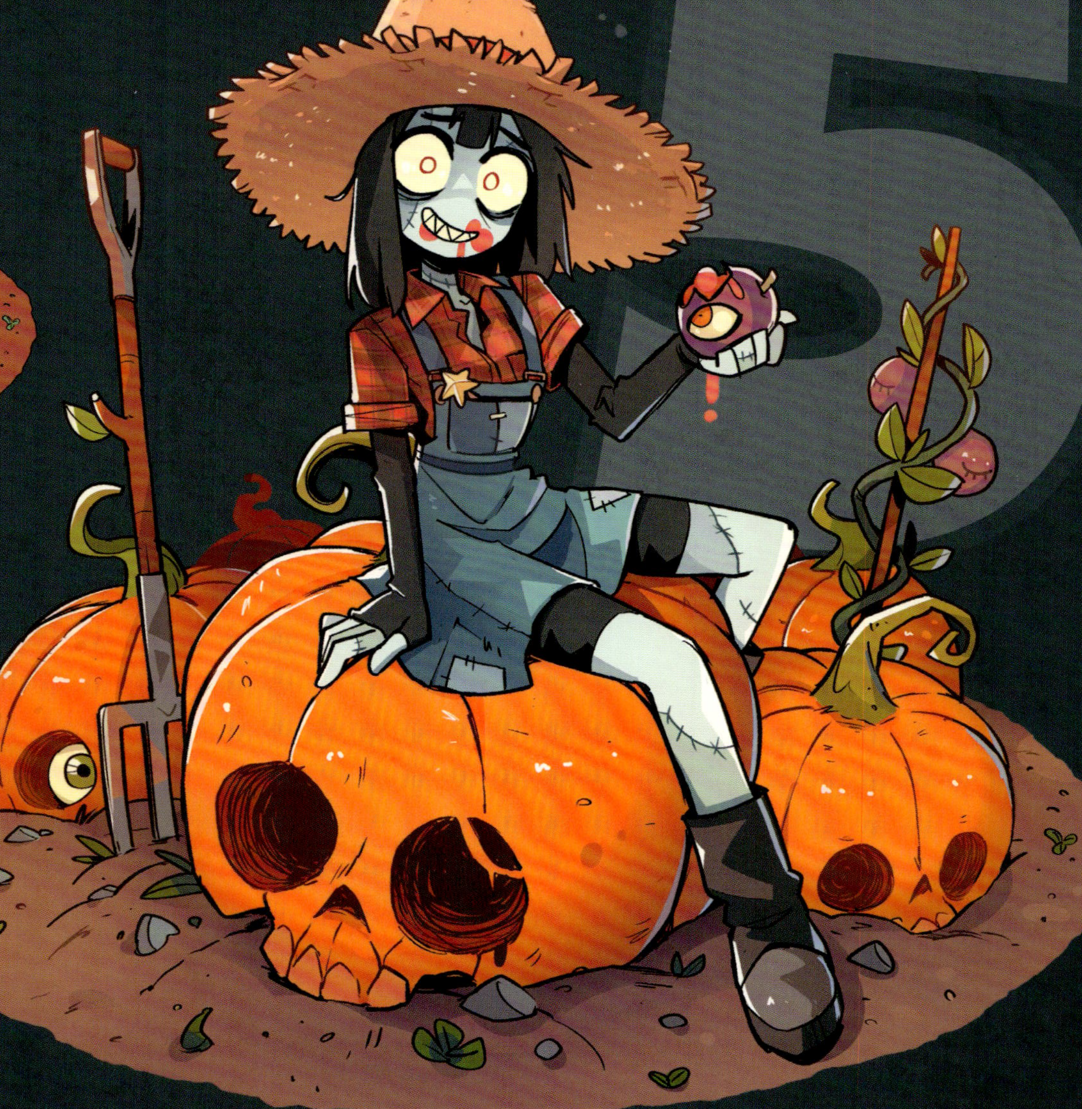

'I PREFER HOW THIS SKETCHY LINE ART LOOKS'

5 The final step is to think of the lighting this scene has, so I add shadows and lights on each element so they look nice and cohesive together. After I finish the render, I paint over some of the line art to integrate it further into the drawing, and it's finished!

HOW I

REAL-LIFE INSPIRATION

Often you can find yourself not knowing what to draw. Real-life events can be a great inspiration for your work. For example, this artwork was created as a part of the annual MerMay challenge and is a tribute to Ukrainian artist Lyubov Panchenko. The mermaid's face and hairstyle were inspired by the artist herself, and the overall design was inspired by one of Lyubov's art pieces.

STYLIZE

Visual art is a great way to express yourself and contrary to popular belief, 'a right way to make art' isn't really a thing. There are general guidelines to particular styles and it's great to know and practise them, but when it comes to self-expression, the only right way to make art is the one that makes you happy. You are going to spend countless hours drawing in your style, so make it enjoyable!

Every artist has their own tips and tricks they've learnt through the years which define their approach to art. Unfortunately, there are no shortcuts to finding your own unique style, only hours of work. Let me show you the building blocks of my approach to art. I've gathered together some of the techniques I use in my work – maybe some of them will resonate with you.

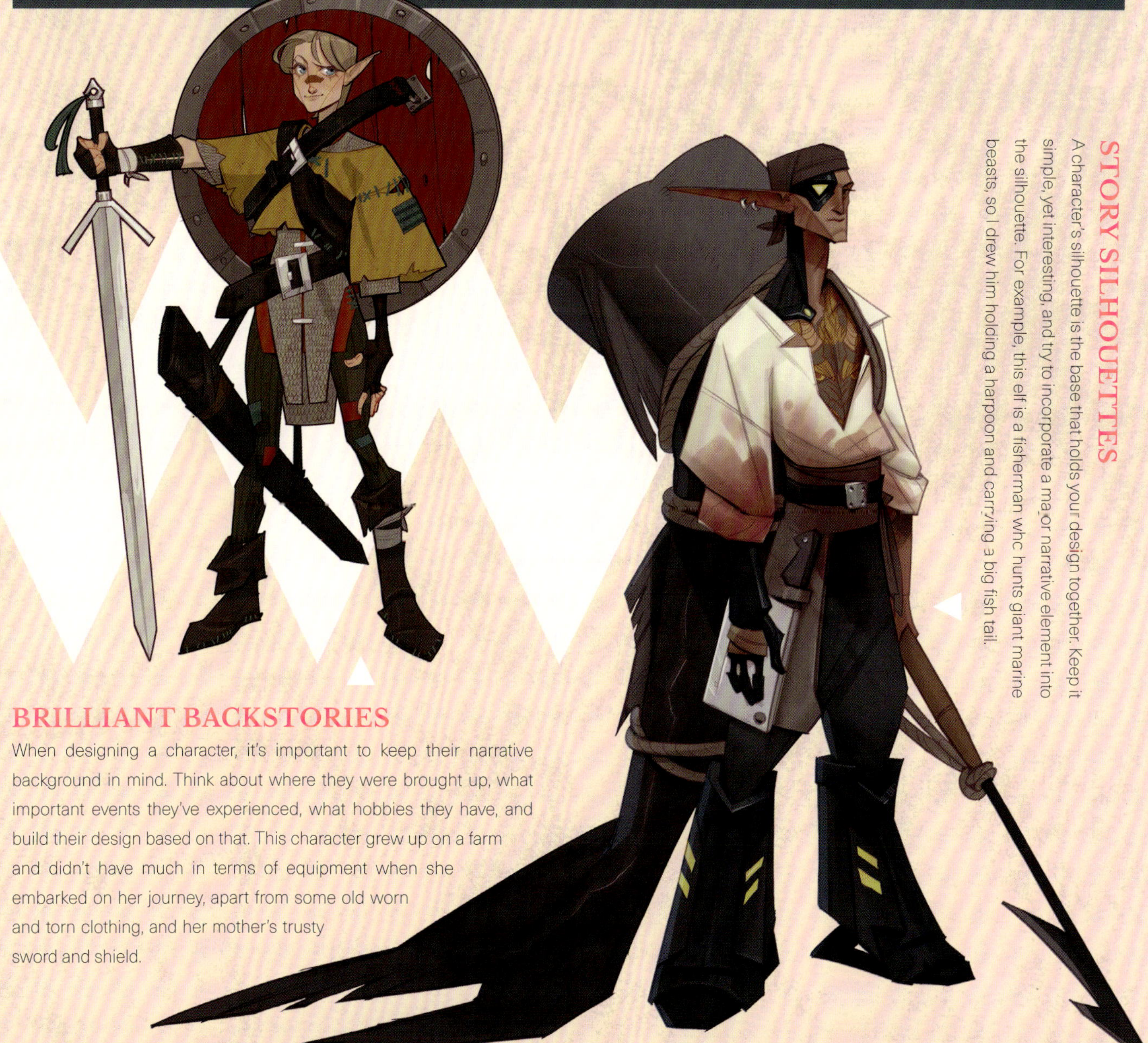

BRILLIANT BACKSTORIES

When designing a character, it's important to keep their narrative background in mind. Think about where they were brought up, what important events they've experienced, what hobbies they have, and build their design based on that. This character grew up on a farm and didn't have much in terms of equipment when she embarked on her journey, apart from some old worn and torn clothing, and her mother's trusty sword and shield.

STORY SILHOUETTES

A character's silhouette is the base that holds your design together. Keep it simple, yet interesting, and try to incorporate a major narrative element into the silhouette. For example, this elf is a fisherman who hunts giant marine beasts, so I drew him holding a harpoon and carrying a big fish tail.

PATTERN POWER

Adding patterns to your designs can make them a lot more interesting. It also creates an opportunity to tell the viewer more about the character: their background, where they are from, their line of work – maybe even foreshadow their fate.

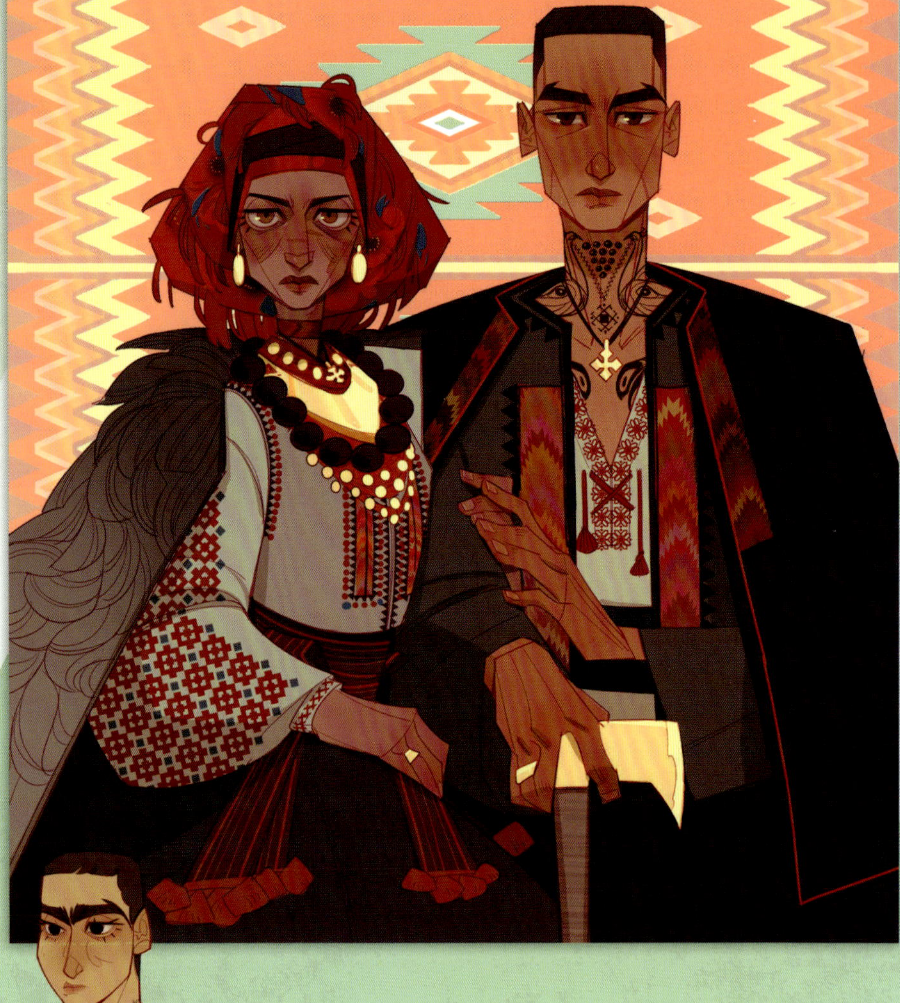

COLOURS TELL A STORY

The colours you choose for a character not only say a lot about who they are, but also about their relations to other characters. Here are two leads from my comic *Bird House* – they are polar opposites in terms of background and overall character, yet they have a lot in common as well. Their designs reflect their tumultuous relationship, with the colours of their clothing being inverted versions of each other.

BUILDING FROM BASIC SHAPES

Sometimes it can be very hard to create a compelling silhouette. The best way to start is to choose a basic shape, such as a circle, triangle, or rectangle, and build your character design from there. This technique will also help with keeping the silhouette clean and simple, because you'll always have that original shape as your guideline.

REPURPOSE STEREOTYPES
Stereotypes in your designs are usually boring and lazy, however using them against type can make a character more compelling. This character's story arc focuses on exploring the way society considers any showing of emotion as negative, embarrassing, and feminine. He is a very emotional person – however, he hides it. As a nod to his 'feminine' emotional side, I gave him a pocket bag and a coin necklace, which are considered stereotypically women's accessories.

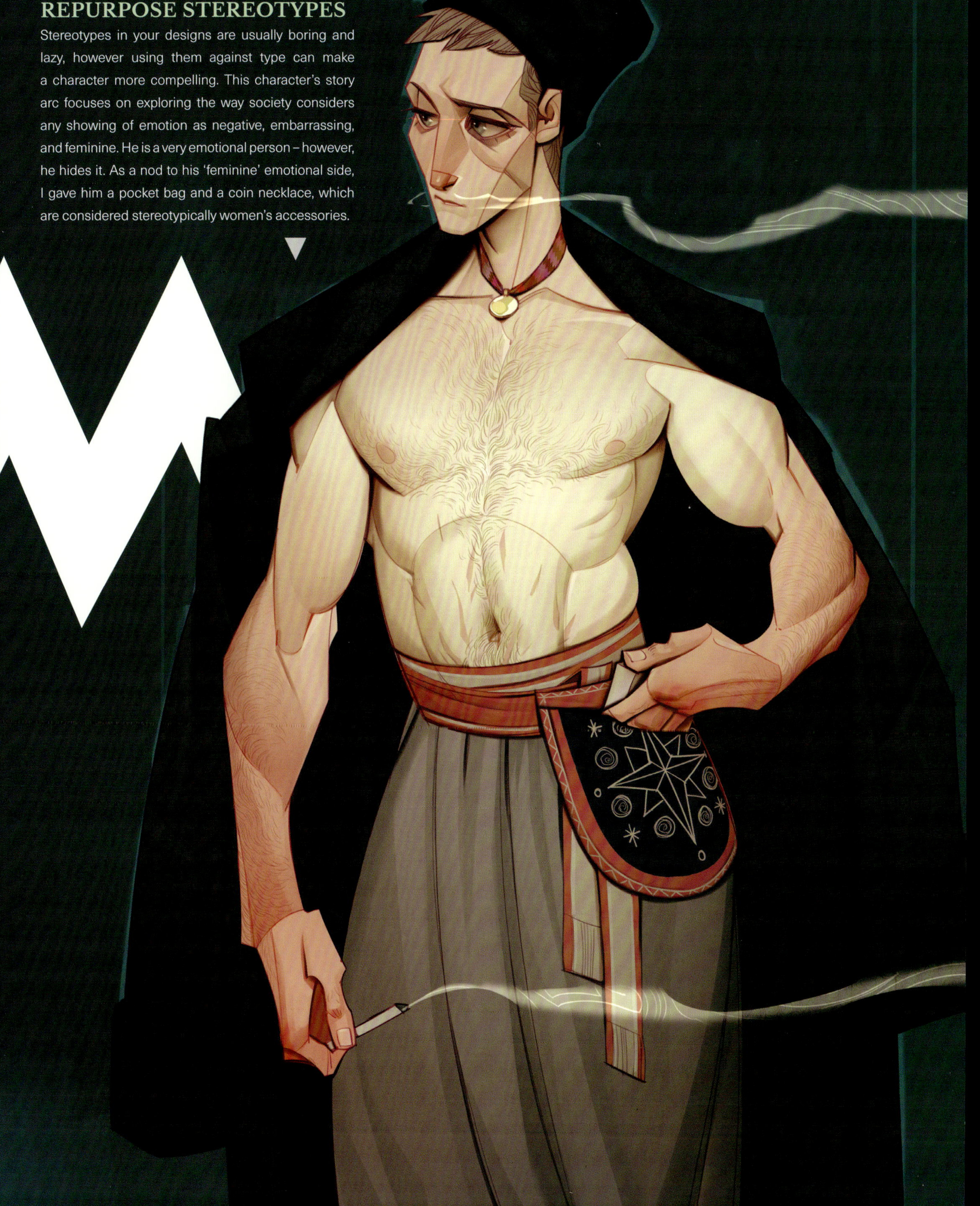

THROUGH THE LOOKING GLASS

KATE PELLERIN

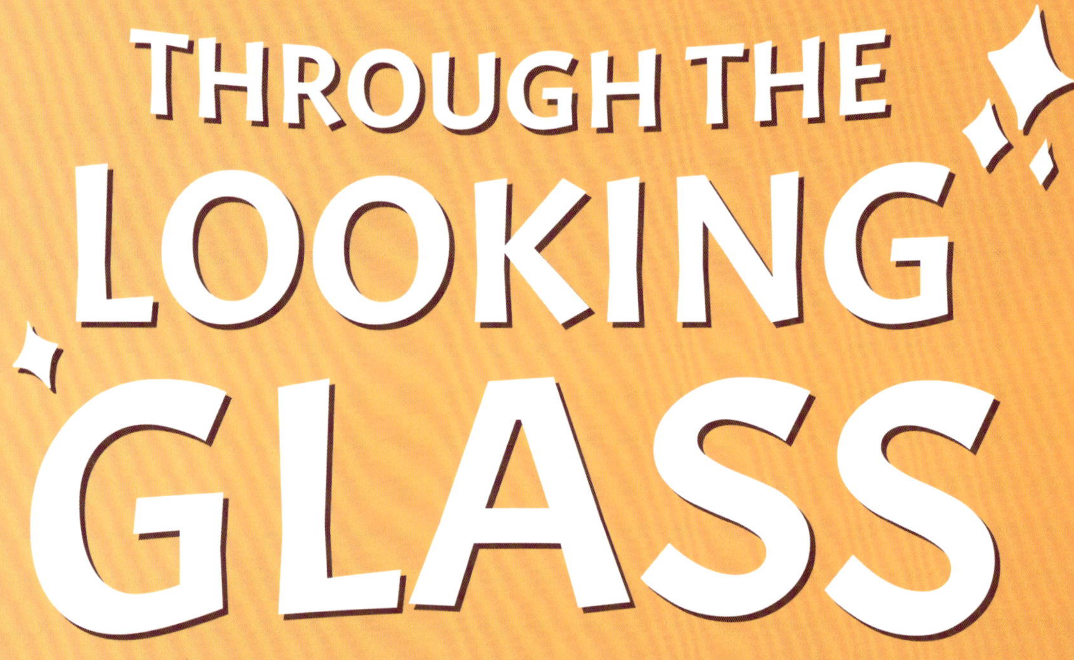

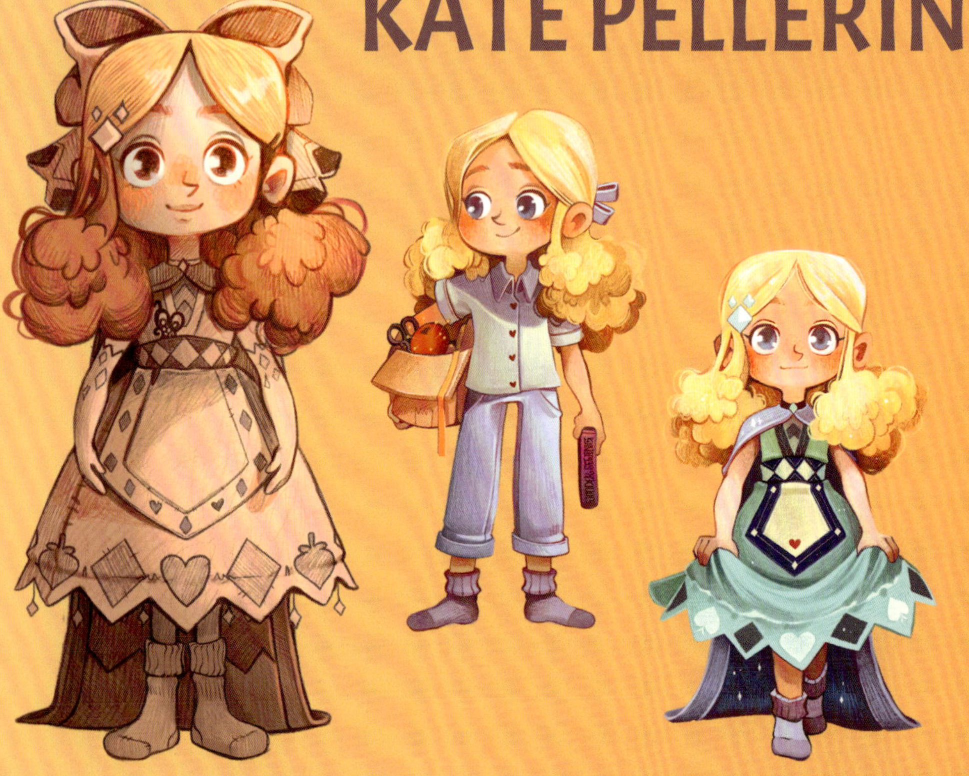

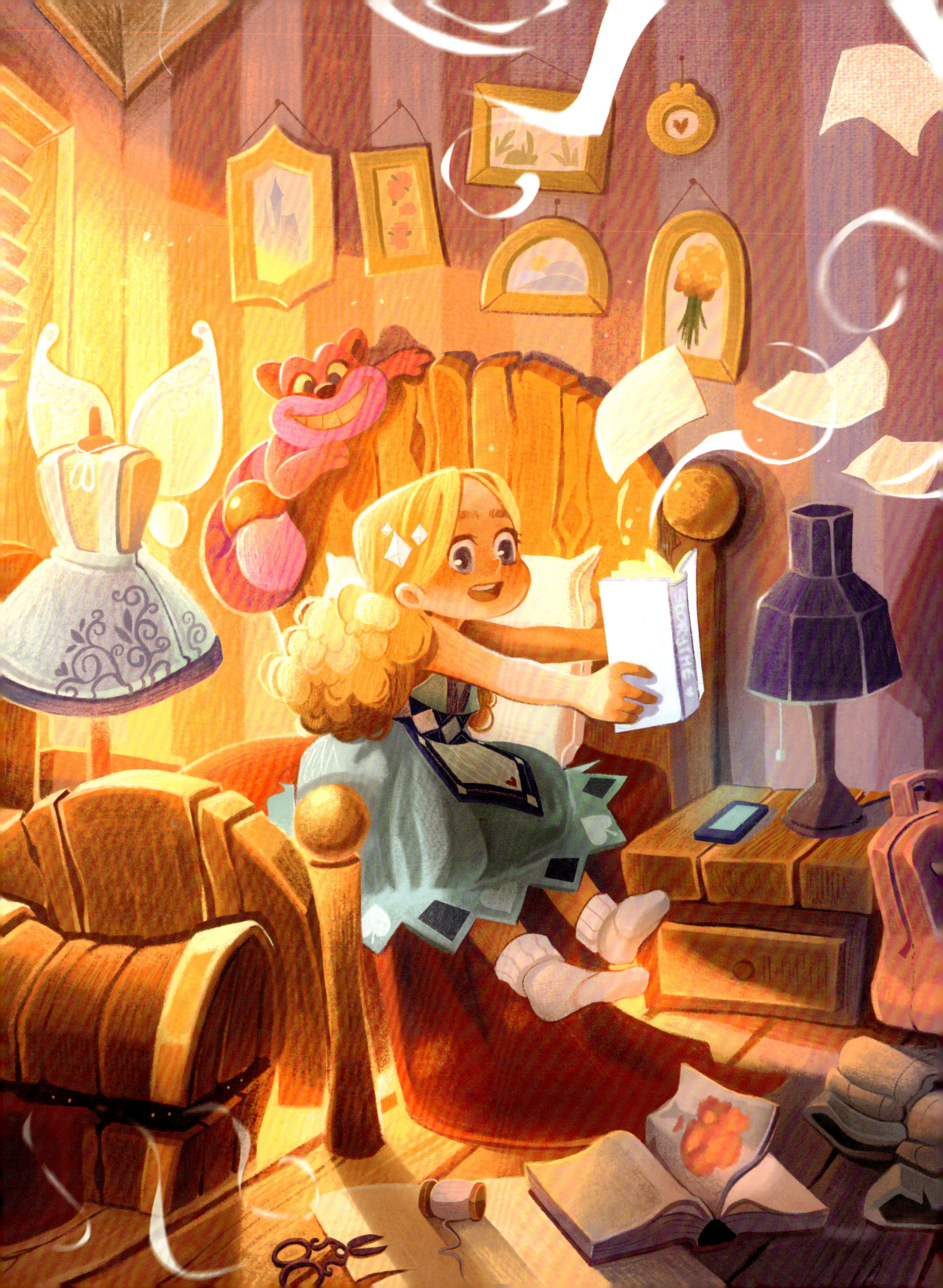

In this tutorial, I want to share my process of reinventing a classic character. I'll be creating my take on Alice, from *Alice in Wonderland*, in a way that feels alive and fun. I want to make sure to keep her base characteristics, but at the same time see how far I can push my imagination to build something new and interesting. I'll demonstrate my process through a lot of character development on Procreate and a bit of sketchbook drawing in the early phases of this tutorial. Without further ado, let's get into it!

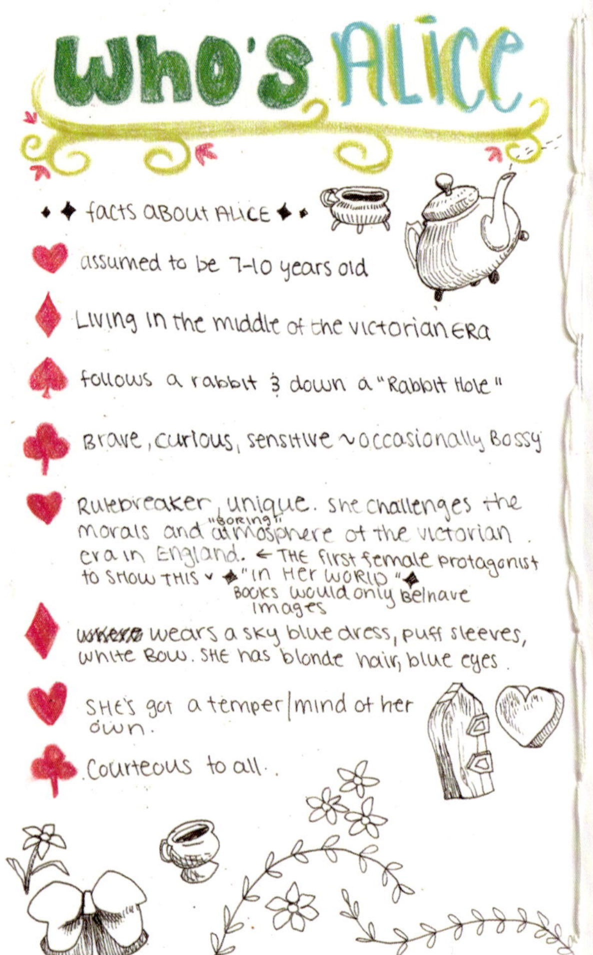

Writing ideas for Alice in a home-made sketchbook

The first thing I do when creating a character design is to figure out who the character really is. There are many questions to ask, such as where they live, what era they are from, what their personality is like, whether they are human or not, and so on. I start by jotting this information in my sketchbook, sticking as close to Alice's story as I can. I like to keep this part analogue so I can have my references next to me, rather than on my iPad screen.

When you are designing a character (and especially reimagining one) I recommend asking yourself what kind of journey your character is on. Figure out what happens to them throughout their story, what important events might take place, and so on.

For reinvented Alice, my goal is to keep her core characteristics and the original message of the story. However, I want to place her new design in a modern setting, instead of the Victorian Era in which the original book is set. So, for this phase I jot down the core characteristics I want my Alice to have, while also looking back to the first step to make sure I stay close to who the original Alice is.

Planning the next steps using a mind map

If anyone asks me for tips to improve their character development, I always recommend starting with studying shape design. At first, shaping silhouettes can be challenging, but it will help elevate your character designs, perhaps more than any other tip.

To warm up, I start working from my comfort shapes: circles. I ask myself if I want Alice to have a firmer or softer head shape. Since she is quite young, I decide on the softer, rounded shape. Next, I play with the nose and ears, adding a bit of personality to these early shape designs.

A series of different head silhouettes to warm up

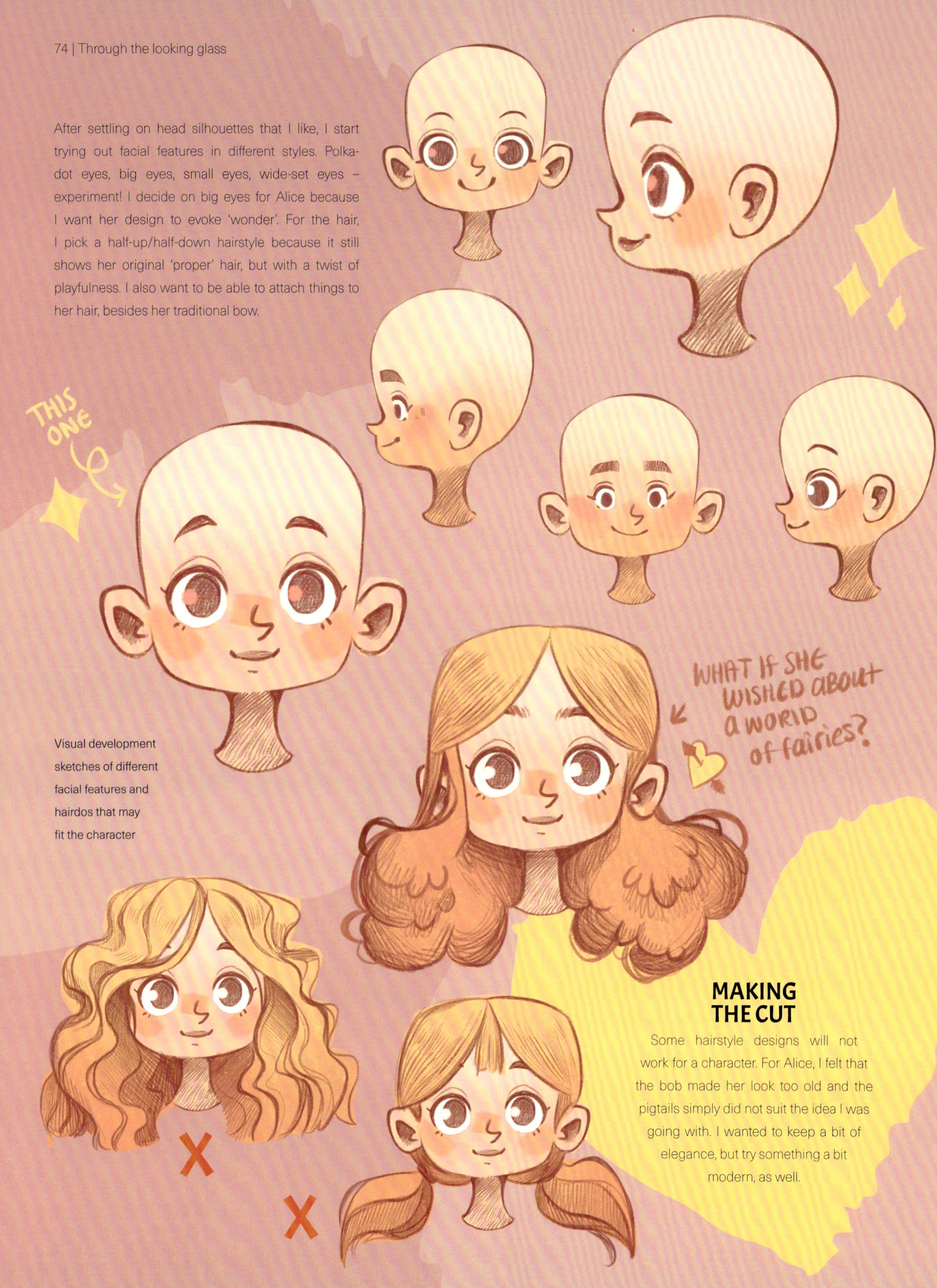

After settling on head silhouettes that I like, I start trying out facial features in different styles. Polka-dot eyes, big eyes, small eyes, wide-set eyes – experiment! I decide on big eyes for Alice because I want her design to evoke 'wonder'. For the hair, I pick a half-up/half-down hairstyle because it still shows her original 'proper' hair, but with a twist of playfulness. I also want to be able to attach things to her hair, besides her traditional bow.

Visual development sketches of different facial features and hairdos that may fit the character

MAKING THE CUT

Some hairstyle designs will not work for a character. For Alice, I felt that the bob made her look too old and the pigtails simply did not suit the idea I was going with. I wanted to keep a bit of elegance, but try something a bit modern, as well.

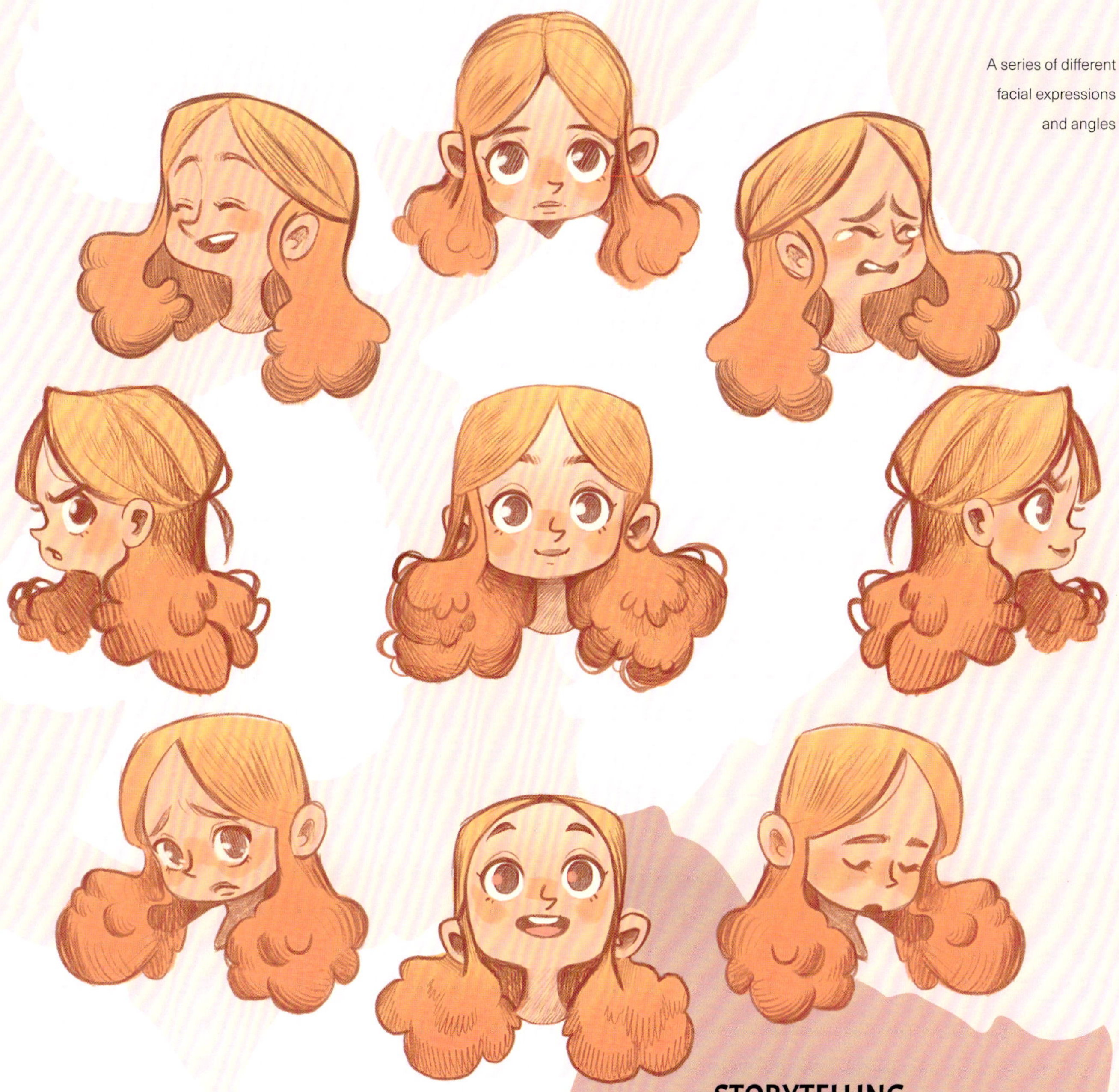

A series of different
facial expressions
and angles

Whenever I design a character, I always use the wheel of expression. It will help you understand how your character looks from different angles and help you practise consistency. My characters always start to drift after a while if I don't complete this step. I keep the wheel of expression next to me as I work, always referring back to it as I draw.

STORYTELLING WITH EXPRESSIONS

When creating facial expressions, it's good to remember what your character's personality is like. Each head rotation can make a certain emotion stronger, so choose wisely. For example, if your character loves to laugh, using the 'looking up' rotations – looking up when laughing will make the laugh seem more intense. If your character is evil, using the 'looking down' rotation and having them laugh will make them look creepy. You may think it would be odd to look down and laugh, but it wouldn't be for an evil character!

With the head of the character done, I can start imagining what the rest of her body looks like. I recommend starting with the head because you can get a sense of who your character is through facial structure and expressions. Once you have that, it makes it easier to envision the character's body. For Alice, I don't want to stray too far from her original design, but at the same time I want to bring through my own style, so I play with different sizes of limbs, picking which ones I think suit Alice best.

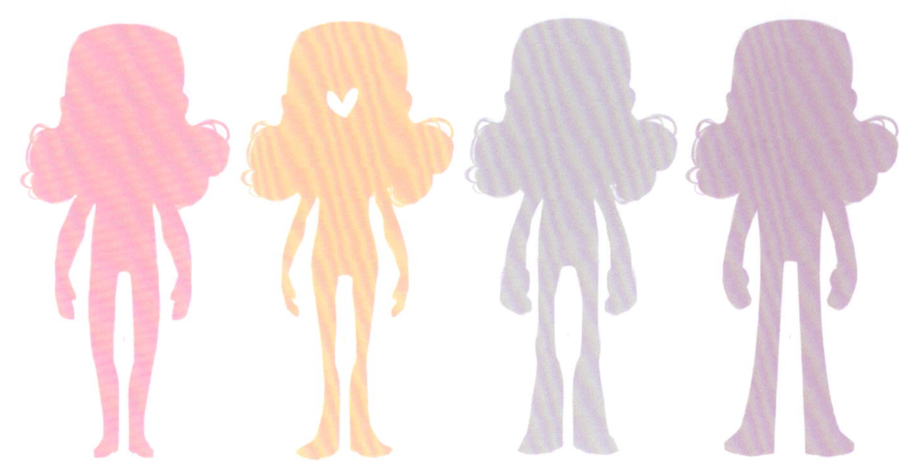

Potential silhouette ideas for Alice

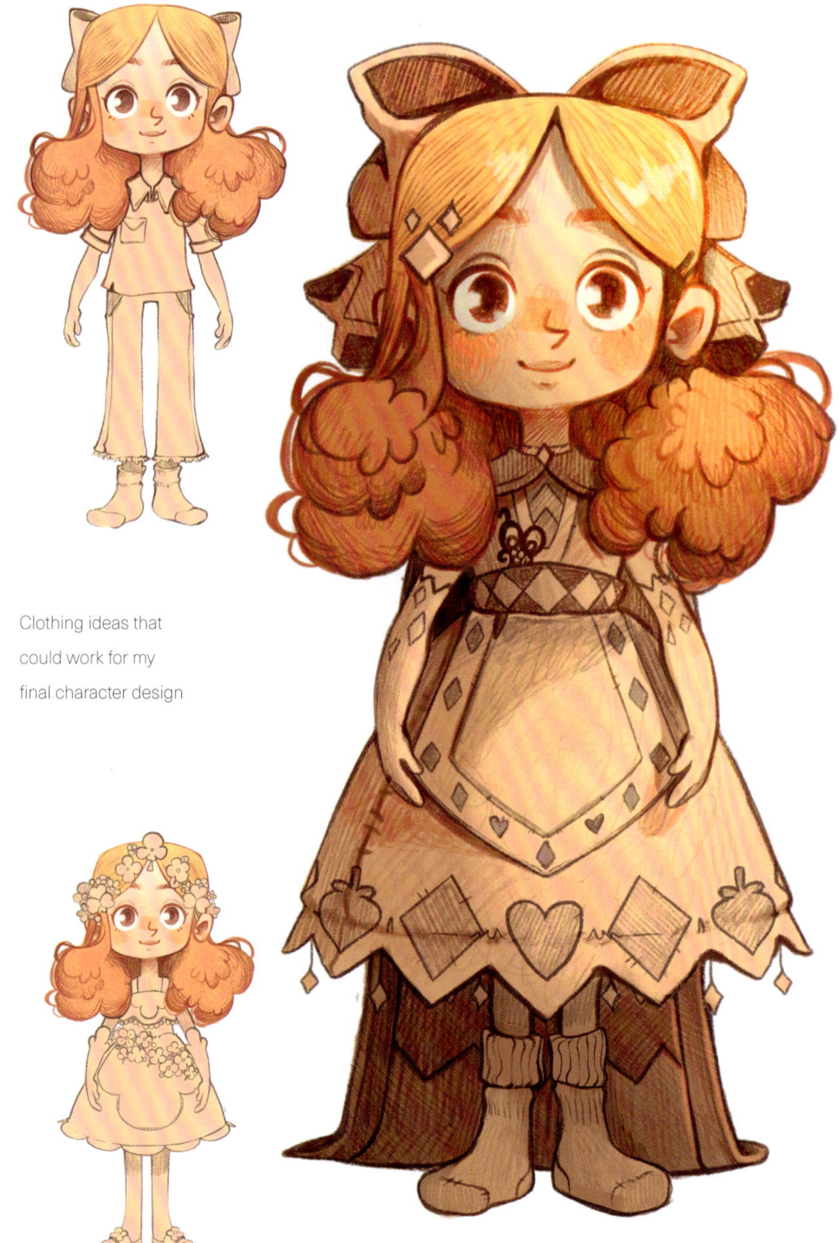

Clothing ideas that could work for my final character design

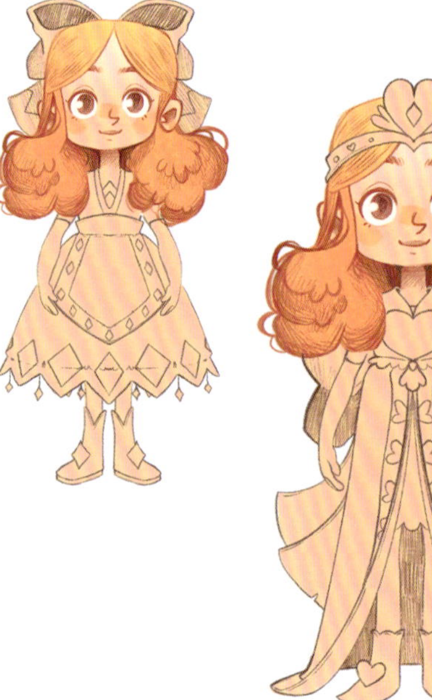

Did you play dress-up games when you were a kid? If you did, then this next step will feel familiar, except we're creating the clothes our character is trying on! Before starting this phase, make sure your character's proportions work – if everything looks good, you can start to dress them up. I want to create one example of clothing that depicts Alice's 'normal' clothes. Then, for the next three examples, I create outfits that Alice might imagine to be the 'perfect' outfit. These outfits are inspired by the Queen of Hearts and other aspects of the original story. I'm imagining Alice creating her own world through sewing.

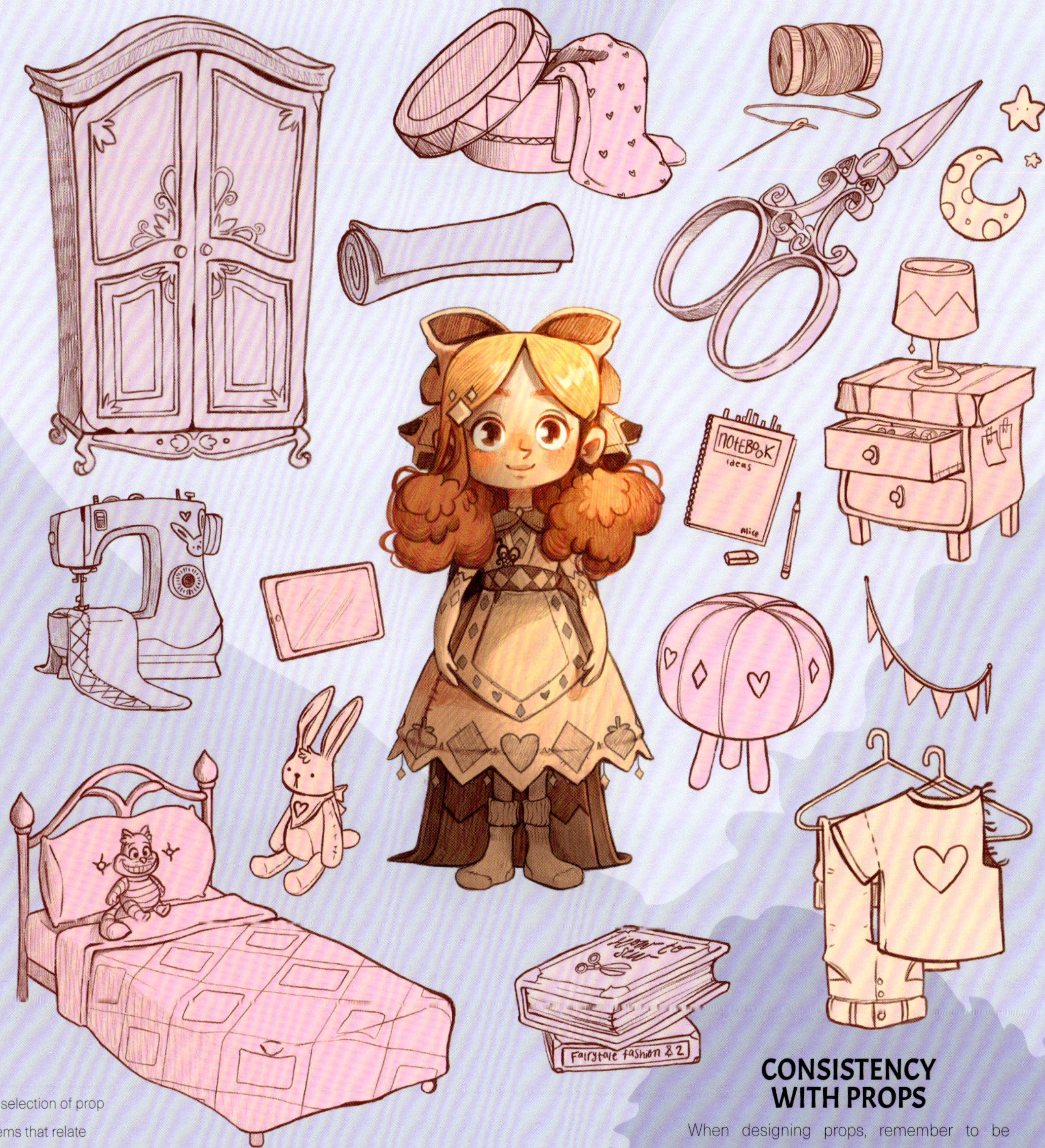

A selection of prop items that relate to the character

CONSISTENCY WITH PROPS

When designing props, remember to be consistent throughout. If you want your props to be cute, you may want to stay with soft or rounded edges. If your props are supposed to feel scary, then use sharp angles. Another way to keep them consistent is to add the same types of patterns to a variety of props. If you use circles, make sure others have the same type of circle, too.

Designing props that fit the character you're creating is another step that I wouldn't skip. Figure out their favourite tea cup, chair, bed to sleep in, and so on – it's a fun exercise and teaches you so much about your character. Designing props can also aid with world-building. For example, I know I want to portray Alice in a bedroom, so I think of props that could be found in such an environment. I consider her personality and where she lives when creating these items, further enriching the narrative.

Next, I work on adding detail to the design by looking at patterns. Often patterns and detailing will be affected by all the research and world-building we did at the start of the process, so keep your brainstorming ideas in mind. For Alice, I want to keep some elements from the original story, so I add some plaid and the symbols from a deck of cards: hearts, spades, diamonds, and clubs.

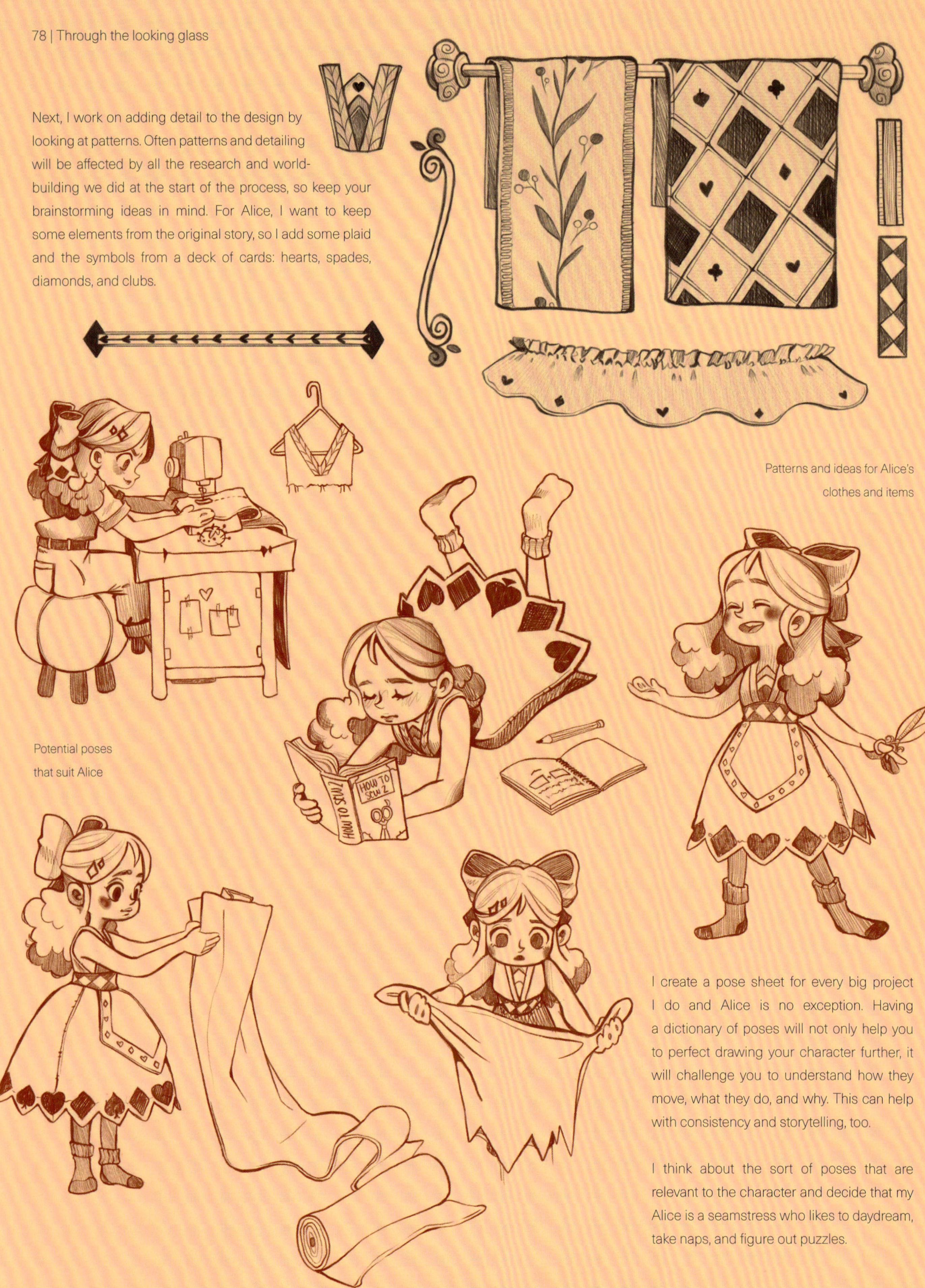

Patterns and ideas for Alice's clothes and items

Potential poses that suit Alice

I create a pose sheet for every big project I do and Alice is no exception. Having a dictionary of poses will not only help you to perfect drawing your character further, it will challenge you to understand how they move, what they do, and why. This can help with consistency and storytelling, too.

I think about the sort of poses that are relevant to the character and decide that my Alice is a seamstress who likes to daydream, take naps, and figure out puzzles.

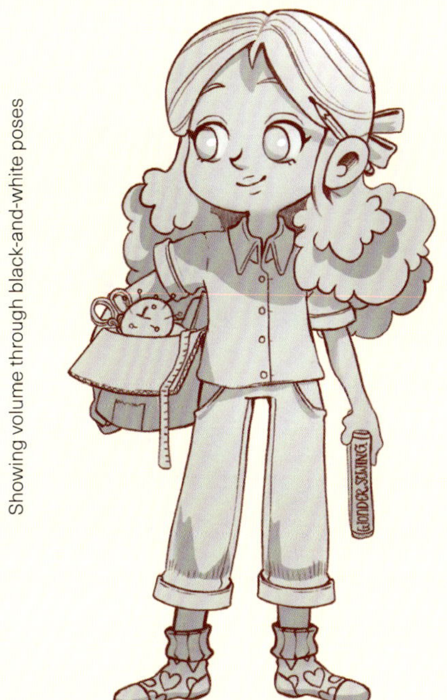

ABOUT to start

mid-process

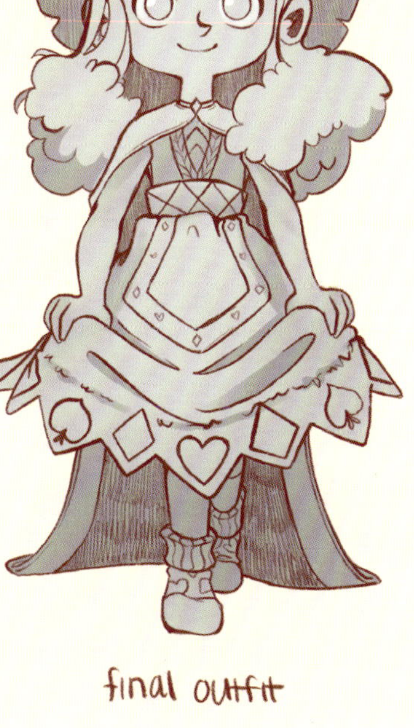

final outfit

When creating any character, it's important to figure out the mass of your character before you add colour. Doing so will allow you to see if there are any problems with your design, in terms of flatness, and will bring your character closer to life. I find that you can add even more story to a character pose through the use of shadow and lighting. Be as dramatic as you'd like!

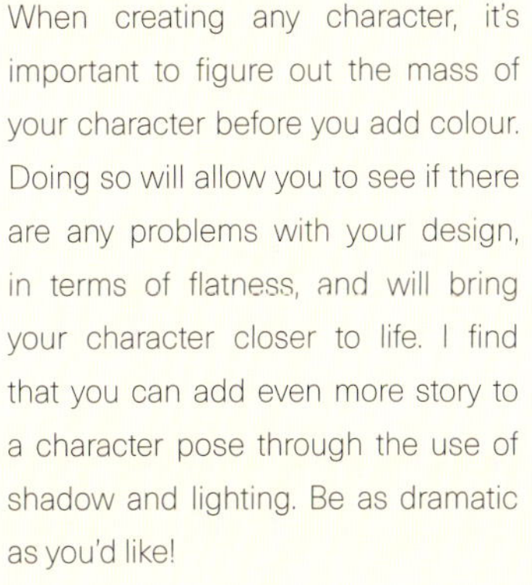

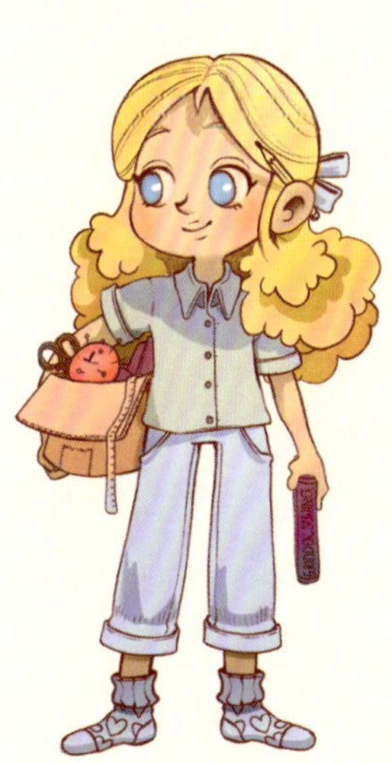

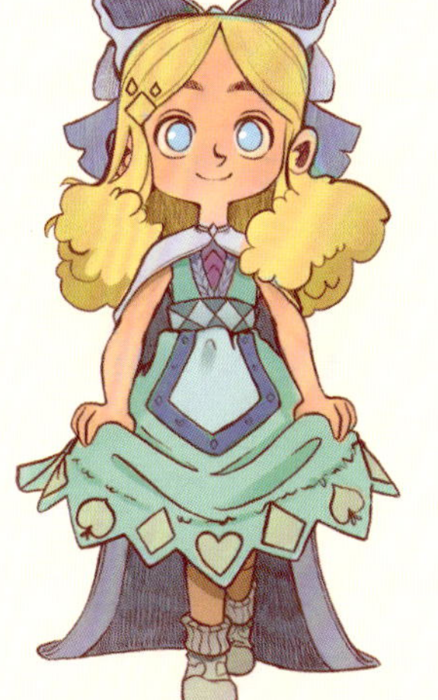

Multiple rough colour palettes for Alice

I always find selecting colours to be the hardest part of creating a character. There are so many colours to choose from, so how do you pick the best one? I narrow down palettes for my characters by doing multiple colour tests (even more than I'm showing here.) For Alice, I want to keep some of her original colours, such as blue and her original blonde hair. I then play with other pastel colours, such as mint green and pink, to find a combination that suits her personality.

Final colour
palettes

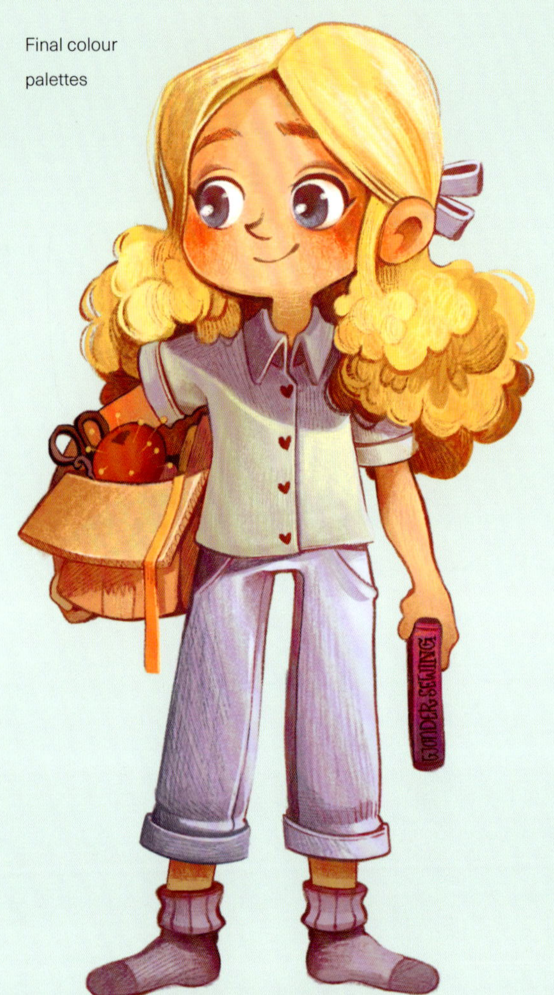

EVERY DAY OUTFIT

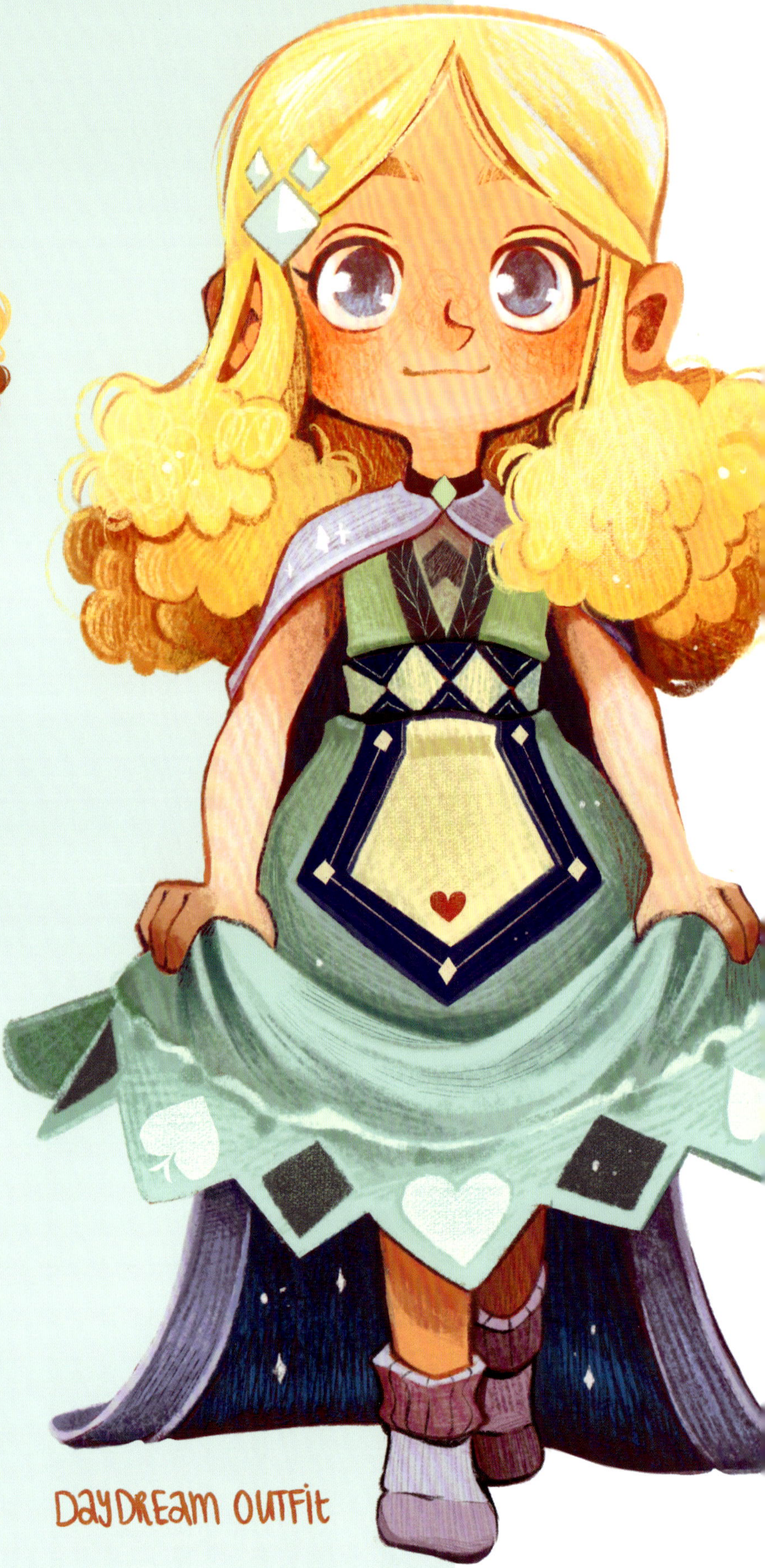

DAYDREAM OUTFIT

I decide to move forward with two different outfits for Alice: her own sewn creation and an everyday outfit. I choose a different colour palette for each, but with some common elements between the two. Both outfits have blues, teals, and purples, which tie them together, even if they don't share the same aesthetic.

When you find a colour palette you like, try to paint your character from start to finish as soon as you can, so you can spot anything you feel needs changing as early as possible. Sometimes adding colour will reveal something I'm not happy with about the design, which sends me back to the drawing board.

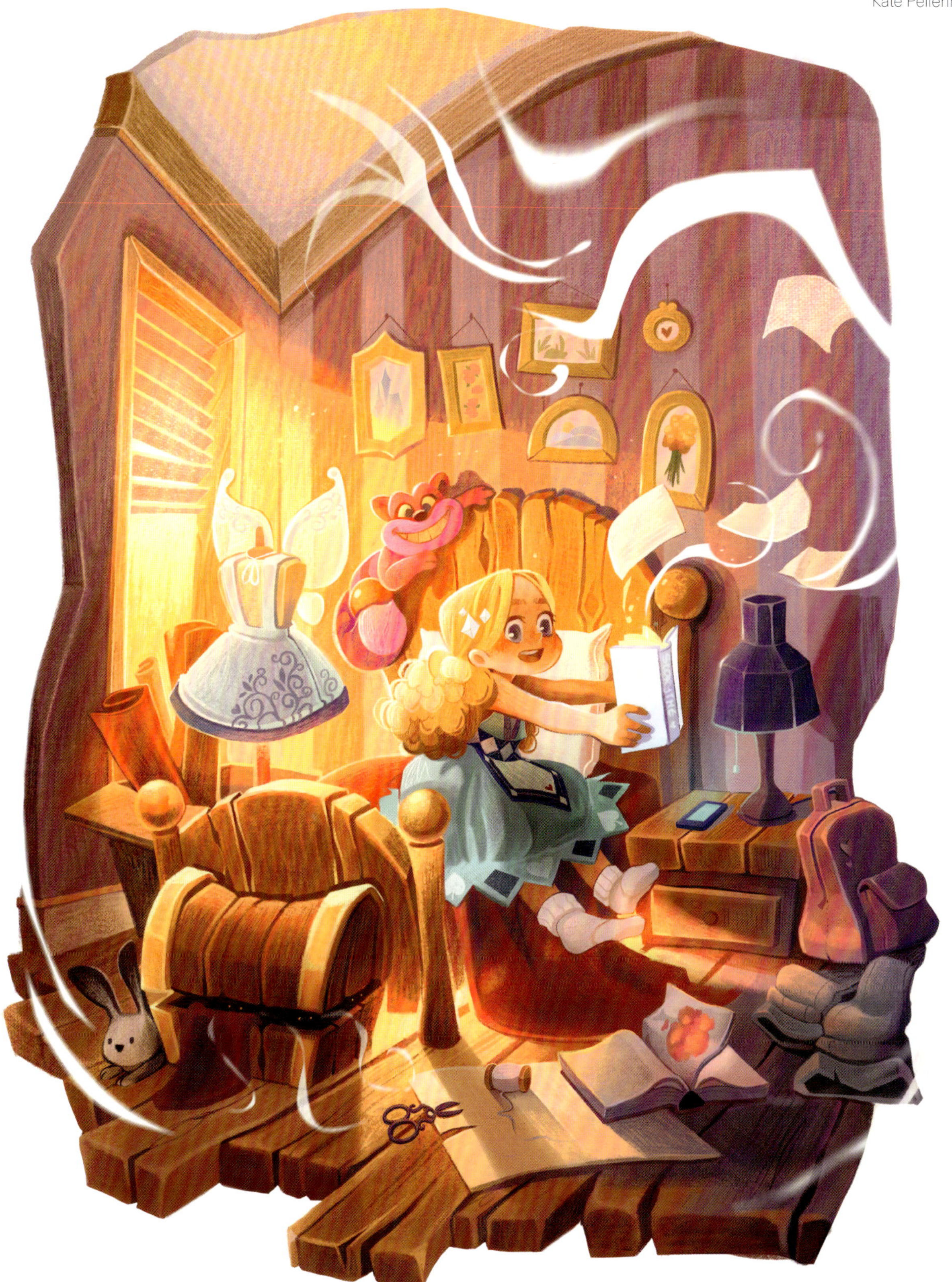

With my version of Alice completed, I can move on to the final step, which also happens to be one of my favourite parts of character design: bringing the character into an environment where they can live and breathe. I want to draw Alice in her bedroom, perhaps after a day at school. She's wearing a dress she's made and is in the process of designing another one for the world she is creating inside her head! Isn't that one of the best parts of being a kid? The part when you come home, throw your backpack on the floor, and play make-believe in your bedroom while the sun sets.

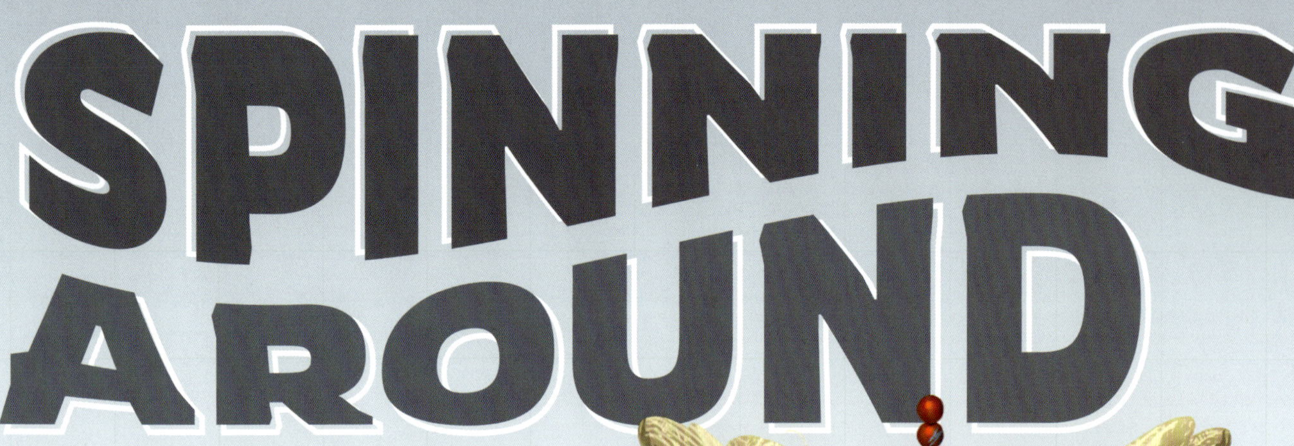

Sheryl Yap takes us step-by-step through creating a character turnaround for animation

Character turnarounds are typically used in animation and character design. They are essential to the production pipeline, as they provide the storyboard and modelling team with a comprehensive view of a character from multiple angles. Turnarounds allow the team to see every part of the character in three dimensions, including all the areas usually hidden by the camera.

In this article, I will be demonstrating how to design a character turnaround that could be used in the animation industry, sharing tips and tricks that will help you work more efficiently.

There are two common poses used when creating a character turnaround: the T-pose and the A-pose. In a T-pose, the arms are extended straight out from the shoulders, forming a 'T' shape with the body. The palms (in three-quarter, front, and back views) are usually faced down, with their fingers extended. In an A-pose, the arms are extended from the shoulders, but are angled slightly downwards, forming an 'A' shape with the body.

While both poses have their own advantages, usually 3D modellers prefer T-poses, as they are then able to see and model what is underneath the character's arms, so that's the pose we'll use for this demonstration. Our character, Uncle Barney, will help us along the way.

There are typically five views in a character turnaround: the front, three-quarter front, side view (if symmetrical), three-quarter back, and back. The most important pose is the three-quarter front view – this is where I usually start as it provides me with enough information to draw the other views.

Don't be afraid to draw loosely when starting on a design. This first rough pass is for you to generally block out your shapes, proportions, and volumes quickly. I start by establishing my ground plane, where Uncle Barney's back heels will be standing on all angles. This is to ensure consistency throughout the turns. As I establish the shapes and sketch them in, I make sure to add a vertical centre line. This helps the character retain its overall shape and proportions throughout the turn. Also, when sketching out the three-quarter view, be aware of the ellipses throughout the body. A common mistake is confusing the ellipses of the three-quarter front with the three-quarter back.

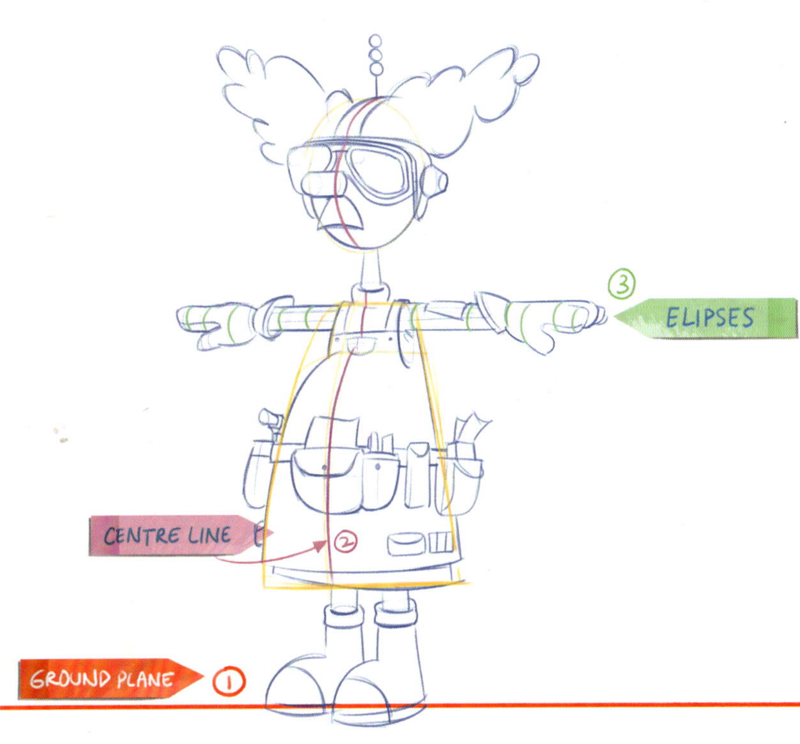

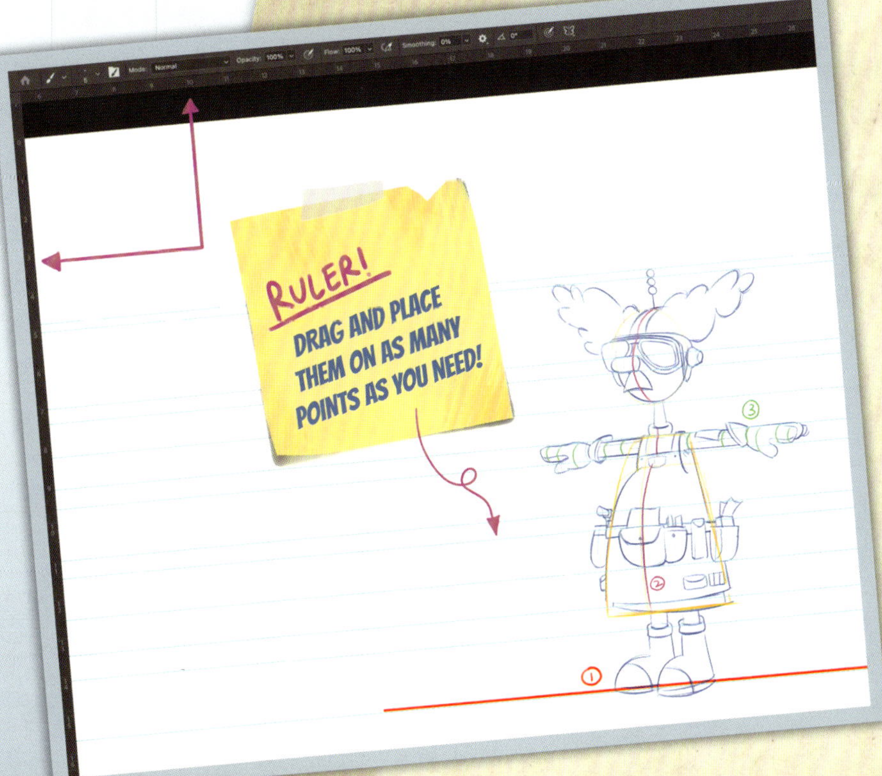

Once the three-quarter front is finished, it's time to start work on the other views. But before I do so, I set up some guidelines. Guidelines are crucial, as they ensure that the character's proportions and details remain accurate and uniform throughout all views. I usually do this by using Photoshop's ruler guides (Cmd+R). With the tool selected, click and place the lines at as many points as you need. I switch the guidelines on and off as and when I need them throughout the rest of the process (Cmd+:)

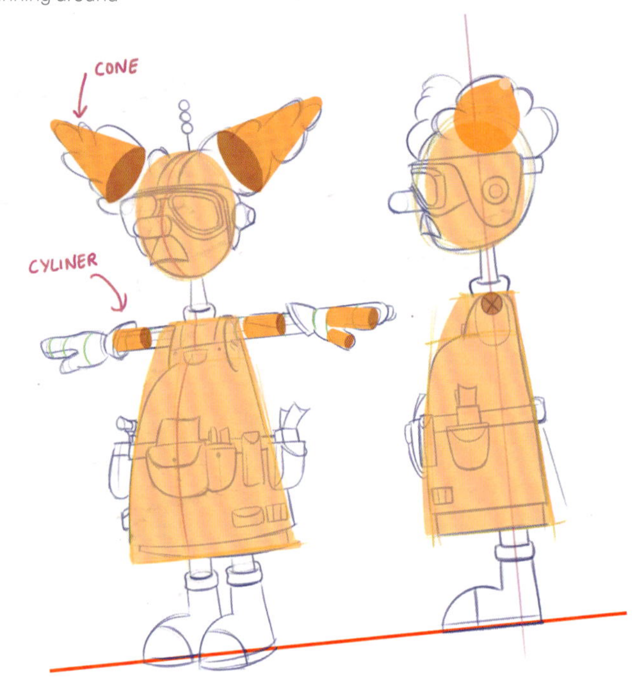

After setting up the guidelines, we move on to the trickiest part, which is translating individual elements into each view. One helpful tip that has made this part of the process so much easier for me is to break down each body part into simple shapes. Once you realize that arms are like cylinders, or that the hair of Uncle Barney resemble cones, you'll be able to quickly imagine how they might look in the different views.

For the back view of Uncle Barney, I take the front view, flip it horizontally, and edit it from there. To keep certain elements (such as legs, necks, and arms) consistent in different views, I make a selection from a certain view, then copy and paste them to use in others.

For side views, oftentimes the arms are not included, as it's essential for modellers to see the side of the body without any obstruction. Instead, I draw a circle with an 'x' inside to signify where Uncle Barney's arm would be.

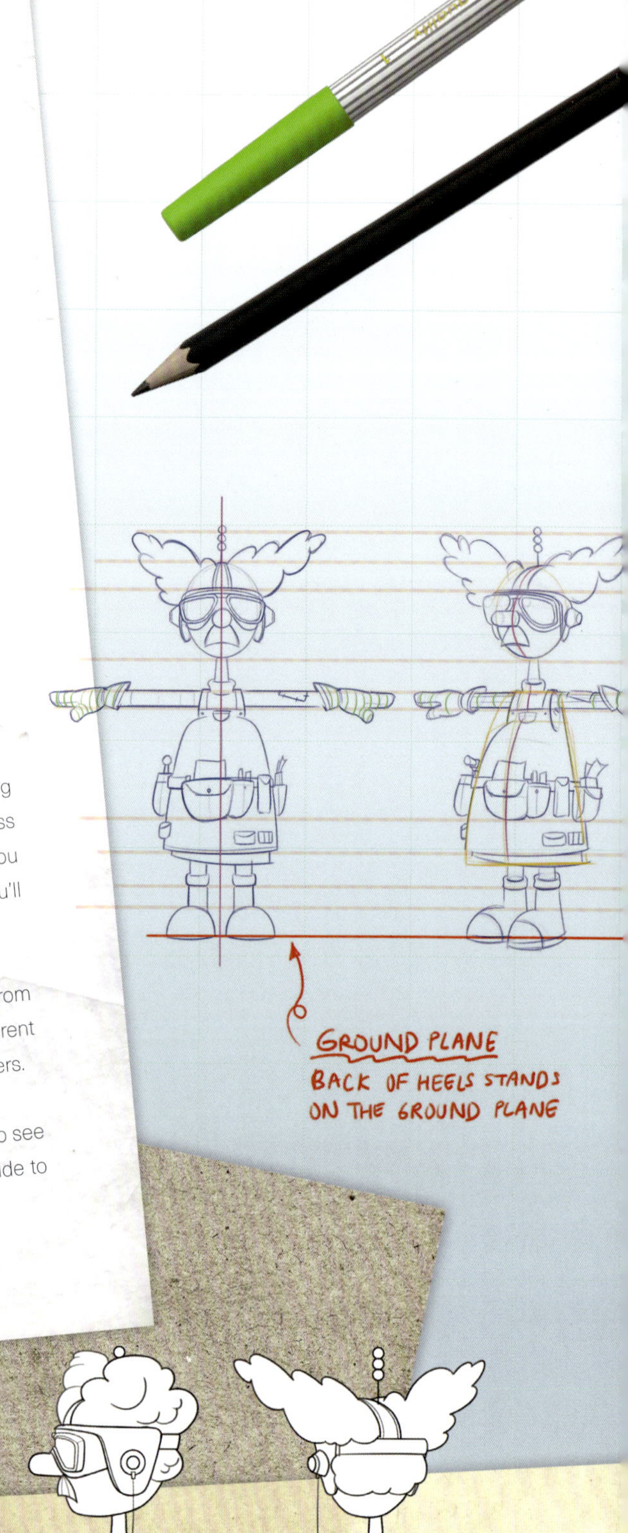

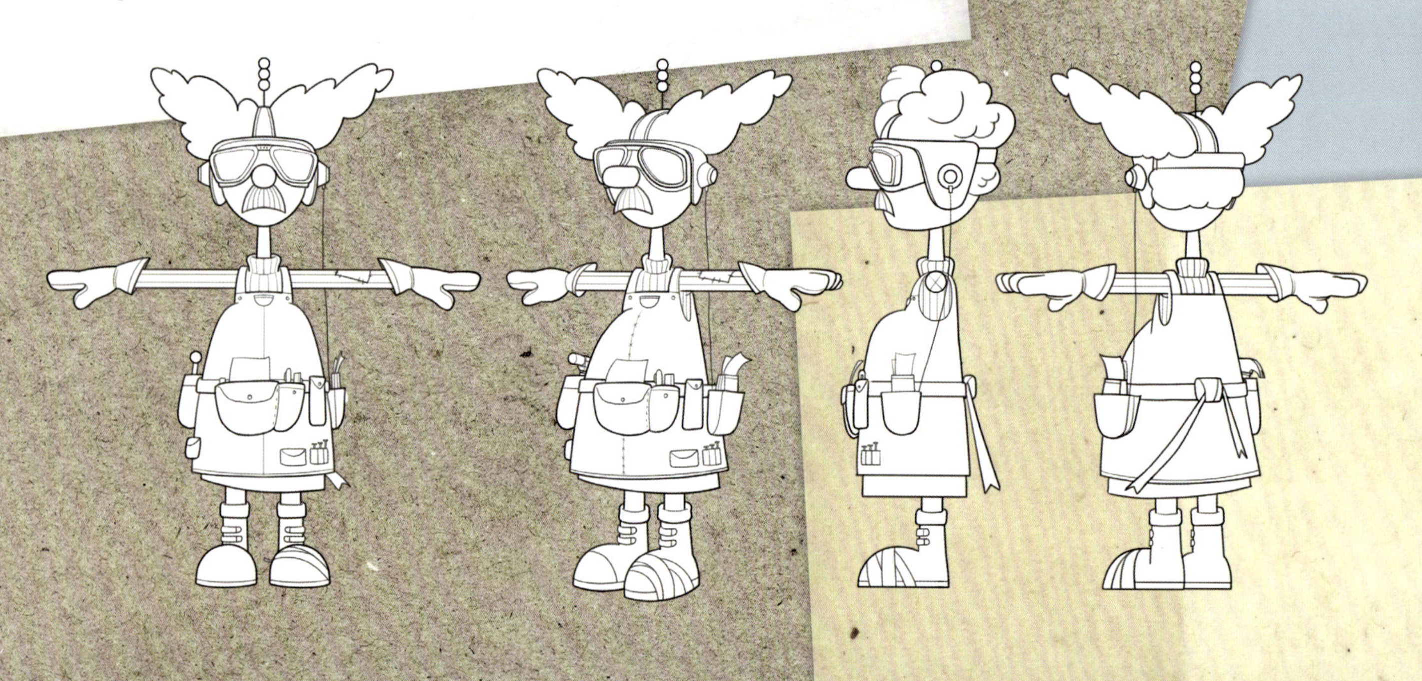

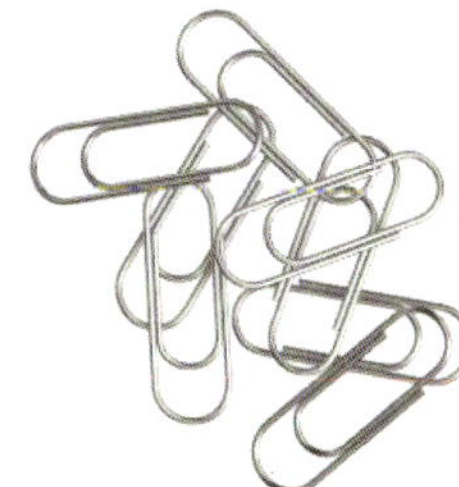

After roughly blocking out the shapes and proportions for all turns, the next step is to switch on the guidelines and check if all elements are aligned with one another. I put together a rough pass showing how Uncle Barney looks from every view. As the character has asymmetrical details I've created eight views, instead of four, to show the differences on either side of the character.

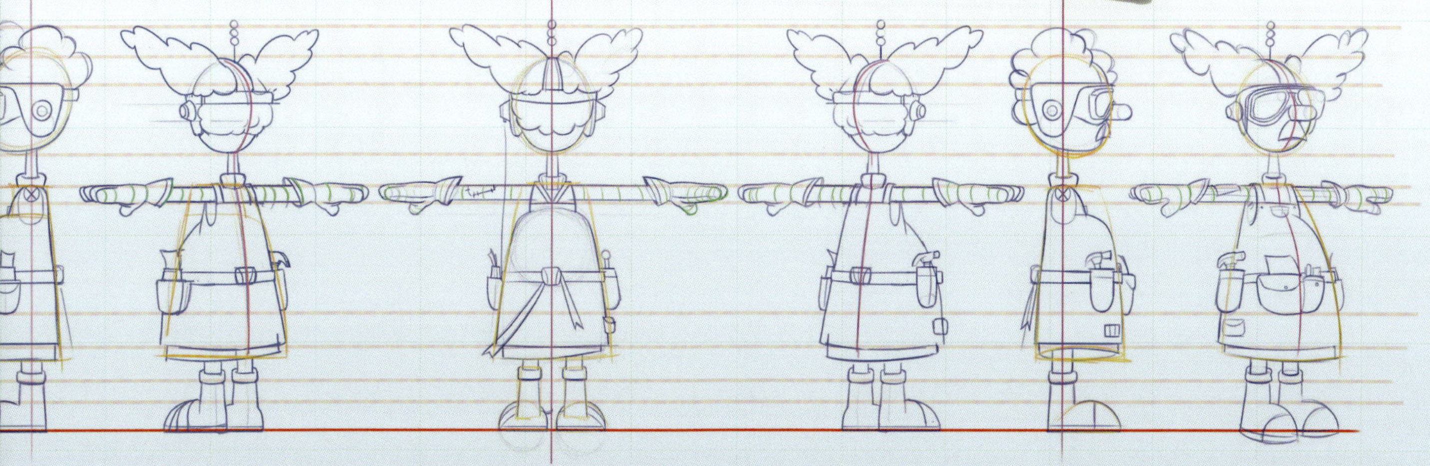

Last but not least, if all views align, it's time to refine and clean up the sketches. Adding details and refining the shapes and proportions is my favourite step. I create another eight-step turnaround to show off the cleaned-up and completed version of Uncle Barney from every angle.

Character turns might appear tricky at first, but if you take it step-by-step and don't rush through the process, you'll get the hang of it pretty quickly.

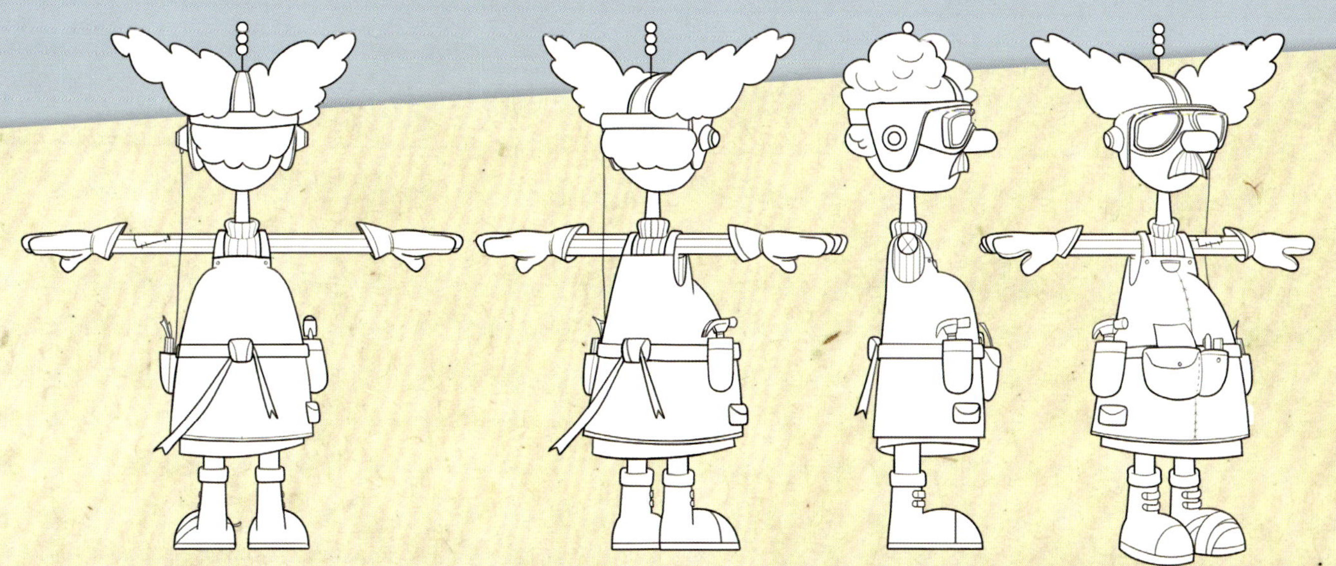

JOSE CICERARO

I'm a multi-disciplinary artist who works in the game industry. Let me share with you the principles behind my character designs and show you how I bring my ideas to life.

01. I started this drawing knowing that I wanted to make some sort of goblin or lizard character. I like to mirror my traditional workflow when I work digitally, starting off with a grey marker sketch. I keep it loose and hunt around for shapes.

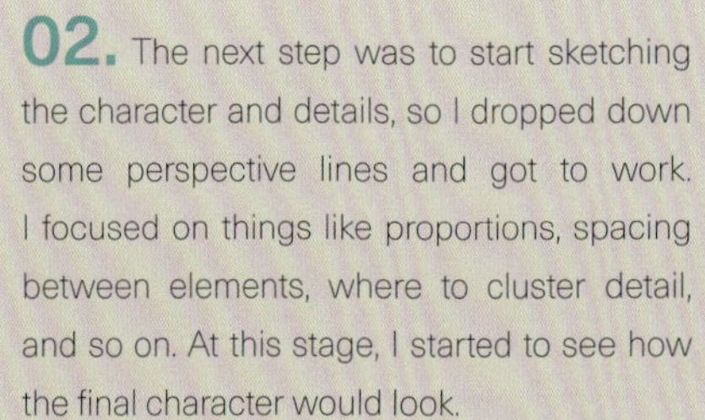

01

02. The next step was to start sketching the character and details, so I dropped down some perspective lines and got to work. I focused on things like proportions, spacing between elements, where to cluster detail, and so on. At this stage, I started to see how the final character would look.

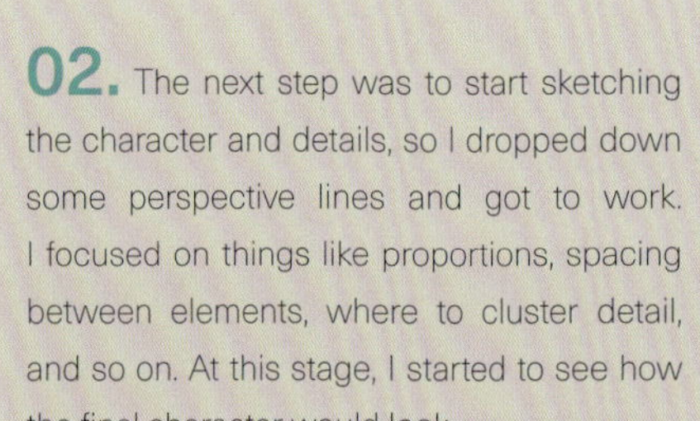

02

03. For this piece in particular, I knew from the start that I was going to try and paint it all on one layer – I know, crazy, right! I started with clean line work, painted all the areas with a flat local colour, and then added highlights and shadow.

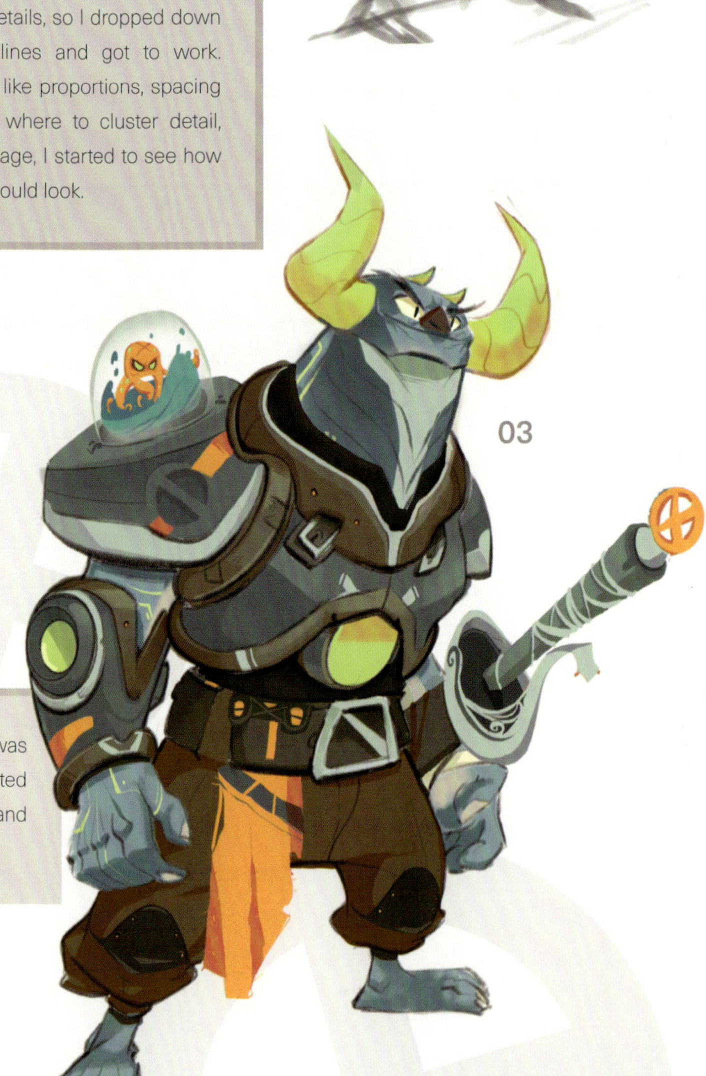

03

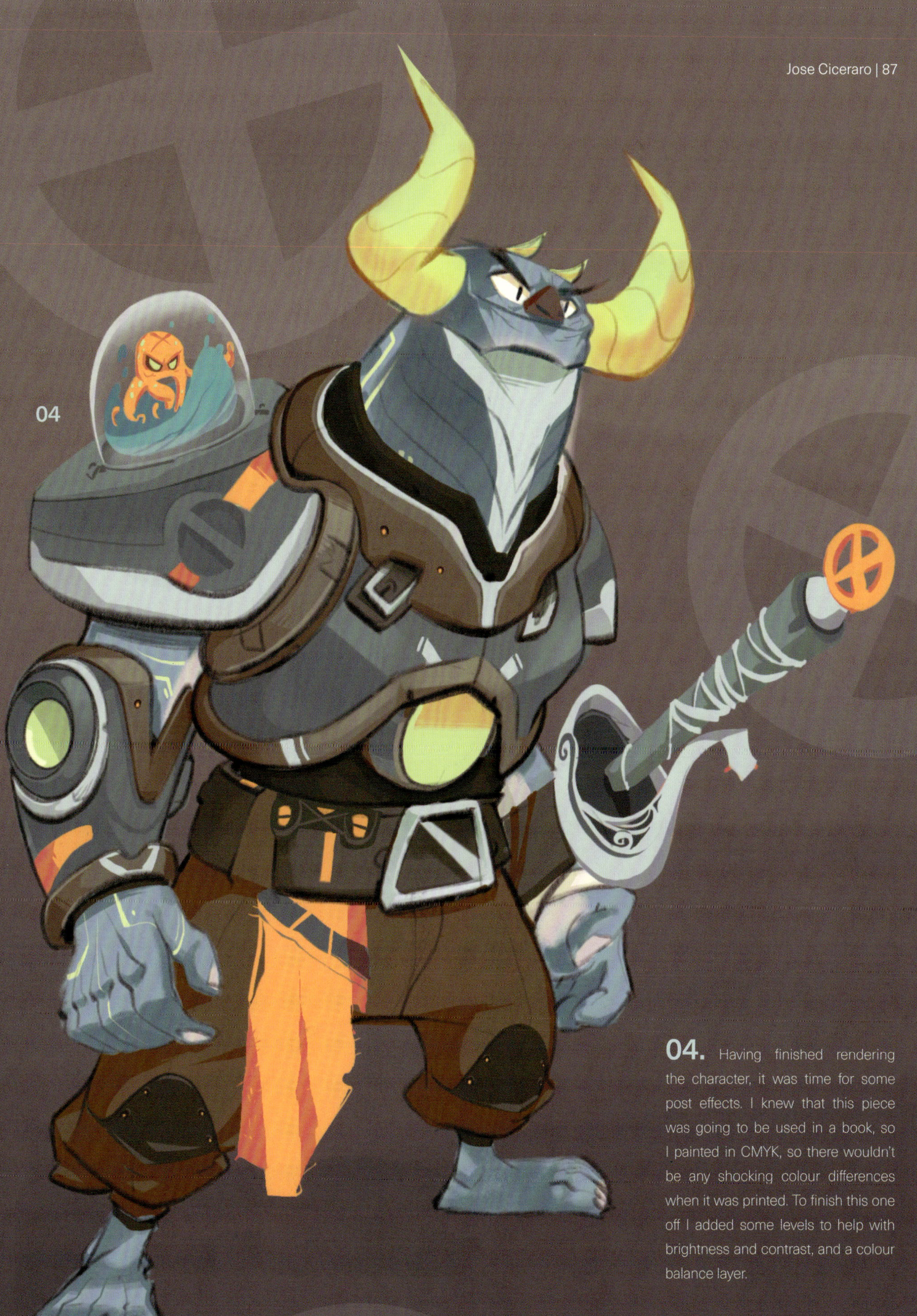

04. Having finished rendering the character, it was time for some post effects. I knew that this piece was going to be used in a book, so I painted in CMYK, so there wouldn't be any shocking colour differences when it was printed. To finish this one off I added some levels to help with brightness and contrast, and a colour balance layer.

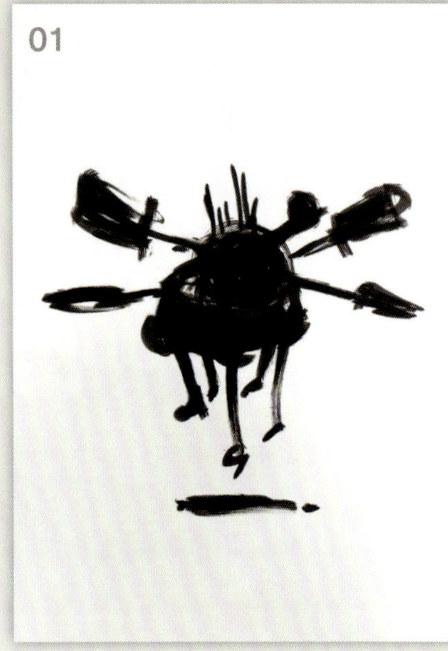

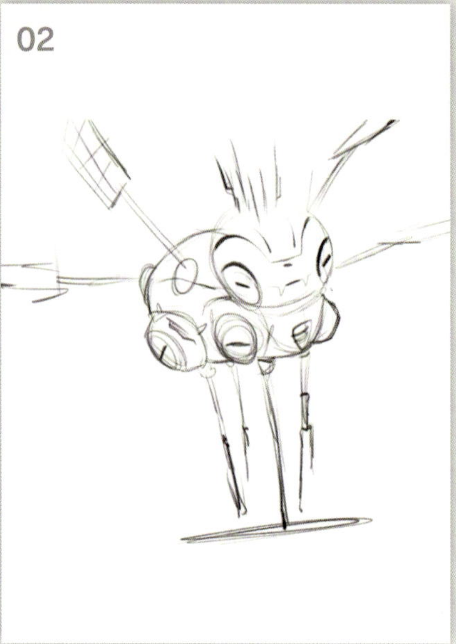

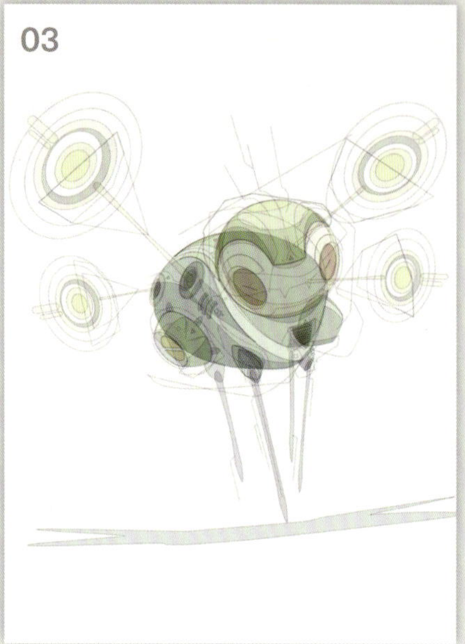

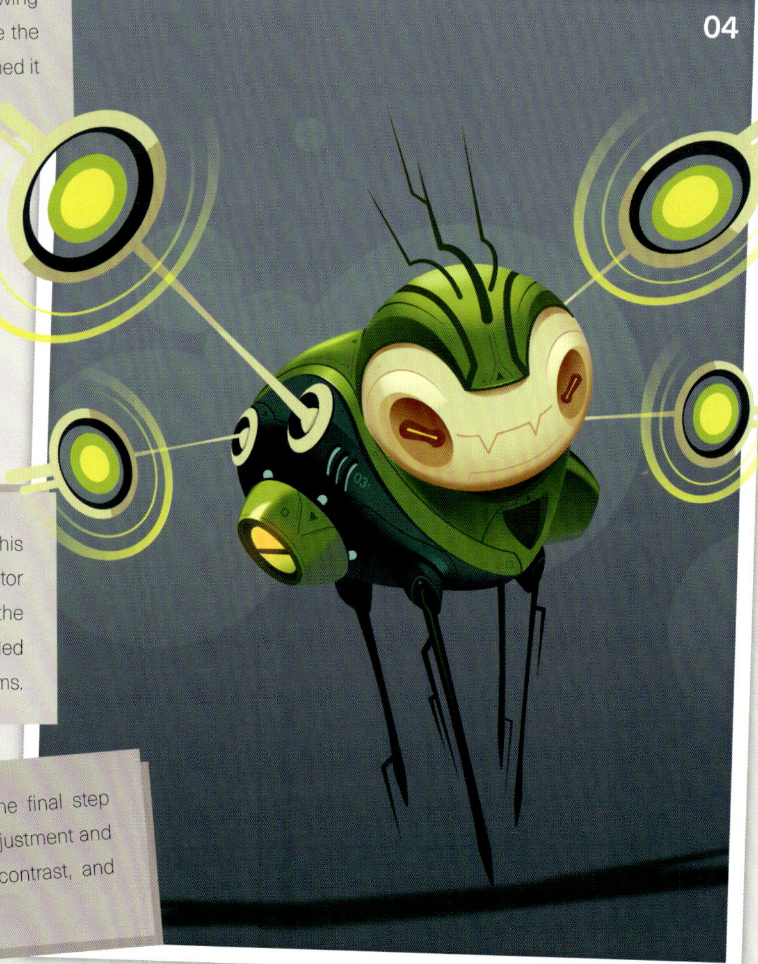

01. I love drawing in a sketchbook – I generate so many fun ideas between its pages. I started this character by drawing silhouettes with a giant poster marker. I find the less precise the tool, the better at this stage. Once I had an idea I liked, I scanned it and got ready to draw.

02. With the silhouette scanned in, I opened Affinity Designer, added another layer, and started sketching, remembering to keep it super rough – I'm not focused on clean line work at this point. I wanted to leave some things up for interpretation as I rendered it out.

03. I love using different methods to make art. For this piece, I decided to create the whole character from vector lines. Using paths and shapes, I started building out the character, using the line work as my guide. I then added shadows and highlights to help round out some of the forms.

04. Now that everything had been rendered out, the final step was to do a little post correction. I tend to use a levels adjustment and a colour balance here – this helps to brighten, add contrast, and harmonize the piece.

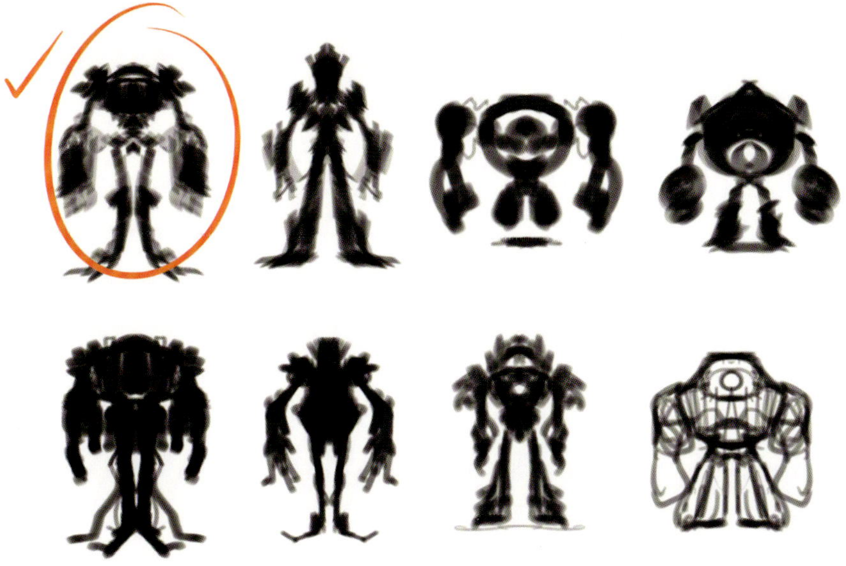

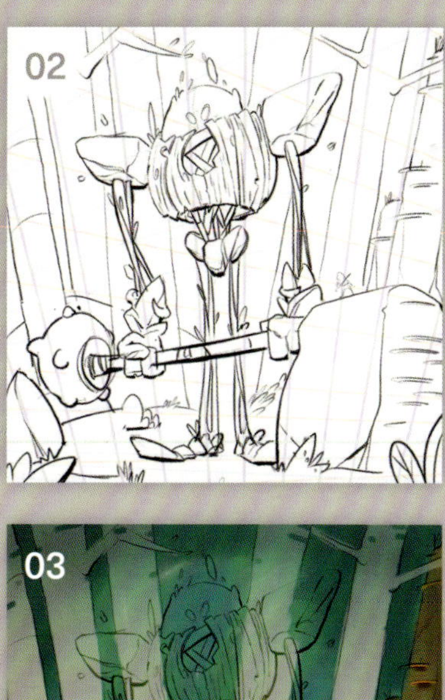

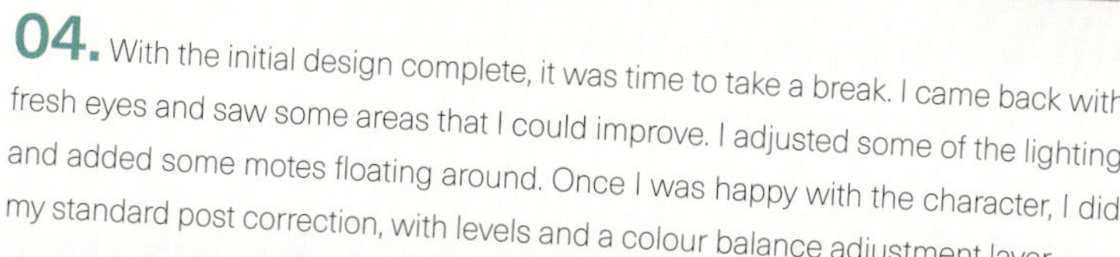

01. I love using the symmetry tool for character and silhouette exploration. Here, I used this method to explore eight different ideas. I wanted to make a robot character. After narrowing it down to my favourite silhouette, I was ready to start designing the character and details.

02. After generating some thumbnails, I worked on a loose sketch. Next, I focused on establishing the right perspective grid and cleaning up the line work. For me, rendering goes a lot smoother if I can figure out all the details in the drawing pass.

03. I already had a palette in mind for this piece – I really wanted to have a strong spot of orange. I worked from the background to the foreground, adding more detail and refinement with each pass. I went through four passes in total: flats, lighting, details, and atmosphere.

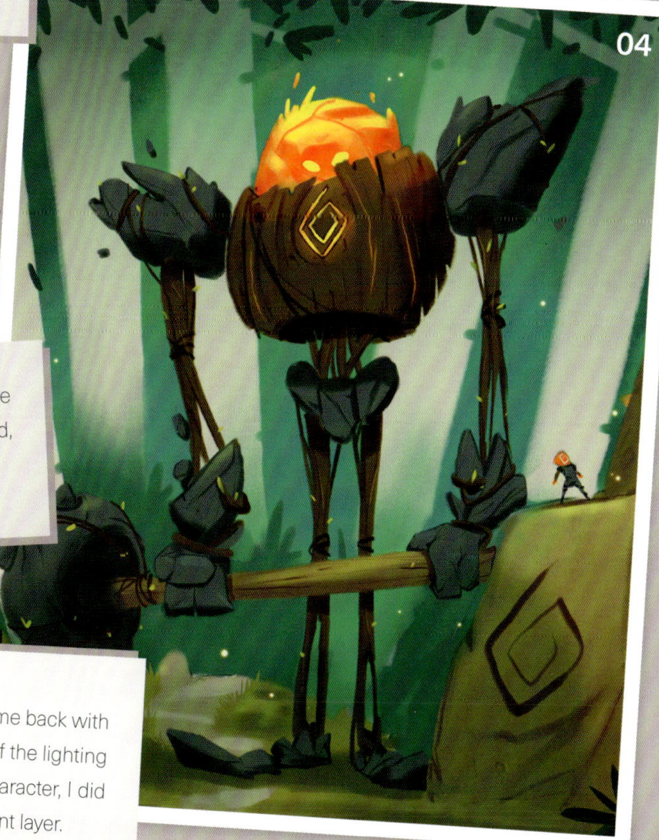

04. With the initial design complete, it was time to take a break. I came back with fresh eyes and saw some areas that I could improve. I adjusted some of the lighting and added some motes floating around. Once I was happy with the character, I did my standard post correction, with levels and a colour balance adjustment layer.

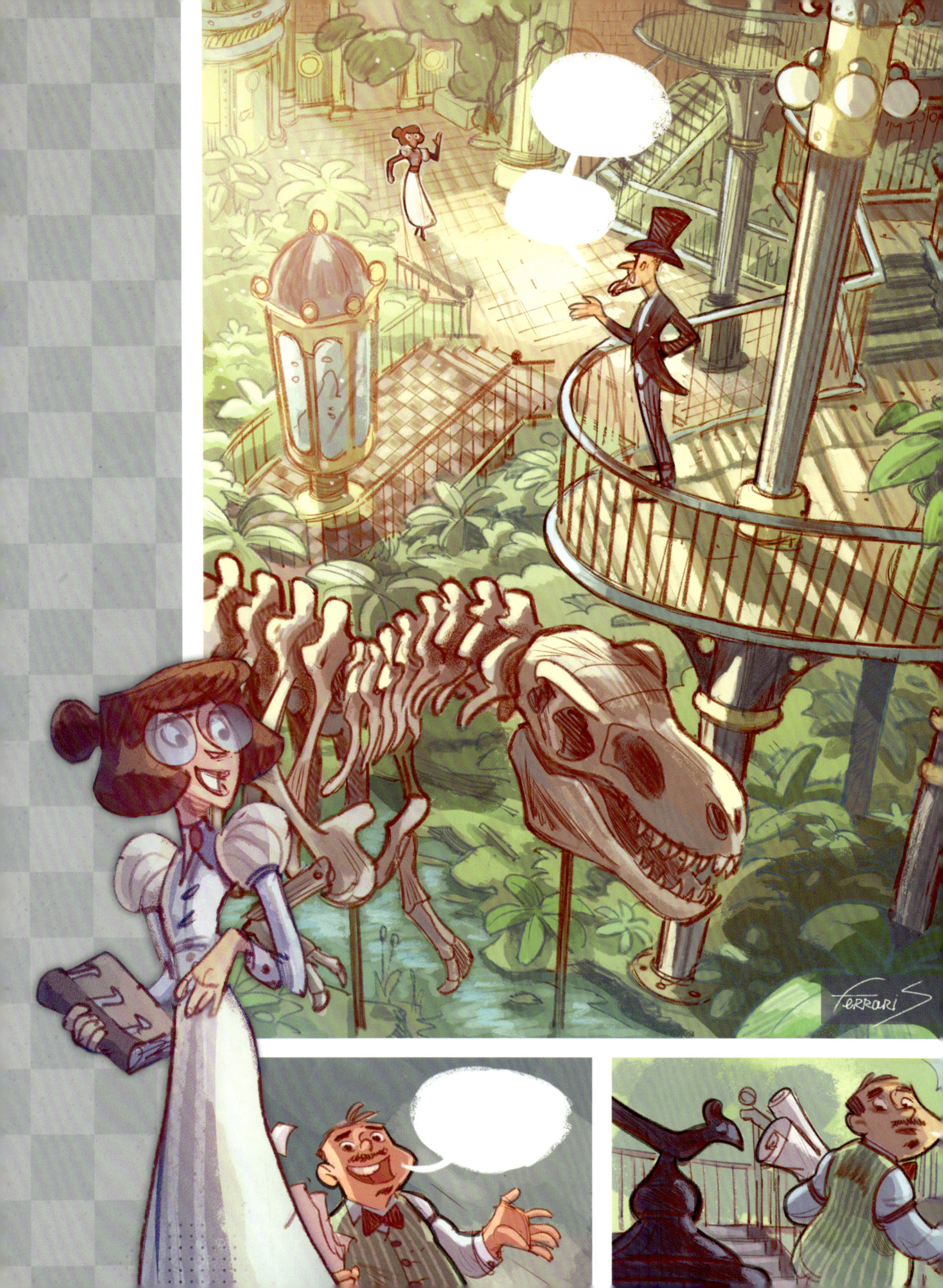

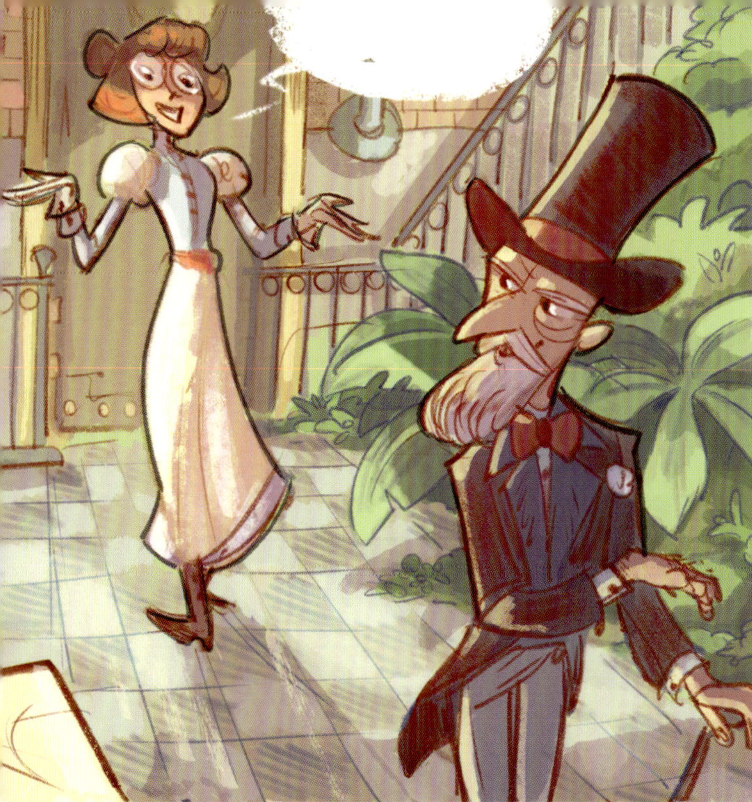
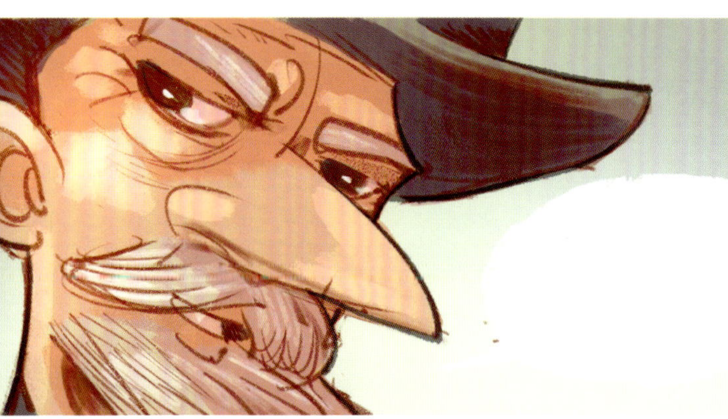
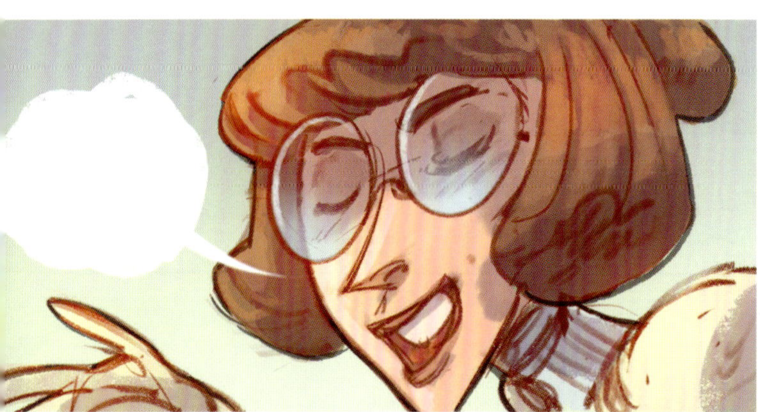
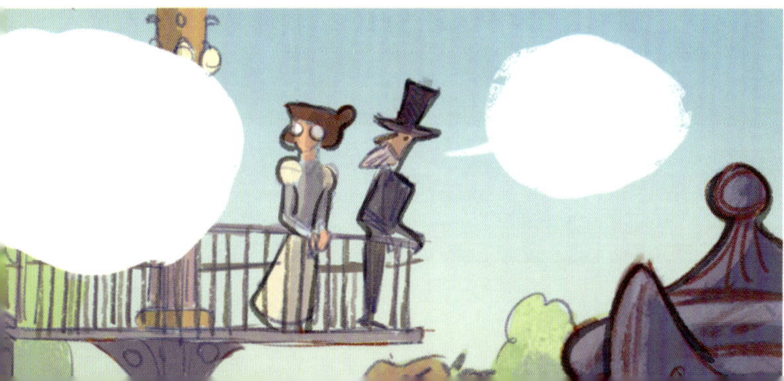

COMIC CREATIONS

MARCO FERRARIS

In this tutorial I will guide you in creating a page for a comic. We will start from the basics and address the main difficulties you may encounter along the way. In the first part of the tutorial we will focus on the design of the characters – we will then move on to the colour palette and the colour script, and finish with the direction and creation of the final page. I created this tutorial to be suitable for drawing and narration styles that are totally different from mine, focusing more on the way of thinking about the page than on technical aspects.

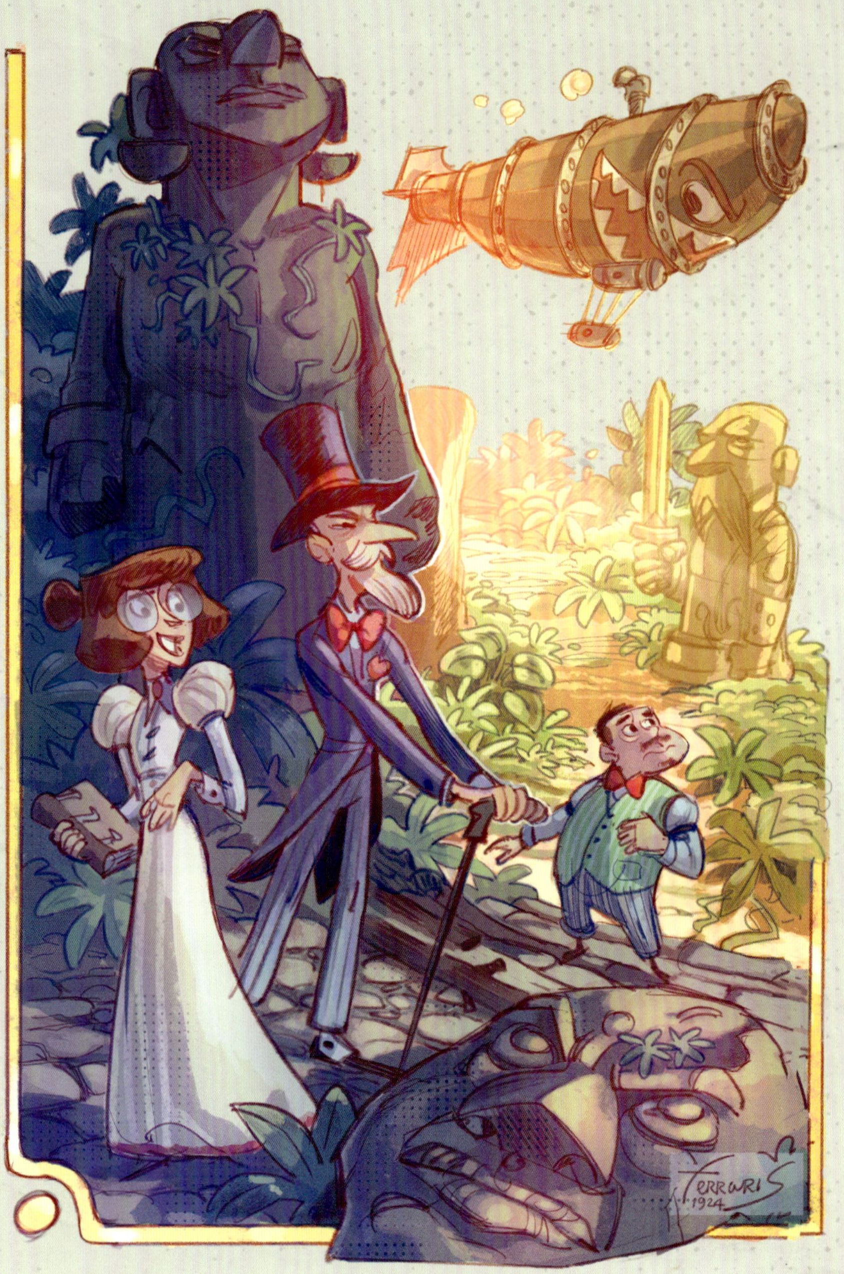

Let's imagine that we have received text from a screenwriter or that we have written the subject for a comic – now we need to draw the main characters. An easy mistake to make early on is with the characters' composition: they should be neither too complex or too similar to one another. From the very start, make sure you focus on using simple and distinct shapes – we will have to redraw the same characters hundreds of times in different poses and it's essential that they always remain recognizable. Playing on shapes also helps with characterization, ensuring your designs are distinguishable even in night scenes, or with very distant shots where the details would not be visible.

In the draft phases we don't need to immediately create a 'nice' drawing

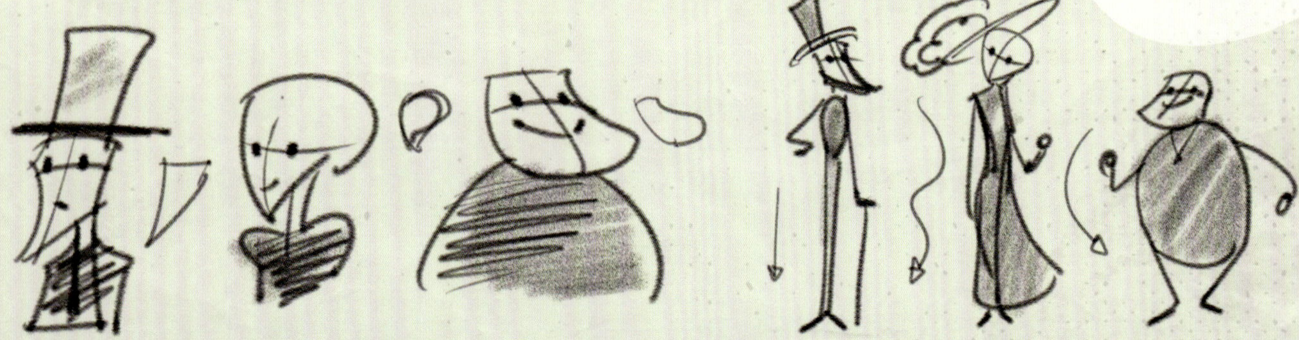

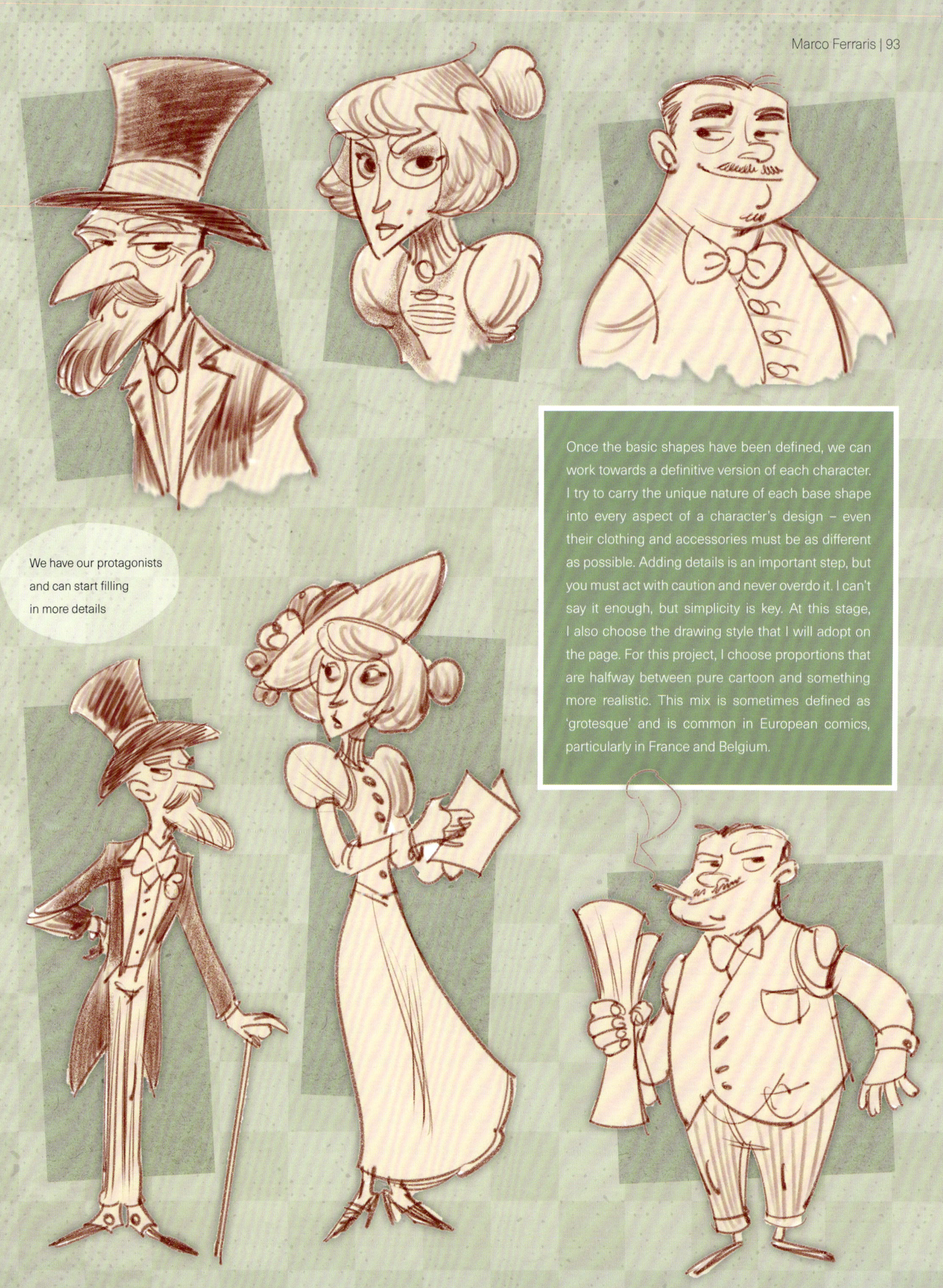

Once the basic shapes have been defined, we can work towards a definitive version of each character. I try to carry the unique nature of each base shape into every aspect of a character's design – even their clothing and accessories must be as different as possible. Adding details is an important step, but you must act with caution and never overdo it. I can't say it enough, but simplicity is key. At this stage, I also choose the drawing style that I will adopt on the page. For this project, I choose proportions that are halfway between pure cartoon and something more realistic. This mix is sometimes defined as 'grotesque' and is common in European comics, particularly in France and Belgium.

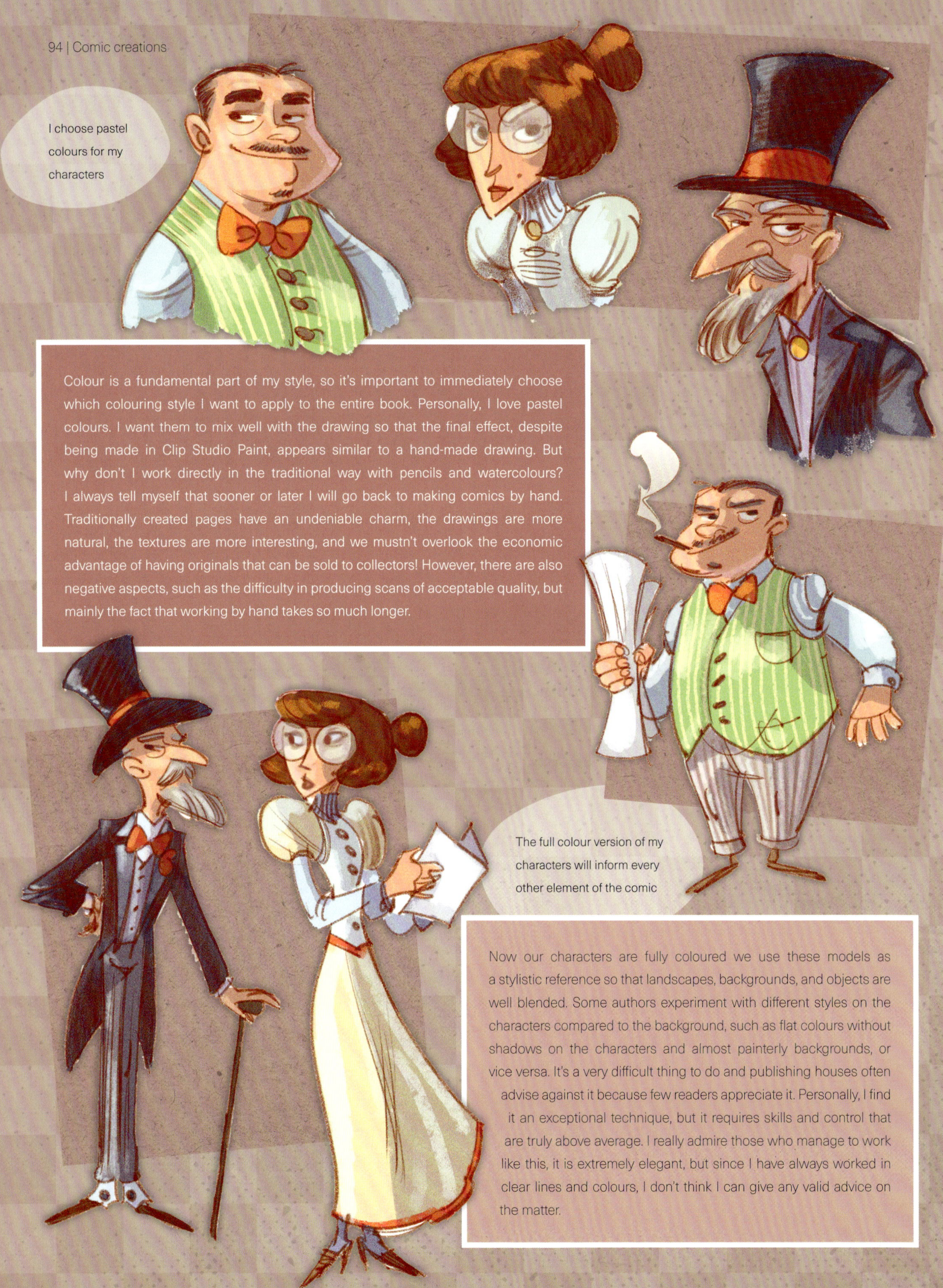

Colour is a fundamental part of my style, so it's important to immediately choose which colouring style I want to apply to the entire book. Personally, I love pastel colours. I want them to mix well with the drawing so that the final effect, despite being made in Clip Studio Paint, appears similar to a hand-made drawing. But why don't I work directly in the traditional way with pencils and watercolours? I always tell myself that sooner or later I will go back to making comics by hand. Traditionally created pages have an undeniable charm, the drawings are more natural, the textures are more interesting, and we mustn't overlook the economic advantage of having originals that can be sold to collectors! However, there are also negative aspects, such as the difficulty in producing scans of acceptable quality, but mainly the fact that working by hand takes so much longer.

Now our characters are fully coloured we use these models as a stylistic reference so that landscapes, backgrounds, and objects are well blended. Some authors experiment with different styles on the characters compared to the background, such as flat colours without shadows on the characters and almost painterly backgrounds, or vice versa. It's a very difficult thing to do and publishing houses often advise against it because few readers appreciate it. Personally, I find it an exceptional technique, but it requires skills and control that are truly above average. I really admire those who manage to work like this, it is extremely elegant, but since I have always worked in clear lines and colours, I don't think I can give any valid advice on the matter.

COLOUR CHECK!

Always keep in mind that some digital colours will be replaced by similar colours when your comic is printed. The replacement colours can be completely wrong, causing serious damage to your designs. You have been warned!

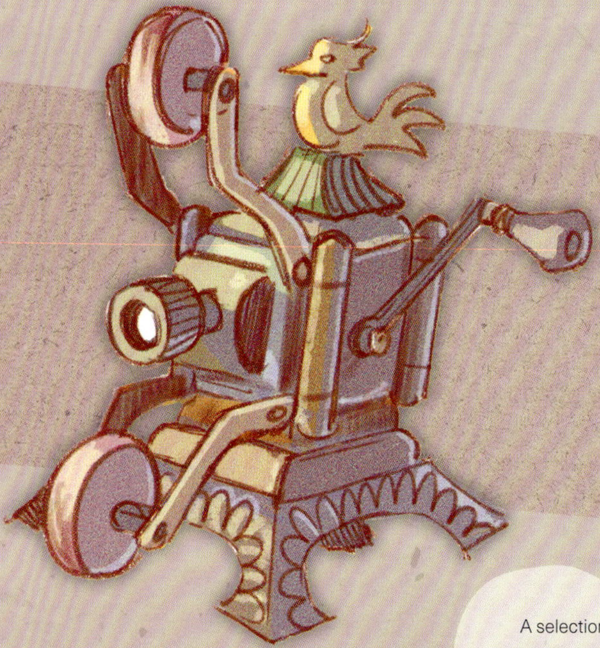

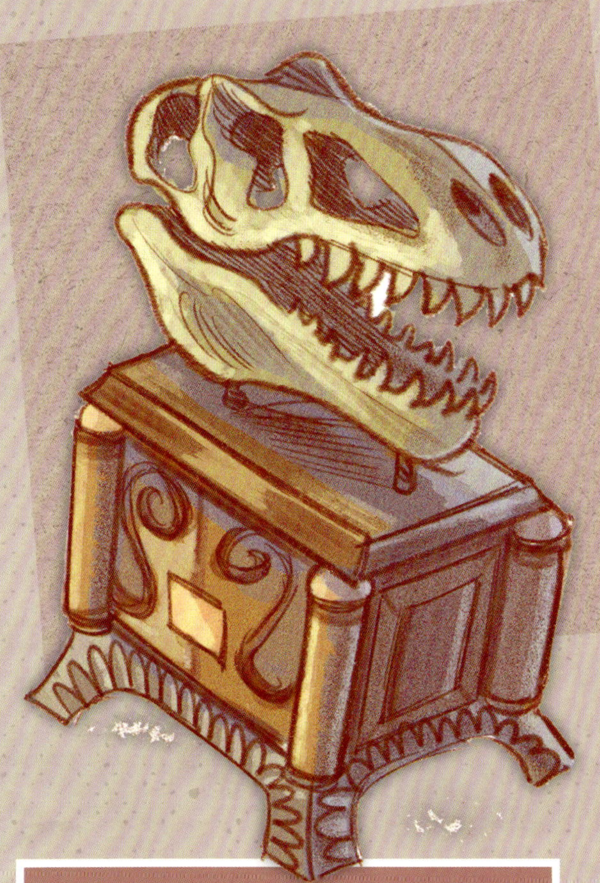

A selection of objects that help define the characters

Finally, we move on to objects and backgrounds. This is one of the most underrated parts of the process, despite it actually being extremely important. We can't add too much text to a comic, otherwise it will read as slow and didactic, so we must apply the famous rule, 'Show, don't tell.' Objects can tell us a lot about the world that surrounds our characters, avoiding the need for unnecessary explanations. I want to give my world a steampunk feel, so I mix different eras and styles to create some objects that help sell my vision. A T-rex skull, a mysteriously shaped aquarium, and a retro film projector tell us about the protagonist: his profession, social class, artistic taste, passions, and hobbies – all very important details.

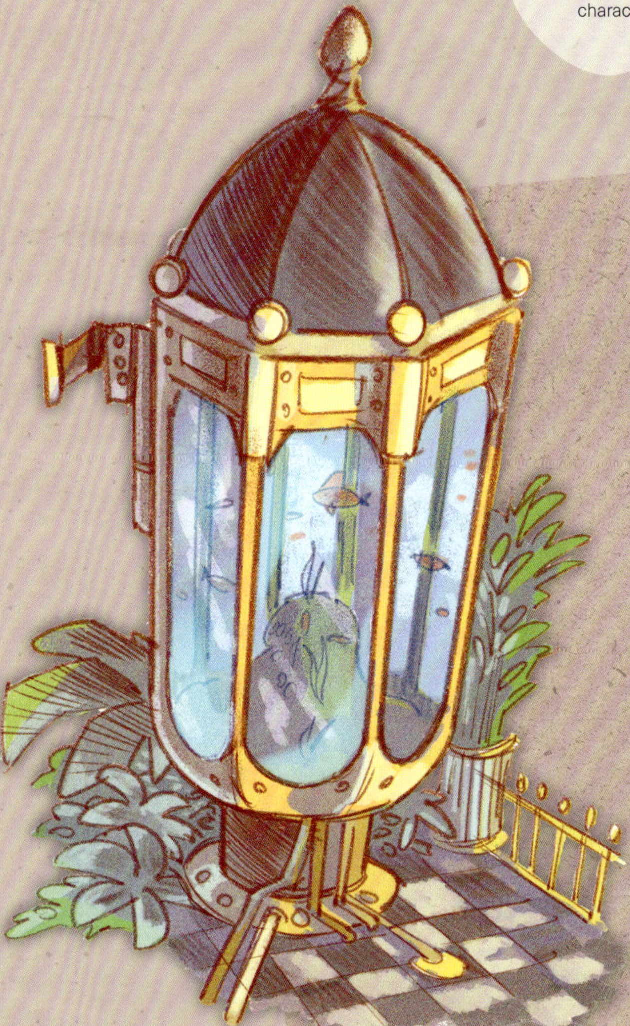

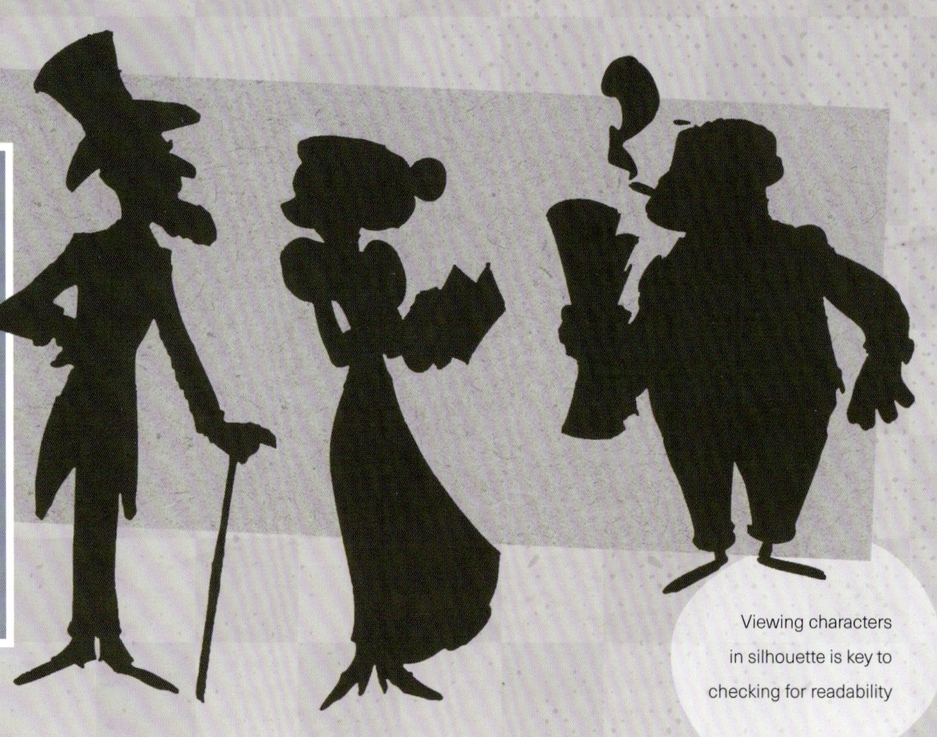

Before I start on the comic panels, I go back to the main characters one last time to make sure they are drawn correctly. I recommend filling each character with a dark colour and looking at them in silhouette. If each character remains recognizable with only their outline visible it means we've done a good job. Even their shadow against a wall will be enough for the reader to recognize them and we can be sure they will be memorable throughout the story.

Viewing characters in silhouette is key to checking for readability

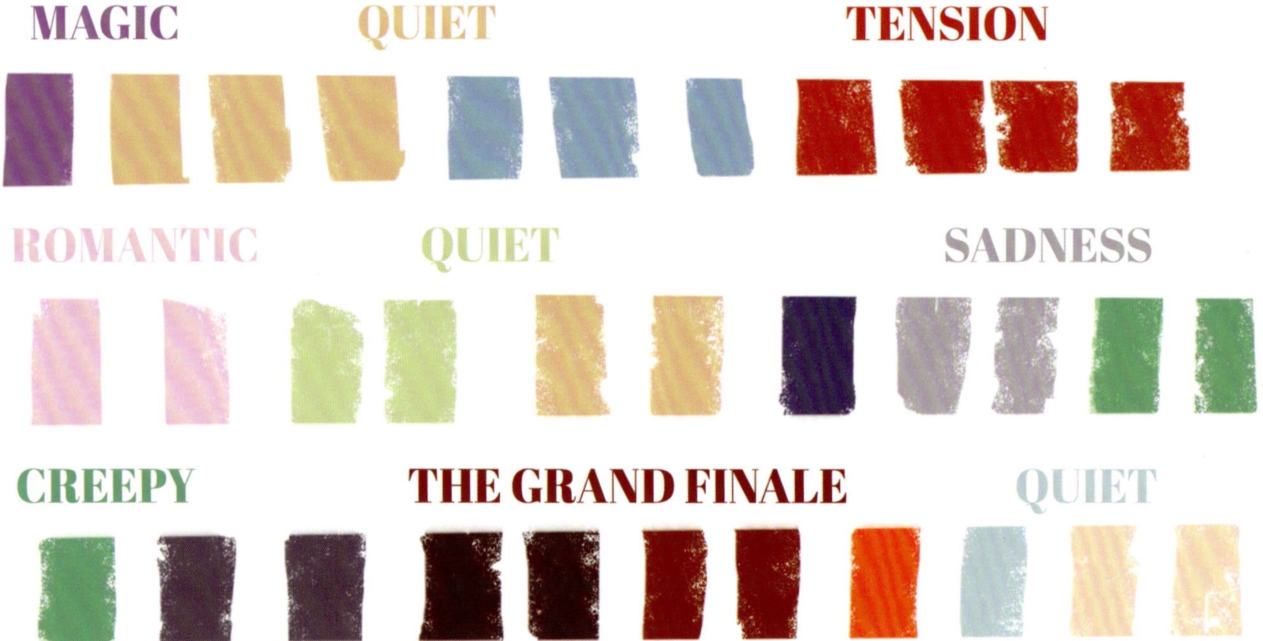

We have now completed the character design phase. Next, I recommend creating a colour script. This means we choose the dominant colours of each page of the book and tell the story in a basic way. What colours should we choose? There are a set of principles to follow so that the colour you choose serves the narrative: action scenes will be red or orange, romantic scenes will be pink or lilac, relaxing scenes will have colours like blue or sandy yellow, purple for magic, green for disturbing situations, grey for sadness, and so on. Each colour has its own meaning for storytelling purposes. I recommend that the book is a crescendo of tension, colours getting darker until reaching the 'grand finale', which will have strong contrasts or dark colours. After this, we return to calmer shades and the story ends.

Each spot of colour represents a couple of pages, divided based on what's happening in the story

Now, let's tackle the first page of our story. First you need to choose the format, although usually the publisher decides this based on their experience or existing catalogue. I'm using a format suitable for A4 and a French grid.

What do I mean by grid? It can be a complex matter, but let's say it's the way in which we will tell our story, how many cartoons per page we will use, and how they will be made. There are many types of grid – the French style is characterized by a high number of vignettes, well suited for books that will be printed on large formats, typically with hardback covers.

I roughly sketch out the action for each panel, showing the characters, positioning, and any key objects.

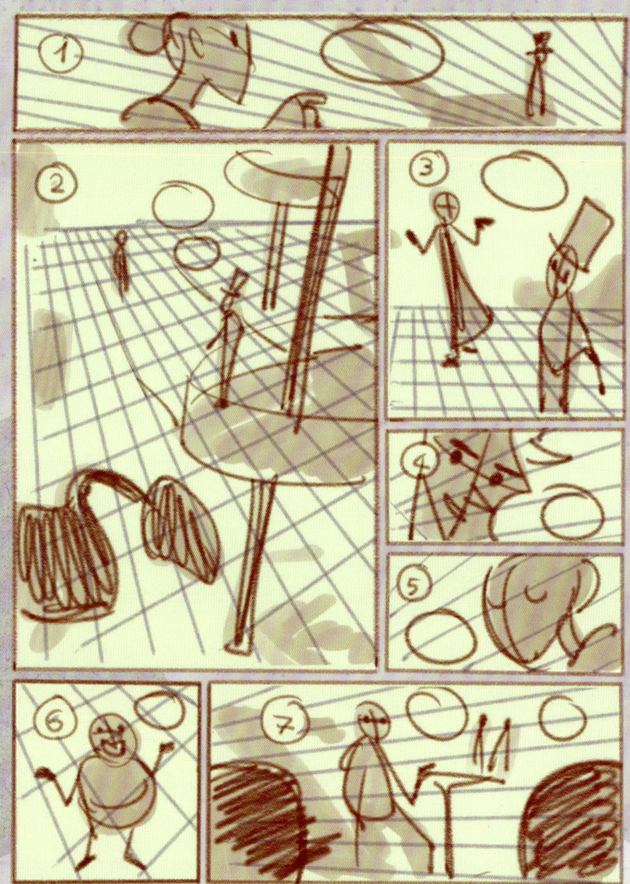

Sketching out each pane of
the first page of our story

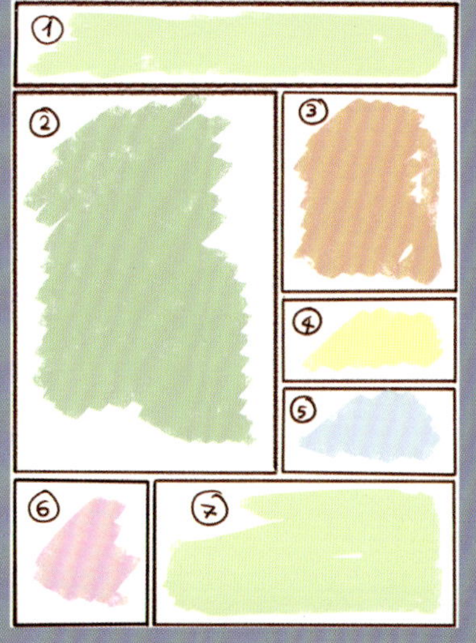

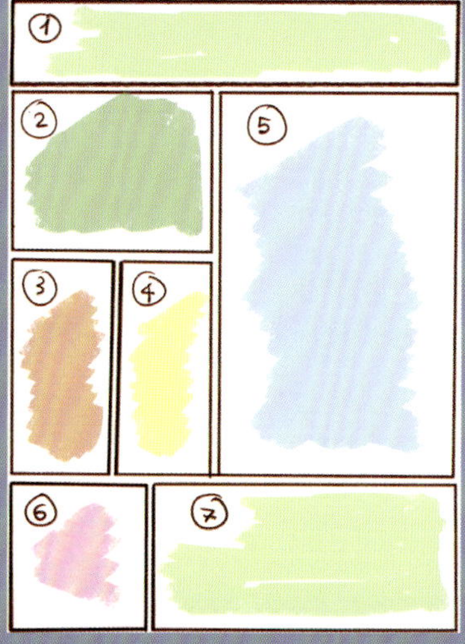

A B

GETTING TO GRIPS WITH GRIDS

The order in which panels should be read is important. Take a look at these two examples – which is correct?

The answer is A. In the West, we always read from left to right and then from top to bottom. In example B the eye would travel from panel 2, to 5, and then 3 and 4. If you place a larger panel on the right, you may also find that readers skip over the smaller panels on the left, so like in example A, always try to put smaller panels to the right of larger ones.

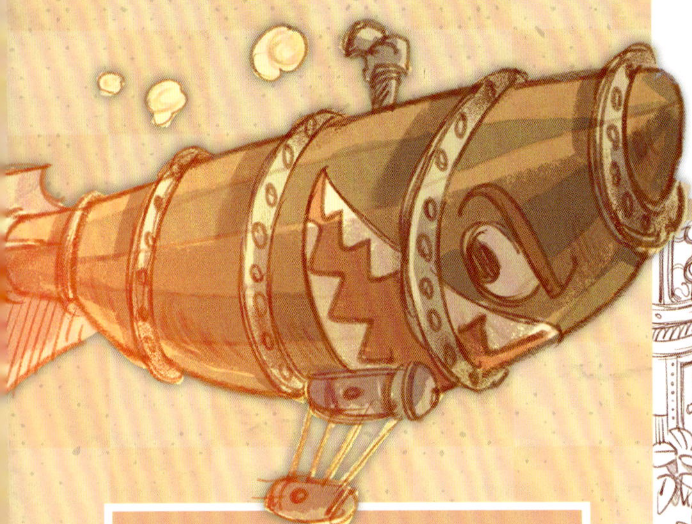

When composing each panel, we use techniques that have been the basis of comics all over the world for years: large panels for long shots and small panels for close-ups. Space and time are well connected in the world of comics. Large panels are 'slower' than small panels which represent fast scenes, such as very tight dialogue with shots and reverse shots, or action scenes in rapid succession.

In comics, direction is everything. The choice of shots allows you to give the right rhythm to the story, highlight the key details, and prevent the reader from getting bored. I find it very useful to include a variety of different shots on the same page – it makes the story much more interesting. Here I will use shots from above, from below, and with particular scenes and cuts.

Now all we have to do is draw the page. If you've worked through all the previous steps, getting to know your characters and so on, then this stage should be almost a mechanical process. Make sure you keep the drawing 'fresh' by not stiffening the lines too much, especially if – like me – you want to create a final effect very similar to a pencil sketch.

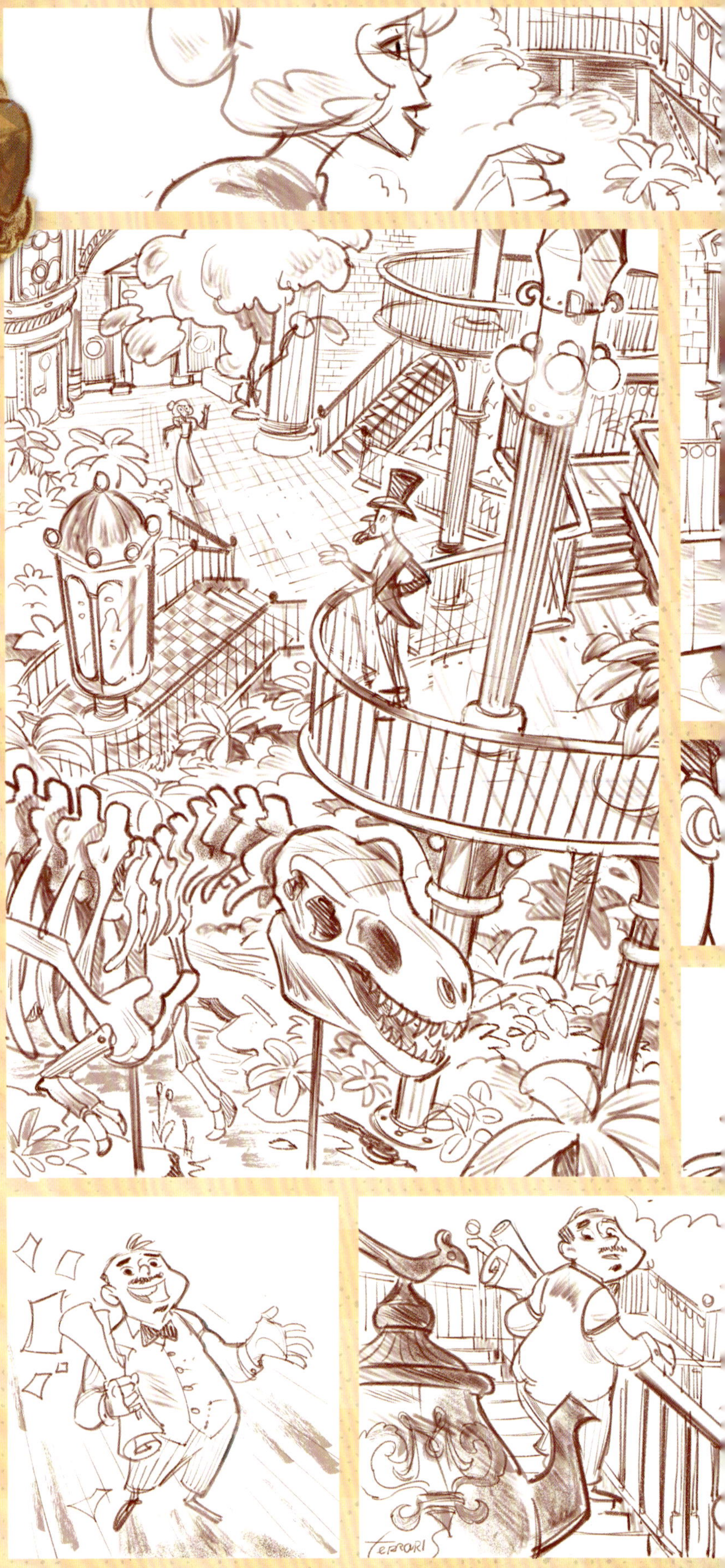

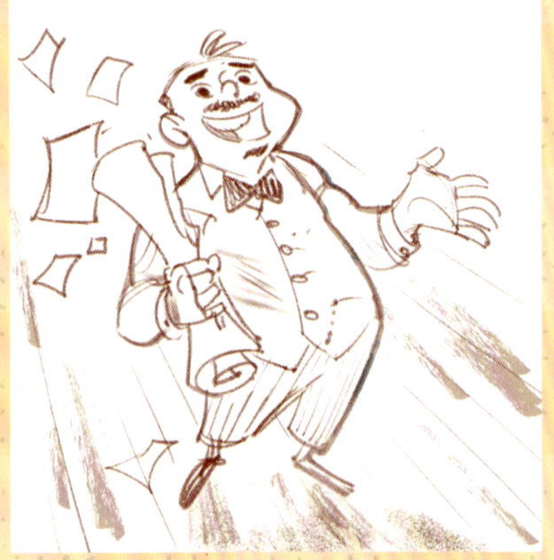

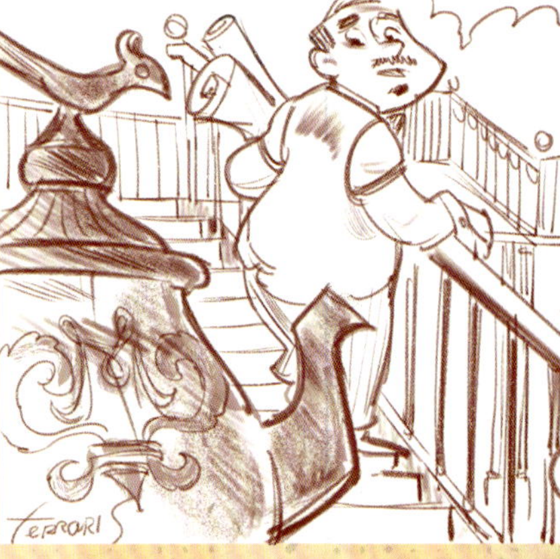

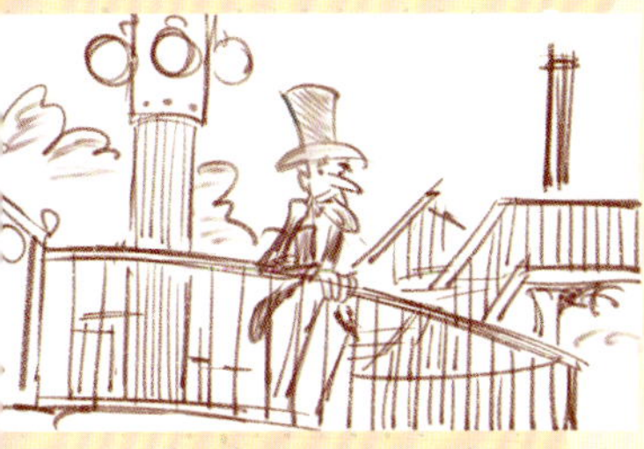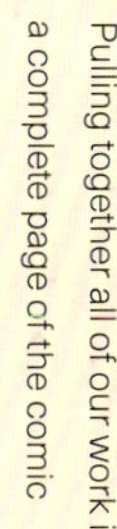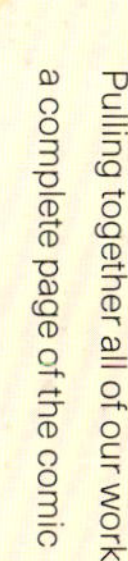

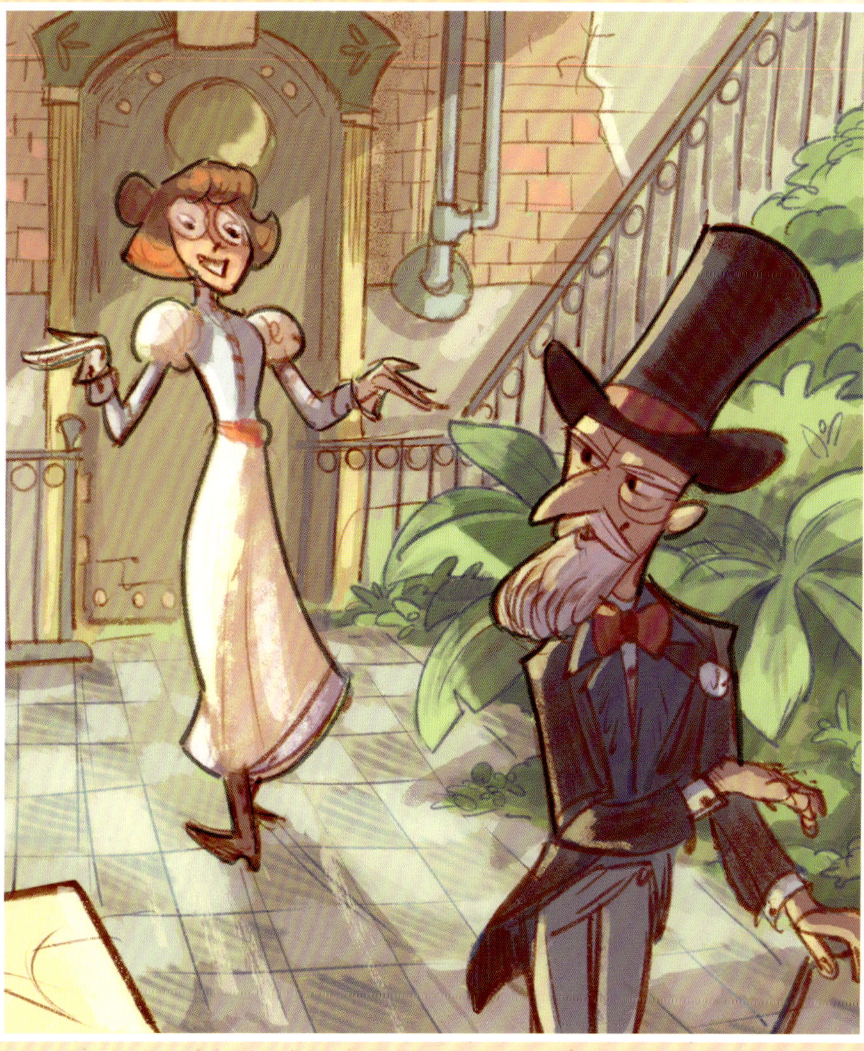

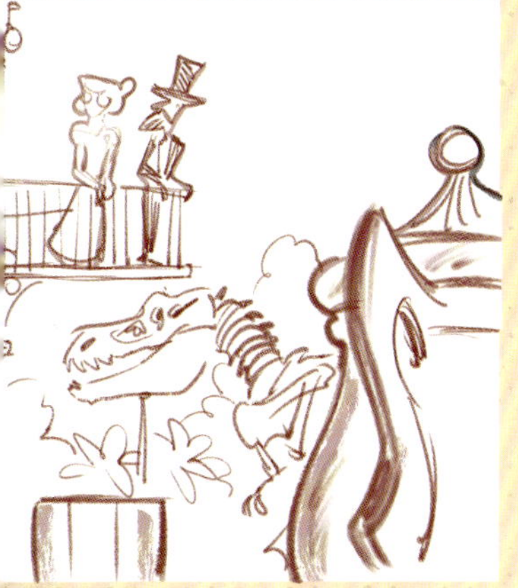

Let's take a closer look at this single panel and analyse the steps for adding the final colouring. I start by choosing a colour palette, insert the spot colours, and add some shadows. In a further layer I add painterly effects and lighting to complete the image. This is more or less my usual technique.

I think the two most important things when colouring comics are readability and atmosphere. By readability I am referring to the fact that everything should be clear and understandable, even without excessive detail and no clear inked outlines. The characters (and any important objects) must stand out from the background.

The atmosphere, on the other hand, is an important part of the story – it helps to convey emotions and is linked to the colour script we addressed previously.

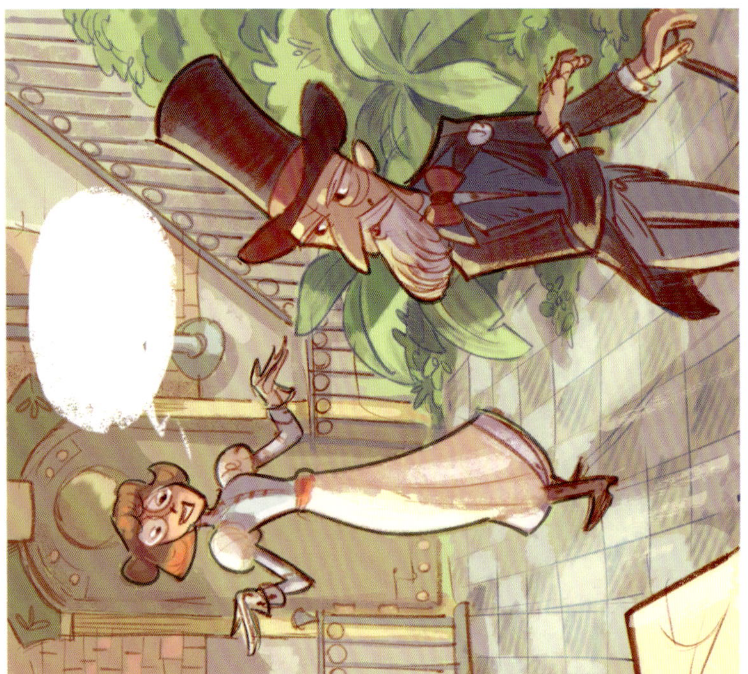
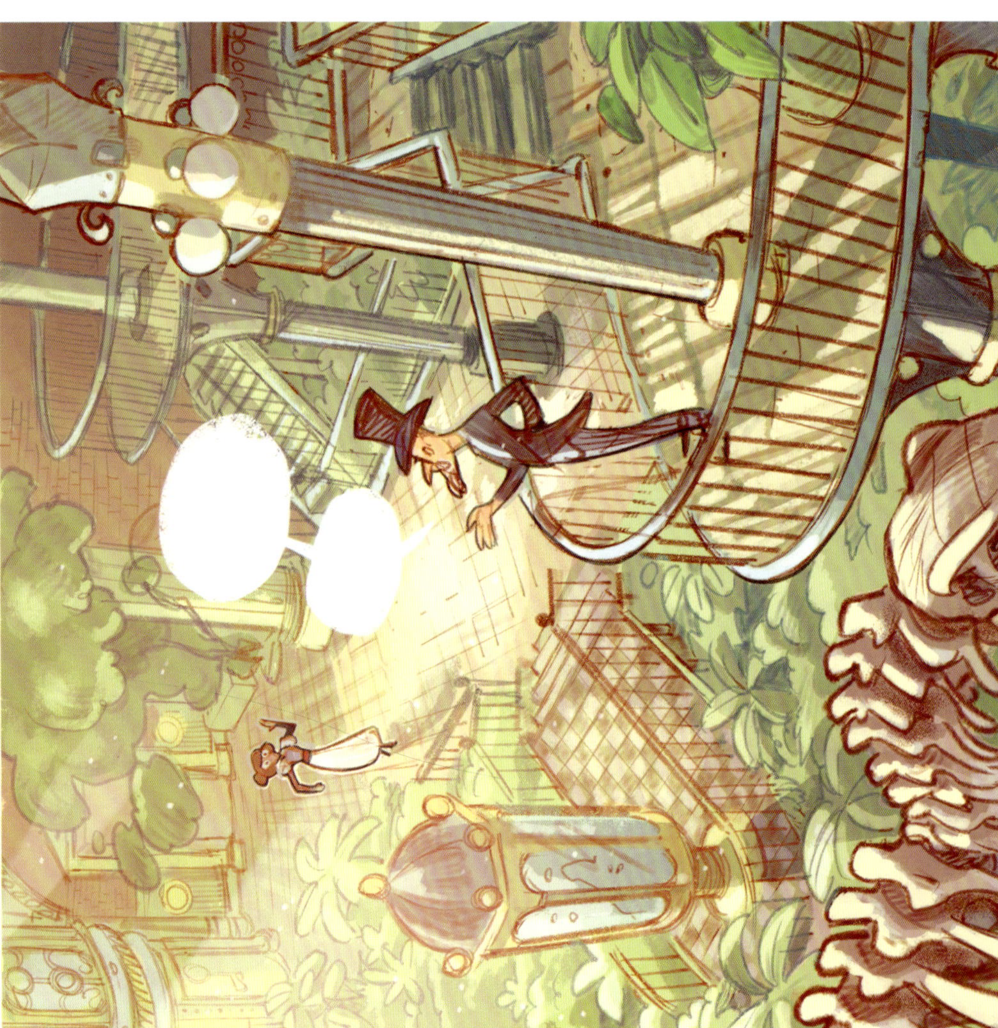

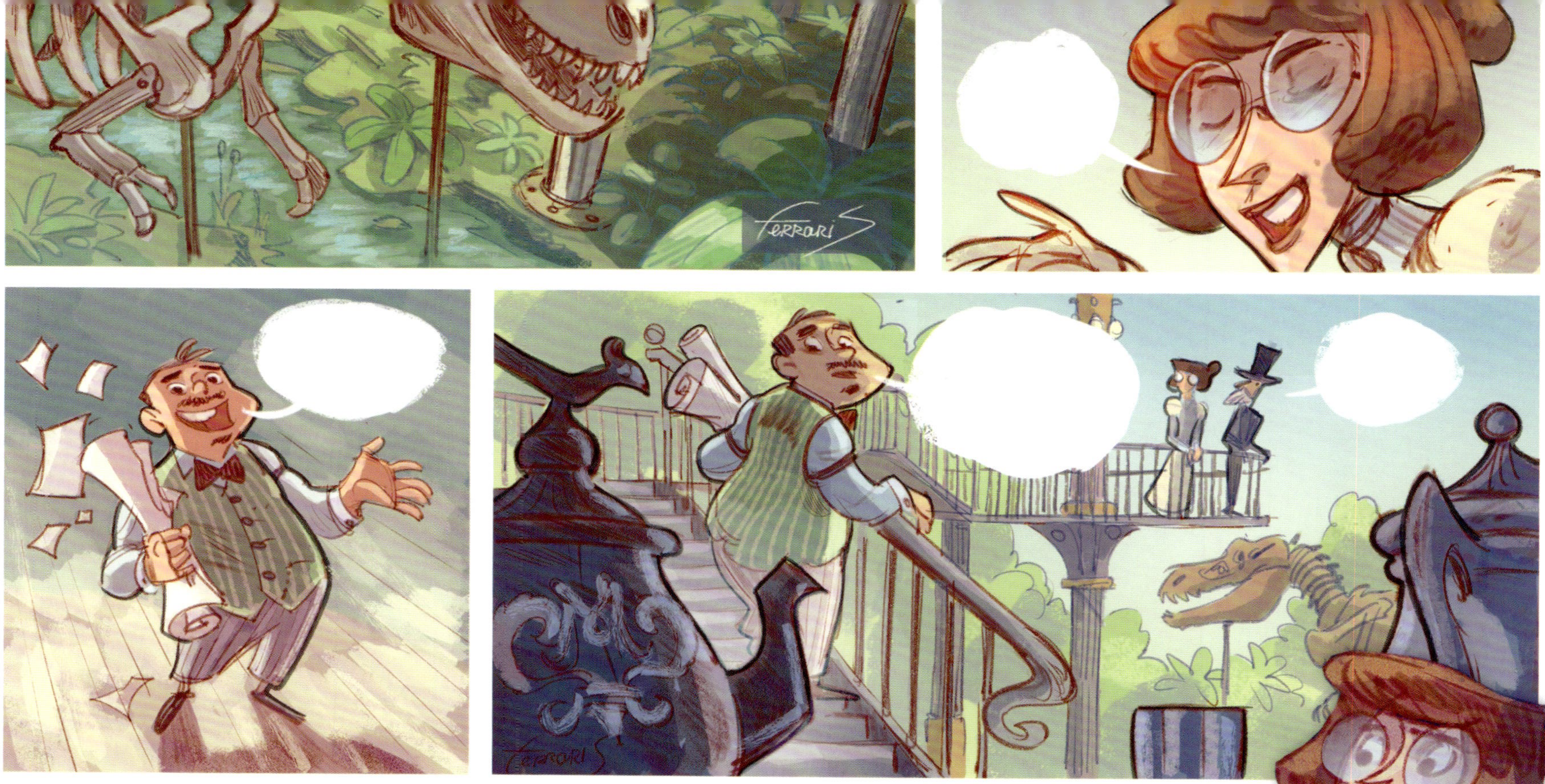

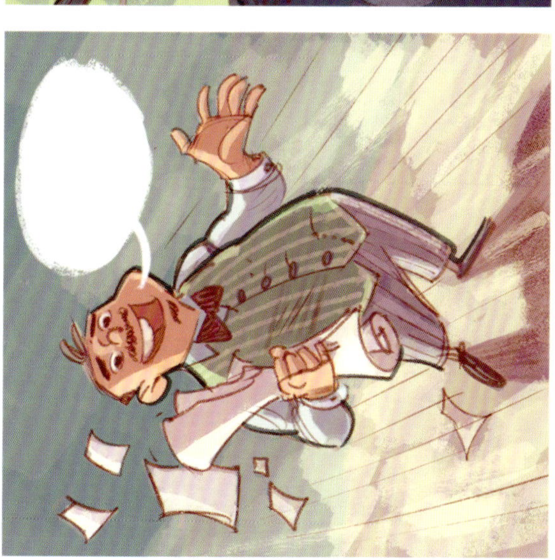

All the previous steps come together and our page is complete. We have the character design, the study of the backgrounds, the direction, the atmosphere, the final colour, and obviously the balloons in which the text will be inserted. Now all we have to do is draw another hundred to finally have our complete book! Making comics is a long and complex process, but also so creative – it's perhaps the only medium that allows you to become the director, costume designer, set designer, and sometimes even author all at once.

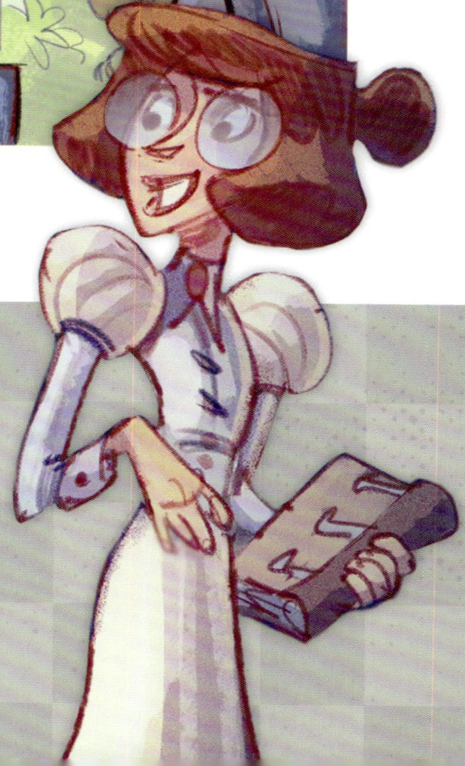

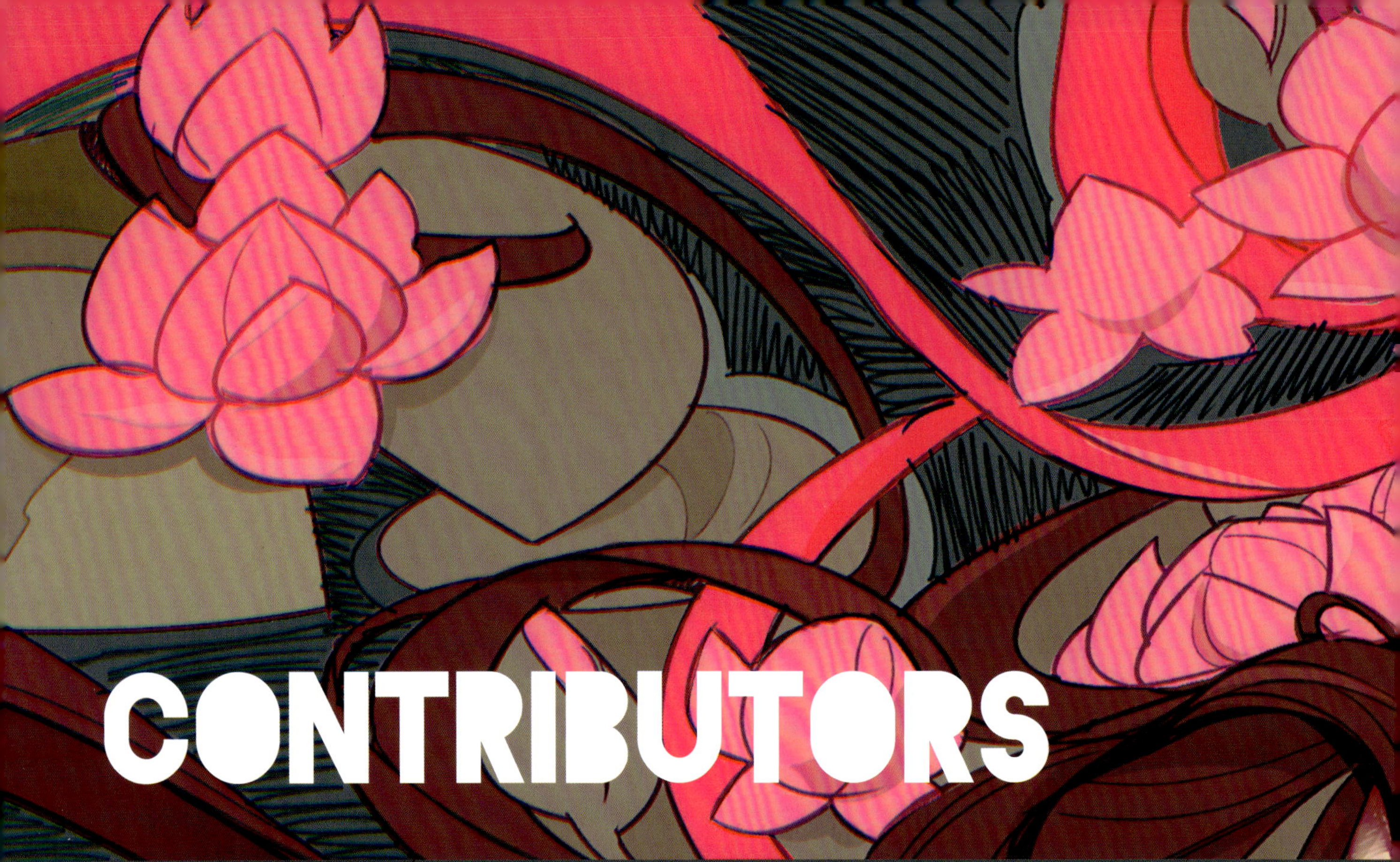

CONTRIBUTORS

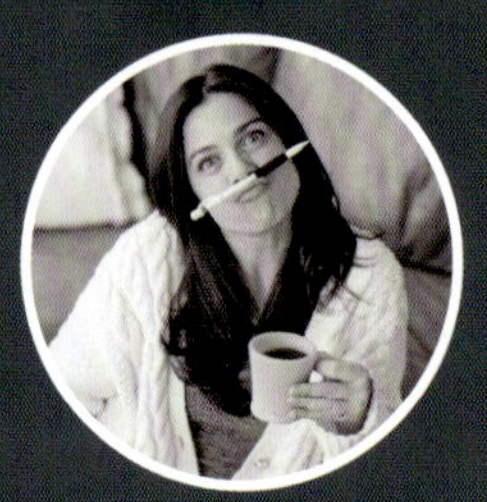

LAUREN BARGER
Illustrator & Character Designer
lbillustrates.com
Lauren is an illustrator with over five years of professional illustration and design experience, with past clients including Sony TV, Ravensburger, and Pixelle.

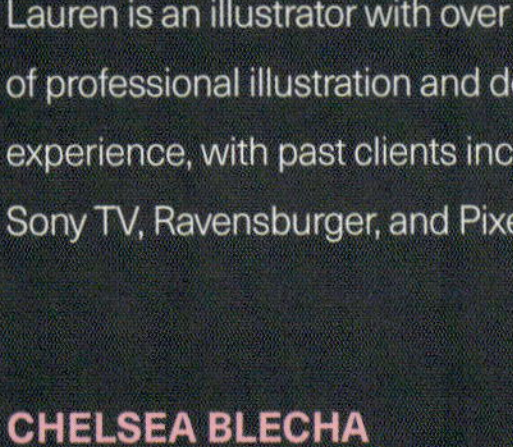

CHELSEA BLECHA
Visual Development Artist
chelseablecha.com
Chelsea is a published illustrator who specializes in colour, light, and mood. She currently lives in Los Angeles and works at Dreamworks Feature Animation.

JOSE CICERARO
Illustrator & Character Designer
instagram.com/superspaceocto
Jose is a multi-disciplinary artist working in games. He loves everything about drawing, design, and UI. More importantly, he loves spending time with his family.

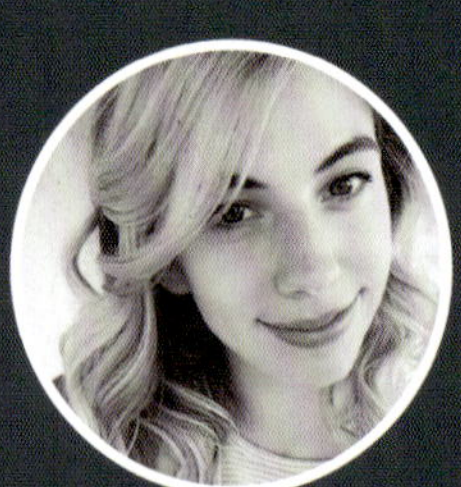

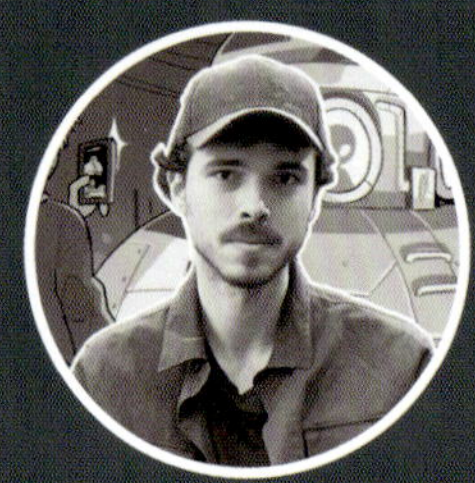

CARLES DALMAU
Freelance Illustrator
instagram.com/carles_dalmau
Carles is an illustrator known for his work for Massive Monster on *Cult of the Lamb* and for the creepy and cute drawings he shares on social media.

MARCO FERRARIS
Comic Book Artist
cara.app/marcoferraris1896
Marco is a cartoonist who mainly draws adventure comics for kids in France and the USA. He usually works digitally, but aims for a hand-drawn pencil look.

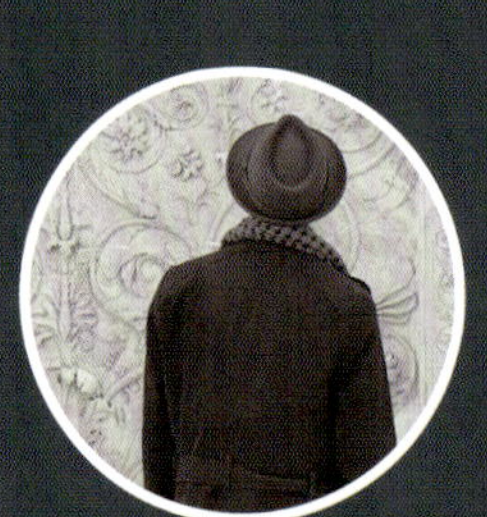

ROMA GEWSKA
2D Artist
linktr.ee/gewska
Roma is an artist from Kyiv, Ukraine, who enjoys drawing fantasy art inspired by her country and culture, and working on projects inspired by Ukrainian folklore

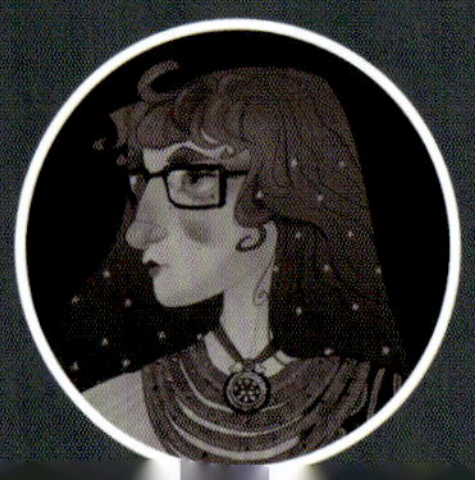

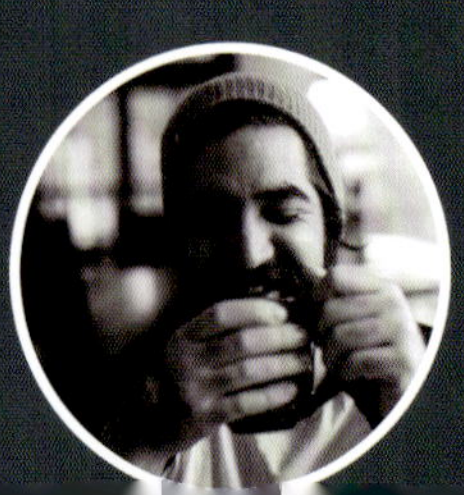

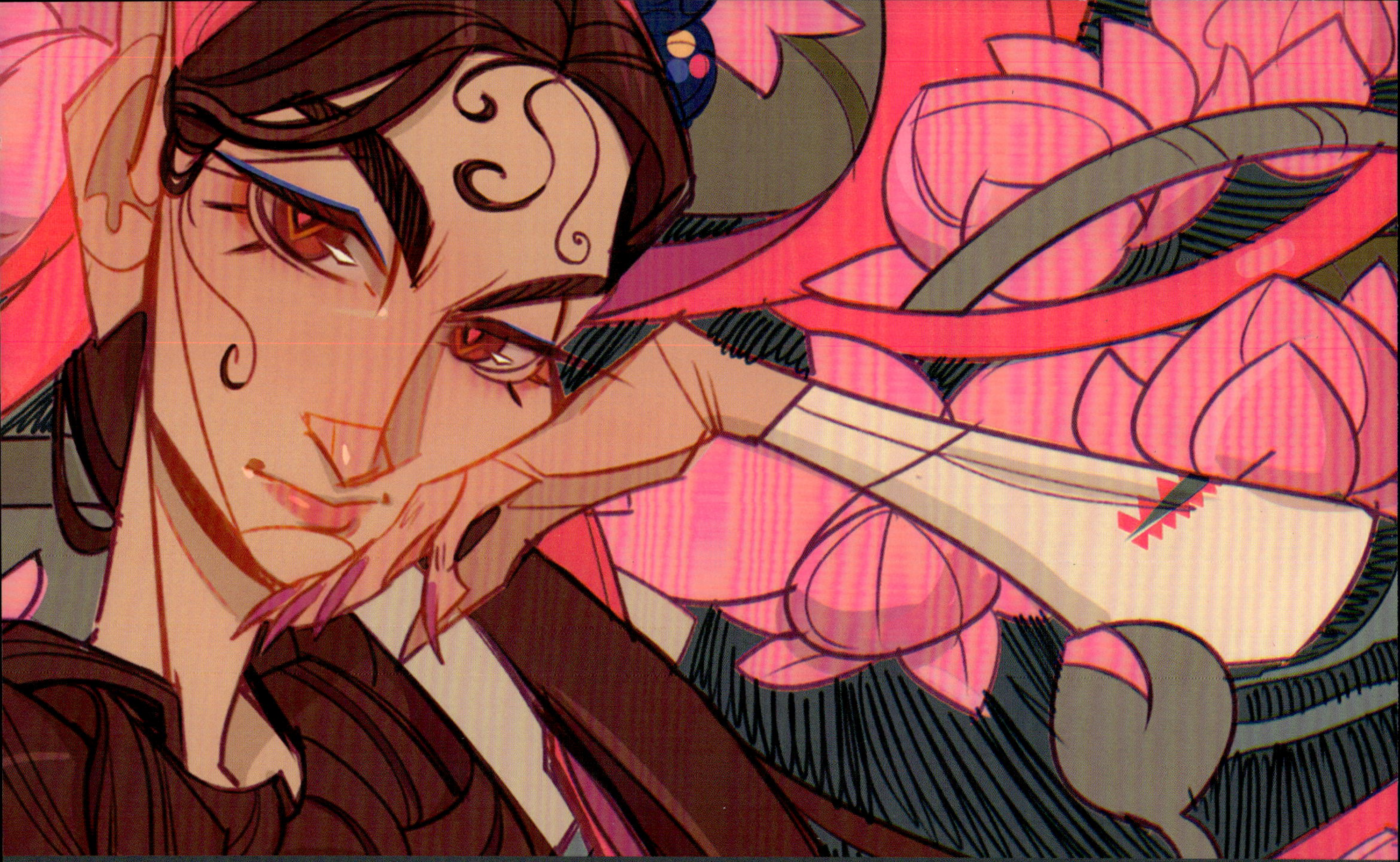

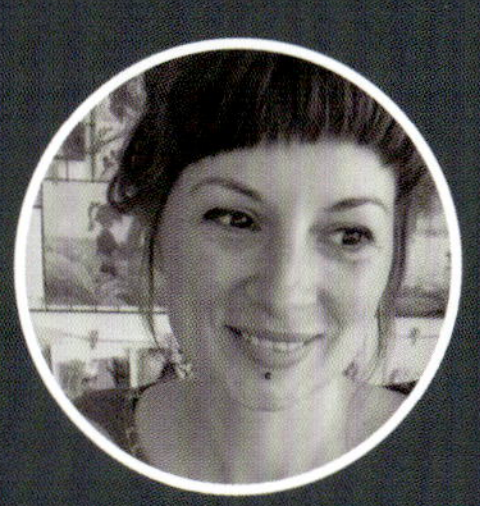

SIMONE GRÜNEWALD
Freelance Visual Development Artist

schmoedraws.com

Simone is a vis dev artist from Germany. She worked in the game industry for over ten years and is now happily freelancing and creating tutorials on her Patreon.

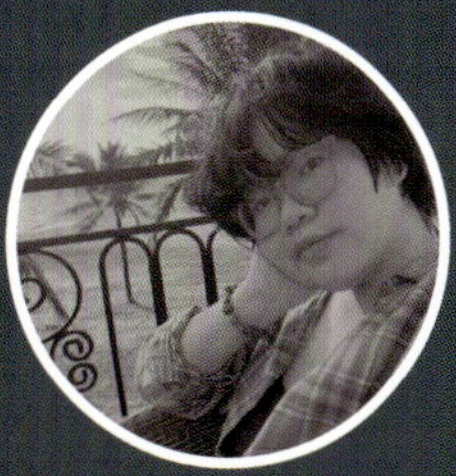

GRACE TRAN
Freelance Artist

artstation.com/gracetran

Grace is a freelance artist, based in Ho Chi Minh City, Vietnam. She has a soft spot for creating fantasy characters and illustrations.

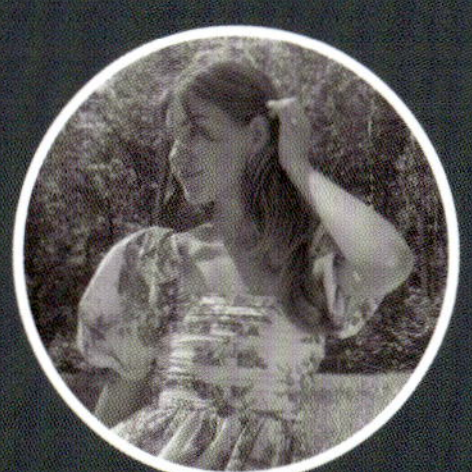

KATE PELLERIN
Freelance Illustrator

poopikat.com

Kate is a freelance illustrator from Toronto, Canada. Her work is focused on whimsical illustrations that capture the playfulness of childhood.

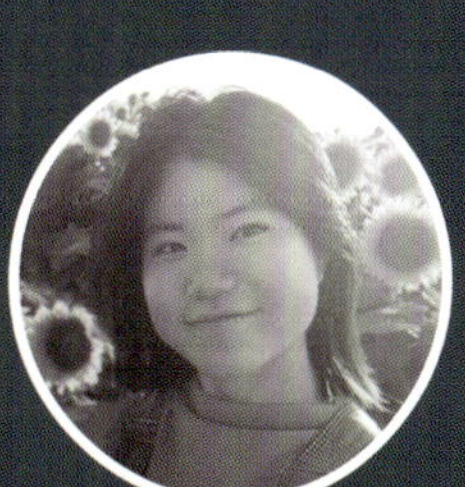

JENNIFER WU
Freelance Visual Development Artist

paluumin.portfoliobox.net

Jennifer is a Canadian visual development artist and character designer. She loves creating imaginative worlds and capturing everyday moments in her paintings.

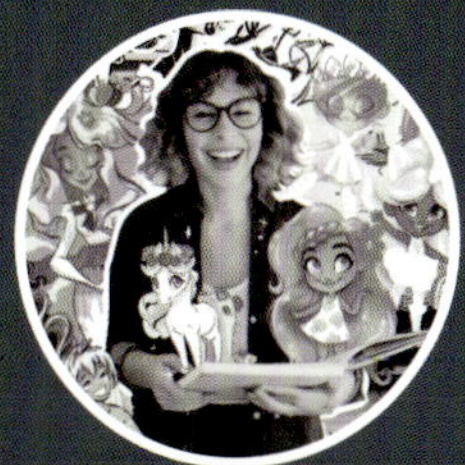

WHITNEY POLLETT
Artist and CEO at Pixelle Studios

wearepixelle.com

With over fifteen years experience in the toy and entertainment industry, Whitney specializes in storytelling, design, and talent development.

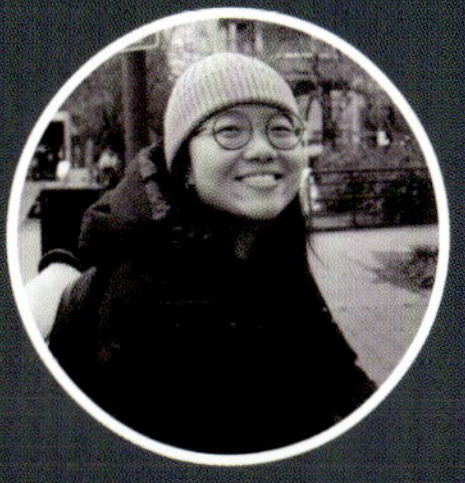

SHERYL YAP
Background Designer at Nickleodeon

sherylyapsl.com

Sheryl is a vis dev artist for TV and animated features. She enjoys telling stories and has worked at Netflix Animation, Dreamworks, Illumination, and more.

Image © Roma Gewska

50%
of net profits donated
TO CHARITY

In 2022, 3dtotal Publishing became successful enough to make a pledge to donate **50% of its net profits to charity**. This continues to be possible due to the incredible support from all our customers, employees, and partners. At the time of printing, we have donated over $1.62 million (USD) to charity.

We focus our giving on three charitable areas: **environmental, humanitarian, and animal welfare**. We use organizations such as Effective Altruism and Founders Pledge to guide who we help within these causes. Some ways of doing good are over 100 times more effective than others, so donating this way hugely increases the impact of our contributions.

**See 3dtotal.com/charity
for full details.**

3dtotal Publishing